Laura Roychowdhury is a social anthropologist and historian who did her dissertation on Anglo-Indians and the railways at the University of Michigan. She has recently returned from Delhi to London, where she now lives with her husband.

THE JADU HOUSE

TRAVELS IN ANGLO-INDIA

Laura Roychowdhury

BLACK SWAN

THE JADU HOUSE
Travels in Anglo-India
A BLACK SWAN BOOK : 0 552 99913 X

Originally published in Great Britain by Doubleday,
a division of Transworld Publishers

PRINTING HISTORY
Doubleday edition published 2000
Black Swan edition published 2001

1 3 5 7 9 10 8 6 4 2

Set in 11/12pt Melior by
Kestrel Data, Exeter, Devon.

Black Swan Books are published by Transworld Publishers,
61–63 Uxbridge Road, London W5 5SA,
a division of The Random House Group Ltd,
in Australia by Random House Australia (Pty) Ltd,
20 Alfred Street, Milsons Point, Sydney, NSW 2061, Australia,
in New Zealand by Random House New Zealand Ltd,
18 Poland Road, Glenfield, Auckland 10, New Zealand
and in South Africa by Random House (Pty) Ltd,
Endulini, 5a Jubilee Road, Parktown 2193, South Africa.

Printed and bound in Great Britain by
Clays Ltd, St Ives plc.

To Joan Bear, for telling me stories
and writing ten books

Contents

Acknowledgements

Fragments of experiences, friendships, conversations and debates fill the pages of this book. I would like to thank the following people whose lives, ideas and words flowed into but are not contained by the boundaries of this story: Mr J. N. Basu, Jeremy and Griselda Bear, Mary Bear, G. Bhadra, Mr S. Bharat, Suparna Bhaskaran, Mr and Mrs F. Blazey, Fiona Burtt, Rohit Chopra, Val Daniel, the Daranjo family, Mr A. K. Das, S. Da Silva, T. Da Silva, W. Da Silva, the D'Cruz family, Nicholas Dirks, Mrs P. Dutta, Clea Finkle, G. Forbes, M. G., Anjan and Sheta Ghosh, Gautam Ghosh, Duncan Hall, the Hastings family, Mr and Mrs E. Hillier, Riyad Koya, Pamela Maas, the Manook family, Rama Mantena, Mr N. Marklew, Harry Menzies, Mimlu and Pobon, Desmond Mitson, Bhaskar Mukhopadhyay, Mrs J. O'Brien, Mr and Mrs Raffiq, Mrs Raja, Gita Rajan, Anu Rao, Mr and Mrs P. S. Roy, Subir, Shaymasri, Sohag and Sohini Roychowdhury, Mr and Mrs R. Rozario, Mr and Mrs T. Rozario, Lee Schlesinger, Aditi Sen, Parna Sengupta, Anne Stoler, Mr and Mrs T. Thompson, Tom Trautmann, Sufia Uddin, Wendy Warren, Tom Williamson, Louis Xavier and especially the Ward family. Indrani Chatterjee has given many gifts to me including the reference which led to the stories of Anna Bella Chakrabarty and Victoria Skinner.

My four years of research in India were made possible by grants from the American Institute of Indian Studies, the Social Science Research Council, the Wenner-Gren Foundation and the University of Michigan. Even before this a fellowship from the Power Foundation started me out on this path.

The book would not have been written without the enthusiasm and faith of Patrick Walsh and Sarah Westcott, who are much more than agent and editor. Deborah Adams, John Saddler, Alison Tulett and Marianne Velmans read the manuscript at different stages and made wonderful suggestions. The cover was designed with inspiration by Claire Ward and Steve Rawlings. Thanks to Duniya for agreeing to be photographed for it and for living up to the symbolism of her name, which means 'the world'. No pages would have existed without my pact with Subhrasheel that he wouldn't read them and that our life together would never be constrained by mere words.

THE JADU HOUSE

Prologue

Some time after deciding to call my book *The Jadu House*, I reopened Kipling's *Kim*. I remembered being told that Kipling had tried to write a realistic novel about Anglo-Indians, which would reveal their plight to a British audience. Yet after many years of false starts and ripped-up plots, he composed an adventure story which would be loved by children and adults for its exotic fantasy. This is how the first page reads:

> He sat, in defiance of municipal orders, astride the gun Zam-Zammah on her brick platform opposite the old Ajaib-Gher – the Wonder House, as the natives call the Lahore Museum. Who hold Zam-Zammah, that 'fire-breathing dragon,' hold the Punjab; for the great green-bronze piece is always first of the conqueror's loot.
>
> There was some justification for Kim, – he had kicked Lala Dinanath's boy off the trunnions, – since the English held the Punjab and Kim was English. Though he was burned black as any native; though he spoke the vernacular by preference, and his mother-tongue in a clipped uncertain sing-song; though he consorted on terms of perfect equality with the small boys of the bazaar; Kim was white – a poor white of the very

13

poorest. The half-caste woman who looked after him (she smoked opium, and pretended to keep a second-hand furniture shop by the square where the cheap cabs wait) told the missionaries that she was Kim's mother's sister; but his mother had been nursemaid in a colonel's family and had married Kimball O'Hara, a young colour-sergeant of the Mavericks, an Irish regiment. He afterwards took a post on the Sind, Punjab, and Delhi railway, and his regiment went home without him. The wife died of cholera in Ferozepore, and O'Hara fell to drink and loafing up and down the line with the keen-eyed three-year-old baby. Societies and chaplains anxious for the child, tried to catch him, but O'Hara drifted away, till he came across the woman who took opium and learned the taste from her, and died as poor whites die in India. His estate at death consisted of three papers – one he called his *ne varietur* because those words were written below his signature thereon, and another his 'clearance-certificate.' The third was Kim's birth-certificate. Those things, he was used to say, in his glorious opium hours, would yet make little Kimball a man. On no account was Kim to part with them, for they belonged to a great piece of magic – such magic as men practised over yonder behind the Museum, in the big blue and white Jadoo-Gher – the Magic House, as we name the Masonic Lodge. It would, he said, all come right some day, and Kim's horn would be exalted between pillars – monstrous pillars – of beauty and strength. The colonel himself, riding on a horse, at the head of the finest regiment in the world, would attend to Kim, – little Kim that should have been better off than his father . . . Then he would weep bitterly in the broken rush chair on the verandah. So it came about after his death that the woman sewed parchment, paper, and birth-certificate into a leather amulet-case which she strung around Kim's neck.

. . . If the woman had sent Kim up to the local Jadoo-Gher with those papers, he would, of course, have been taken over by the Provincial Lodge and sent to the Masonic Orphanage in the Hills; but what she had heard of magic she distrusted.

My book too is full of Anglo-Indians, poor whites, railways and the magic of museums, Masonic lodges and birth certificates, but this time it is not the story of Kim's search for his identity. Instead it is the tale of the unnamed half-caste woman and her distrust of this magic. In Calcutta and the railway colony at Kharagpur I met her descendants, who shared her scepticism, and I listened to their tales. While searching for their life stories I reshaped my own. If I could speak to Kim now, I would tell him, cut the string that ties the amulet around your neck containing those certificates, birthrights and papers, for they dissemble. They may make you a man and help you reclaim a glorious British inheritance, but they will never allow us to know the name of the 'half-caste woman' or the truths of our past and present.

1

Kharagpur Tales

Acrid diesel and jasmine steam from the damp monsoon earth, jarring in the still air as the fan clatters to a halt. Its mechanical clicks cease, no longer marking the seconds passing in the night as regularly as a clock. In the lull of the power cut the other rhythms of Kharagpur that were hidden by the whirring of the fan and the glare of the strip light rise from the corners of the old railway inspectors' guest house. Since this room was built a century ago so many railway officers and travellers have slept here, writing their names and titles into the ledger where Subhrasheel and I had scribbled ours two days ago. 'Student, Presidency College' and 'Ph.D. researcher, University of Michigan' had seemed odd next to 'travelling ticket examiner', 'journalist' and 'ball-bearing salesman'. The accommodation had been provided by the Assistant Additional District Manager, who for unexplained reasons of his own assumed that we would be comfortable sharing a room. In his office decorated with gleaming polo trophies, he had calmly smoothed the dandy polka-dot handkerchief flourishing from the pocket of his immaculate suit while he read my letter of introduction from the Divisional Manager in Calcutta. Ignoring Subhrasheel, with precise etiquette he shook my hand, ordered tea and then a peon to show us the way to the guest house. In the piercing sunlight the long, low building with its endless veranda leading into separate sleeping compartments had the neglected air of an abandoned railway carriage rusting in a siding. At first we were a little self-conscious about sharing the close quarters, but the events of the last few days and our relaxed friendship have helped us to forget formalities. Yet now our conversation dwindles into silence as we feel the presence of the past around us. Shadows gather and murmur, obscuring the cracks in varnish, brown stains on the whitewashed walls and mouldy silvering on the mirror. It is impossible to make out the passing of years.

The room becomes alive with rustlings that could be cotton saris or silk crinolines sweeping across the floor, but are probably just rats chewing the stained mulberry-velvet curtains. The humidity grows heavier, drawing sweat to the surface of the skin. In the deep darkness the mahogany Victorian dressing table and twin beds with mosquito nets draped over their elegantly turned columns loom larger. They take on a fullness of shadows as black as the ancient heaps of coal-ash that villagers still scavenge through on the outskirts of Kharagpur. When they dig through them, charcoal-grey dust billows from the earth and now the same clouds seem to be filling this room. In one corner, a cane lawn chair with long wooden arms creaks as if someone is sitting down. It was specially crafted so that officers could stretch out their legs while they waited for servants to pull off their boots.

When Kipling was a young journalist hunting for stories along the railway tracks perhaps he had stayed in this guest house too. It would have looked much the same as it does now under the cover of darkness. Long before he became a grand man of letters, Kipling earned a meagre living as a writer of traveller's tales for the *Pioneer*. One of these was set in Jamalpur, a railway colony built in the 1860s that was just like Kharagpur. Kipling was fascinated by the order of Jamalpur, describing it as a perfect English village, so pristine it looked as if it had been placed under a glass case. Preserved in this museum to industry and the benevolence of the Raj, all the classes of Indian subjects had been set to work in discrete tasks: Bengalis in accounts, iron-working castes in the workshops, low-caste labourers in the line-gangs and Eurasians and Europeans in the running staff. All of them were supervised by British superiors, who led them on the march to progress. Eurasians and railwaymen imported from Ironbridge, Dublin and Glasgow found a home from home among the well-appointed flower gardens, mock-Tudor bungalows and Railway Institute dances.

This account secured Kipling popularity, fame and a regular income. It was published in the first volume of A. H. Wheeler and Co.'s Indian Railway Library. Thousands of copies were sold in their bookshops, which could be found in every bustling station across North India. It provided diverting reading for civil servants and their wives while they travelled to their posts. Critics in London and India praised Kipling's story for its realism. But other, later writers had different views. Saratchandra Chattopadyay described a work camp of railway linemen as a nightmare of plague and death. Tarashankar Banerjee charted the corruption of an *adivasi* village as men and women were drawn into work on the railways, losing their virtue as wages flowed into their pockets. Prabat Krishna Mukherjee saw colonies as places full of ghosts. And here, now, in Kharagpur, without the fan marking time and surrounded by the fullness of shadows, it is these ghosts that I can hear haunting Kipling's museum of industry.

For a moment the whisperings are drowned out by the Hindi announcement for the Madras Express from the nearby station, famous for the longest platform in the world. The train screeches over the junction. Its lights sear the room, glinting on the lone green eye of a signal lamp watching from where it is hung up on the wall. Leaping from beneath his mosquito net, Subhrasheel seizes the candle and matches suddenly visible on the dressing table. Again I feel heavy and slow, as I have done so often while following him through the crowds of Calcutta, chasing a bus or one of his myriad friends, from black marketeers to commerce students wielding mobile phones. He is always in movement, words streaming from his lips, fingertips unfurling ideas from the air and slipping through the waves of his hair in an attempt to will it into restraint. But his dark eyes that he jokingly calls his snake-eyes are perpetually still and waiting. They are now lit up by the flickering candle flame.

'I hate it here, Laura. I hate you in this place. All the railway officials rush around treating you like royalty and me as your faithful servant. I feel as if I'm in a bad film sequel, *The Return of the Raj* or *Heat and Dust II*.'

Smarting from his words, and worried that our growing friendship is under threat, I want desperately to reassure him.

'I hate it here as well.'

'How can you? It's awfully convenient for your research that everyone becomes respectful at the sight of your British manners.'

Wincing at his barbed parody of an upper-class English accent, I try to think of a way to convince him that the last thing I could enjoy is a return of the Raj. I haven't come here to revive Kipling's English village, but to draw forgotten ghosts out of the shadows. Some months ago in the India Office Library, I had read about Victoria Skinner, an Anglo-Indian woman whose descendants lived in railway colonies like Kharagpur. Now, after Subhrasheel's caustic comments, I find her story echoing in my mind, and I decide to tell him about her so that he will understand why I could never feel nostalgic about the Raj.

George and Helen Skinner lived in Meerut before the 1857 Rebellion. George was the Christian illegitimate son of a soldier, Helen probably a Muslim who had converted to Christianity. They had a daughter, Victoria, who sometimes attended the local missionary school or whiled away the hours listening to her mother reading from Urdu storybooks. George, like his father before him, fought for the British Army and died in the Rebellion. Helen and Victoria lived on their own until 1867 when Thomas John, a clerk in the judges' court, moved in with them. He and Helen had fallen in love, but he was already married. There was no bar on Muslim husbands having multiple wives. So, with a pragmatism that showed the strength of their passion over their religious conviction, they converted to Islam and married.

The Skinner relatives started to gossip about the arrangement and feared for the well-being of Victoria in such a household. They urged Helen to send her daughter to a proper Christian school in the hills at Simla. Such schools were designed to provide girls with a British education in music, domestic skills and deportment so that they could become respectable wives and dame-school teachers in railway colonies. Helen agreed to send her, but Victoria ran away back to her mother and stepfather, saying that she wanted to live with them and be a Muslim. This was too much for the relatives who brought a case in the High Court against Helen, arguing that her home was immoral and unchristian. The court awarded guardianship to the headmistress, Miss Scanlan, and packed Victoria off once more to the hill school where she could have only rare visits from her mother. Helen was devastated, as was Victoria. So Helen appealed the case.

The judges decided to uphold the earlier decision on the grounds that religions in India coexisted as separate communities with distinct laws affecting every relation of life. They argued that differences of religion and community governed all domestic usages and social relations. Therefore a mother could remain a legitimate guardian only as long as she brought up her child in its father's faith. The judges ignored all the evidence in Victoria's life that, in some Indian houses, traditions mingled. Victoria and Helen's love for each other was cast aside so that Victoria would have the benefit of British manners.

Victoria was faced with a painful choice: to forget either her mother or her father. Before the court ruled she placed in evidence a statement of what it felt like to be riven in two and to have her memories divided by impossible choices.

My own feelings alone have prompted me. I wish to remain a Mussulmani. I would not be persuaded to become a Christian because it is from my own conviction that I am a Muslim. I am in the purdah by my own free will. I went up to Simla with my mother and Mr John. They wished me to go to school and pressed me very much to go, but I would not consent. I wish to return to my mother.

There was a picture of my father, but I had heard that it was strictly forbidden to keep pictures by our religion. I therefore destroyed it with my own hands. The picture was on paper in a frame with glass. It was destroyed soon after we returned from the hills. I heard that to keep pictures was prohibited, after my return from the hills, from a preacher who came to the house and preached a sermon. No one advised me otherwise. I had long thought of becoming a Mussulmani, but when I was young did not understand the different religions. When I returned from the hills I turned my attention to it.

Many years ago in a dusty courtroom Victoria's words had been read out by a pleader in front of indifferent judges. Now they echo in the darkness covering us, but this time I want the conclusions drawn from her case to be different. So I ask Subhrasheel, 'Was Victoria's choice to become a Muslim driven by religious conviction or by her love for her mother? Did she rip up her father's picture because she truly believed it was idolatry? Was it because she wanted to forget his Christian, British parentage that meant she would be packed off to a school she hated, far from her mother? Whatever the answers to these questions, it is clear that Victoria only paid attention to distinctions of religion and community once meddling relatives and the law had intervened. Her free will was taken from her so that she would acquire the proper deportment of a British woman. Now do you see? How could I relish the respect of railway officers when it is founded on such sacrifices?'

The fan haltingly whirrs into action and the signal lamp sends a faltering green beam across the room. The current is back, but it wavers below a voltage strong enough to power the strip light.

Subhrasheel shrugs his shoulders, casting off Victoria's story: 'All of that was so long ago. Besides, I only said I hated you to distract us from the load-shedding, to provoke conversation.'

With Subhrasheel, I never know whether our conversations should be taken seriously. He snaps his fingers, suddenly changing a confessional mood into a more playful one, leaving me spinning. I try to keep up with him as he spirals off: 'All my friends in college are more concerned with whether they are up to date with the latest VJ's fashions on MTV than with this ancient history. Why do you care about the Anglo-Indian past? Why did you come all the way here to hunt for it? You may be British, but you didn't have any relatives in the Raj.'

23

These questions have turned in my mind for a long time and I'm still not sure how to answer them. Of course, there are academic reasons for coming here, but are they enough to explain why I was willing to leave behind in the US my husband, Maurice, for a year or so of research? Maurice with his calming smile that I had first kissed in the middle of a Hallowe'en party full of drunken students. We were the only two people there who had not dressed up as fantasy alter egos for the occasion. There were no costumes or façades between us. And it was his unwavering honesty that I continued to admire and love. I treasured the stability of his character even more because it was so hard for him to maintain it in the flux of his life. He had travelled from the Ivory Coast, leaving behind his family and culture, to study oceanography in the US. Not a rich kid who had pulled strings for a scholarship, but a young man who had spent his early years in a remote village next to the border with Liberia. Together we faced the newness of America and forged something distinct, distant from both our pasts and the reality around us. I wish he was here in Kharagpur with me, then he would resolve my confusion. He would reassure me that my research on Anglo-Indians and the railway colonies they lived in was purely a career move that tangentially dealt with the issues of race that sometimes surfaced in our lives in America. But sitting opposite in the green half-light is Subhrasheel, who wants to ask questions, not provide answers. Once my earnest explanations are flowing he will probably announce again that we are just passing time. Hesitantly I begin to speak, fearing that Subhrasheel will mock me again, that he is not really after the truth, only an entertainment that will turn our attention away from the stifling, humid air weakly circulating round the room.

'It's true, I didn't have any relatives in the Raj, but

my reasons for coming here aren't that simple. Maybe it all goes back to my grandfather.'

For as long as I can remember my mother's father was like an Old Testament patriarch, stroking his long white beard, making strange predictions about the future and recounting unfamiliar versions of the past. All of his life he had obstinately chipped away at conventional wisdom, leaving behind his strictly god-fearing family to go to art school. Expelled for painting lines on a naked life-model to illustrate his theory about a mathematical art that didn't rely on inspiration, he drifted into a bohemian world of Russian ballet dancers and followers of the esoteric Eastern philosophies of Gurdjieff. But he never really found a rigid theory to replace the hellfire religion he had learnt as a child. Rather he spun out a randomly chosen series of heresies. He filled my mind with bizarre ideas about the connections between the pyramids and Pythagoras. His chosen haunt was the British Museum and he took me there often, placing my hands on the sculptures out of sight of the guards, and encouraging me to stretch my mind and think of other worlds.

My grandfather also loved to recount the family's scandals and adventures. His own father, a sober engineer, had been sent to Haile Selassie's palace in Ethiopia to install electric lighting. Laughing, he conjured up the scene: the prudish Scot surrounded by the pomp and circumstance of thousands of glittering chandeliers in the middle of the desert. In contrast to his father, my grandfather didn't want to take technology to the continent of Africa. Instead he studied the artistry of the Benin bronzes and filled his home with delicately crafted Nigerian boxes. One of the memorable sculptures he carved was of an African woman singing, head gazing proudly upwards. He relished its combination of classical Greek form and unconventional subject. I often wondered if this admiration was really a homage to his love affair after my grandmother's death with an ambassadress from Ghana. His library was full of censored texts. A manuscript of *Lady Chatterley's Lover*, which he had been given by the woman who typed up the first copies for D. H. Lawrence, lay on the shelf next to the latest addition, *The Satanic Verses*. Once he explained the roots of his sceptical heresies to me: 'Don't ever believe anything you are told. When I went to school I was taught Britain was great, the proof hanging on the wall in a blood-red map of the Empire, but now we know it was a bloody lie.'

How could I not be influenced by his view of the world? My father's family were, in contrast to this, more enigmatic about their past. My grandmother and her two sisters were brought up in one of the Chinese treaty ports, Foo Chow. Sometimes I heard tantalizing snippets about ayahs, bungalows and pirate attacks on the river. My suffragette great-grandmother had been forbidden to marry a Jewish man and in revenge had run away to Foo Chow and married a Dutch customs officer. But these long-distant memories were drowned out in the daily round of my grandparents' running a fruit farm in Sussex.

One of my great-aunts inherited a bungalow from a cousin who had been a pathologist in Nigeria. His house was littered with the tools of his trade. My father took a few of these, including some bright scalpels in a small leather box, and used them in model-making. Often I would sneak a look at the gleaming blades for the frisson of horror they produced. I wondered what ghoulish dissections they had performed and where they had travelled. Yet, like the Sussex branch of my family, they wouldn't yield their secrets.

At the age of ten I left my state school for the marble grandeur of St Paul's Girls' School. Its halls echoed with the laughter of beautiful, fair-haired girls talking of ponies and balls. Gold-embossed plaques boasted lists of pupils who had achieved scholarships to Oxford or Cambridge. As my classmates grew older they dreamed of travelling to the furthest reaches of the old Empire. Most were drawn there by photographs of grandparents playing cricket and polo in Lucknow. Celia Johnson, an old girl, had recently given her last performance on television in Paul Scott's *Staying On* and the school was abuzz for weeks with nostalgia for the Raj. They wanted to go there to experience this nostalgia, and to be transported as far as possible from Britain by a taste of India's exotic charms. Throughout my time at St Paul's I felt at odds with the place, my grandfather's story about the map of Empire and the 'greatness' of Britain reverberating in my mind. I often thought of my old state-school friends as well. Angela Husain, whose mother brewed Caribbean-Indian curries on her kitchen stove. Andrea Chen, whose mother was Irish and father Venezuelan-Chinese. Najma Razzaq who had arrived with her family newly impoverished by the Pakistan-Bangladesh war. St Paul's was remote from these realities, yet believed itself to be the very heart of Britain. Everywhere I turned I seemed to be taking part in a grandiose hallucination, among people un-prepared to accept other pasts and versions of Britain.

In my rebellion against the blindness of St Paul's, my grandfather's example was my inspiration. Wandering the galleries of the British Museum and gazing up at the monumental sculptures, I continued to look for the other realities he had pointed me towards. Like an eighteenth-century antiquary collect-ing fragments of civilizations from all over the world, I covered the walls of my room with drawings of Assyrian winged beasts and prints of country estates. Piled up to the ceiling in a corner were learned-looking texts. Next to them hung gold Victorian picture frames filled with mirrors in which I could see myself reflected. I wanted my room to be a British Museum too. I began to dress like an eighteenth-century gentleman, in a rich purple and turquoise brocade coat, with my eyes smeared with gold make-up. I tried to trace the roots of European civilization in the mysterious faces of Oriental beasts. And if I studied India, I thought, perhaps I could finally reinvent myself as an expert and descendant of a different civilization. I would at last be beyond the narrow classifications of so-called British pedigree.

At Cambridge, where I followed generations of Paulinas to study Archaeology and Anthropology, I realized that academia didn't always allow a shape-shifting freedom to reinvent oneself and, if anything, the notion of Britain I was trying to escape was reinforced. My college, New Hall, was apart from all of this, a modernist Islamic dome built in the 1960s that held a healthy irreverence towards the older colleges. But this only served to make the contrast with the rest of the university more visible. We were nowhere near its centre. That lay beneath the apses of ancient dining halls and rooms where, in line with hundreds of years of tradition, servers and bedders were ordered around by students learning to be privileged. State-school and private-school students alike donned tweed and ball gowns and punted to Grantchester, and I was even more embedded in a hallucination of Britain.

After Cambridge, the University of Michigan was exhilarating, replacing British intellectual grandeur with entrepreneurial optimism. For the first time I felt as if I was outside some honorary harem of academia – though the University of Michigan's Disneyland bubble of enterprise was another kind of fantasy. Travelling from its opulence to the abandoned buildings and no-go zones of Detroit contained other lessons. But here at least colonial history and its connections to Britishness that my grandfather had told me about all those years ago were openly debated.

My grandfather died soon after I started my studies in the US. Even though his stories had become wilder and less coherent as he aged, I felt his absence deeply. Back in London, helping to clear up his books, I opened up *The Satanic Verses*, curious to see if he had ever actually read it. Underlined on the page and festooned with his wavering old-fashioned italics was the sentence, 'The trouble with the English is that their history happened overseas, so they don't know what it means.' It seemed like a message left for me. When I returned to the US, I hunted through library shelves looking for a research project that would continue his inheritance. When I saw the 1890s pictures of Kharagpur I knew that I had found it.

Kharagpur was in rural Bengal, yet each picture showed a stage-set English village. There seemed to be a desperate refusal of India in every frame. The grainy black and white images were full of mock-Tudor bungalows, billiard rooms and apprentice houses decorated with silver sports cups. The houses for Indian workers, across the railway tracks from European and Anglo-Indian quarters, were concrete boxes, more concerned with utility than with making their inhabitants feel at home. And I was even more curious about those who lived in the midst of this scenery.

Kharagpur had been built to house Eurasian railway workers and engine drivers exported from Britain. In its homes and English-medium schools generations who had never seen the white cliffs of Dover were taught to dream of them. How did they reconcile the India which lay just outside the colony with these memories of places they had never been to? They lived under the shadow of an ideal England, reading about its Anglo-Saxon kings and turning their tongues around the declensions of Latin rather than Hindi or Bengali. I longed to find Anglo-Indians who had lived under the shadow of this façade and had chipped away

29

at the plaster and daubs of paint until it was criss-crossed with cracks. In these fissures that let in the Indian sunlight I hoped that something new had been created; a place of unorthodox tales like those of my grandfather. The more I read the more I treasured Anglo-Indians' multiple names: Eurasians, Firinghees, East Indians, Britasians, Indo-British. Most of these names had been imposed on them by Raj administrators, who tried to compose regulations to pin down their identity. The most recent classification was Anglo-Indian, which had been written into the law books in 1919 and referred to all individuals who had a European ancestor in their male line of inheritance. But what fascinated me about these names was that they constantly shifted. This suggested that the mixed parentage and multiple cultural affiliations of Anglo-Indians defied easy definition. I wanted to put faces to these names. When I read Victoria's story, I became even more determined to speak to her descendants.

Subhrasheel has been listening patiently, but now his bed creaks as he sits up to say something. But my story hasn't finished yet and I don't want to lose the connections I am making for the first time between different elements of my life, so I continue: 'There is one more thing I should tell you about – another unexpected message like the one my grandfather left in *The Satanic Verses.*'

On the eve of my research trip to India, I revisited the British Museum for an evening lecture. A friend introduced me to a member of the museum staff, an expert in Roman coins, who sought my help in explaining something that puzzled him. His department often received letters from India enclosing Imperial medals and coins that had been in the family for generations. The letters suggested that the British Museum, not India, was the place where these remnants of the Raj belonged. One recent letter was from a workshop foreman who lived in Howrah, a small railway colony in Calcutta. So I asked for a copy of it. Words jumping lines from the efforts of a bazaar scribe's old typewriter, the letter read like this:

Dear Sir,
Your esteemed Museum has a very high reputation worldwide. It is the centre for history and preserves the past with the science and technology at your disposal. That is why I am writing to you from here. In my family's possession for two generations has been this medal awarded for loyal services rendered during the railway signallers' strike of 1890. We have no need of it. It has no value in my family. We are Hindus descended from our native place not far from here called Panaghar. This is not part of our past. It belongs in the British Museum as British heritage. You can ascertain its value to your national glory and dispose of it as applicable.
Thanking you for your attention
P. Ghosh

I could not forget this letter. Sitting in his railway quarters, Mr Ghosh had also dreamed of the British Museum. Yet strangely his image of it was the reverse of my youthful, exotic imaginings and my grandfather's sense of the place as a repository of other worlds. For him it was a symbol of the grandeur of British learning, part of the Imperial map that had been up on the wall in my grandfather's classroom. The artefacts that belonged there were not Benin bronzes or Indian Gupta-period sculptures, but the insignias of Raj rule that Mr Ghosh wanted to banish from India.

Winding towards the end of my story, I say to Subhrasheel, 'Had I got it all wrong hunting for an escape from Britishness in the halls of this place?

Obviously, the answer lay in India. I decided that on reaching Calcutta I would try and find Mr Ghosh to ask him why he had spent a good part of his month's salary on sending a registered parcel to the museum. More importantly, my sense that the clues to British history lay overseas, in India, was confirmed.'

I realize that I have completely forgotten my fears about Subhrasheel's playful questioning and have rushed onwards until my life is twisted into unfamiliar filigrees of connections. Telling him these thoughts in the half-light is an intoxicating pleasure. But now I have come to a halt and look expectantly across at Subhrasheel, hoping he will spin out another thread. He doesn't disappoint me. Stretching out on my bed, behind the veil of the mosquito net, I listen to him.

'I have a story for you too,' he says. 'It will tell you something very different about dreams of British pedigree from that letter that so fascinated you in the British Museum. My grandmother married into a Noakhali landlord family, wealthy on the profits of the permanent settlement passed by the British in the eighteenth century. What a scam it was, with all the aristocratic rural trappings so loved by your eighteenth-century gentleman. The landlords paid a tax to the British Government which they had the duty of raising from the peasants who worked the land. The peasants paid the landlords in rice and grain, which they then sold back to them at a profit. They were minting money in the name of the British and got to live in a noble style to which they soon became accustomed. The British loved all of these dealings with the squirearchy. They argued it gave stability to the countryside. Village India began to look suspiciously like feudal England.

'But my grandmother was less concerned with this mystery than with where her new husband disappeared to at night. She'd heard that his elder brothers kept Eurasian slave-girls at their beck and

32

call, tasting beer and other delights in Anna-Maria's *para*. Her husband, though, seemed not to leave the confines of the huge family compound, which when she first arrived had felt as big as the fortress gates to the ruined city at Gaur. She knew what her fate as a new wife should be: petty fears about overcooking the rice; teasing from sisters-in-law; mild flirtations with younger brothers-in-law; cuts from the tongue of her mother-in-law. This she had expected from her addiction to Tagore's short stories and rumours carried back home by her elder married sisters. But she couldn't quite accept that her husband, who seemed as handsome and devoted as a Tagore hero, would frequent illicit houses of liquor and pleasure. After all he had chosen her for her beauty and fair skin rather than for any of her family's qualifications, which were still a source of meal-time bickering. He surely didn't need other diversions than her round fair face and sweetly plump arms. She'd secretly read a Bengali translation of *Bluebeard*, but these scandals of murder and multiple wives didn't happen in good Hindu families. But then husbands weren't supposed to disappear at night leaving their auspicious wives for Firinghee women. She had to know. So she followed him one night, skirting the servants' huts, a hive of gossiping tongues, with trepidation. Like Bluebeard, her husband was carrying a key and walking towards a door near the edge of the stage where they mounted clay models of the goddess for the local villagers during Durga puja. She cursed her white and red night-time sari that was already beginning to show mud stains. How would she explain this in the morning? But now her curiosity was too much. She found herself beside the unlocked door, clenching the keys tied to her sari so they wouldn't make a sound. Hoping the loose padlock wouldn't drop, she pushed the door ajar.

'There was her husband with his oil lamp raised

aloft, the light and his beautiful face magnified a thousandfold, the room's earthen walls transformed into pools of reflection by hundreds of British gold-framed mirrors. She realized then that she should not disturb him, so fascinated was he by his image caught in the frames. He traced his features on the surface of the mirrors and touched the cupids, Corinthian columns and ivy leaves surrounding the glass. He looked triumphant, as if he had finally found his secret identity reflected in these flights of Victorian fantasy that should have been gracing a ballroom.

'My grandmother felt feverish and scared, for this was even worse than the discovery made by Blue-beard's wife. Despite his outward show as a good Bengali husband, he found his real, secret self in these foreign mirrors, so out of place in the family's rigid daily adherence to Hindu traditions. He crept away at night from her attempts to conform to the role of a perfect Bengali wife, to find himself reflected in visions of British taste and elegance. He was being unfaithful not only to her but perhaps also to India by loving these mirrors more than her. What were they doing at the centre of her Bengali life? What had they to do with her husband? What was all this talk of good lineage that had made her life hell during the first months of marriage since she could not live up to the family's upper-caste traditions? Her husband found himself here, not in the daily round of pujas or the lists of forebears recited during their marriage. He formed his secret self in a British image.

'Mr Ghosh cannot banish Britain from India by returning Raj history to the British Museum. It's not as easy as that. My grandmother could have told her husband that the secret, British self he saw in the mirror was an illusion, but he would have still been fascinated by what he saw. After all, how could British-manufactured glass, wood and gold leaf not be real, all those years of craftsmanship and history distilled into one object? On the other hand my story could be a lie, told to pass the time. Who can vouch for it apart from a dead Bengali woman? Just as the exotic Orient and India hovered around your grandfather's and your own quest for identity, British civilization lingered around my grandfather's secret dreams of himself.

'And now it's your turn again. What happened when you reached Calcutta? Did you find those clues to British history you were looking for?'

The bedposts rattle with my laughter. Sitting up, I untwist the purple chiffon *dupatta* that has become tangled around my neck and stare at its crumpled demureness. Yes, I found those clues, but in the most unexpected of places. Strangely they revealed as much about the Indian present as they did about the British past.

2

Bengali Lessons

I'm heading in an autorickshaw for the Founder's Day service at St James School. The spluttering vehicle decorated with a photo of Tower Bridge and the words 'Joy Ma', rattles past Lansdowne Road, Palm Avenue, Tivoli Court, Kathleen's Cake Shop and parks filled with cricket teams. Ladies pick their way over potholes and clutch flowery handkerchiefs with which they mop their brows. Holding umbrellas aloft to shelter their complexions from the still-blinding mid-afternoon sun, they ignore the crowds seething around them. When the autorickshaw speeds up, a cooling breeze bearing noxious grey fumes twists my purple chiffon *dupatta* round the black steel bars and yellow nylon cover of the vehicle. The safety pins attaching it to my *kameez* aren't helping me to remain as demurely covered as the brightly dressed matrons.

Mrs Gupta, my landlady and Bengali teacher, had taught me this trick. A month ago I arrived in Calcutta and moved into a small flat on the ground floor of her husband's towering concrete family home. Three generations live here. Her husband's mother presides over the top floor. She is always dressed in the white sari of a widow and her day is punctuated by worship in the family puja room. Delicate white filigree patterns of *alpana*, painted by Shakuntala, Mrs Gupta's daughter who is studying for a master's degree in microbiology, lead down the stairs to the third floor. Here Mrs Gupta's twenty-five-year-old son, Ashok, lives in the rooms he will occupy with a future bride who will be picked for her beauty, homeliness and caste credentials. On the second floor, Jonny, the family's pet Alsatian, sniffs around the kitchen door and turned legs of the vast dining-room table looking for scraps of food on the blood-red floor. But he is never admitted to Mr and Mrs Gupta's bedroom or Shakuntala's, which is lined with science textbooks and fluffy animals. This part of the house is separated from the ground floor by the portcullis of a padlocked gate. The stairs, splattered with shocking-pink dye left over from last year's Holi celebrations, wind down from the gate to Mr Gupta's office. Here at street level he conducts an ill-defined business supplying parts to engineering firms with the help of Raghu, a mournful, scruffy odd-job man. Behind the office is my flat. Its barred windows give on to a tiny garden shaded by a jackfruit tree and each day returning from Calcutta's streets I am grateful for this peaceful view. Mr Gupta and his son ignore me most of the time, just offering polite words of greeting. Shakuntala seems suspicious of me. I had tried to gossip with her about boyfriends and college life but she had answered my friendly enquiries with the curt statement that she was much too practical to believe in romance. She had no time for it with all her studies and anyway once it became important her parents would find a suitable match. She locks herself up in her room with the heavy textbooks and girlish toys, emerging only to be driven to college by the family chauffeur or for meals prepared by her mother.

Mrs Gupta, in contrast to the rest of the family, is full of generous concern for my welfare. She brings me small gifts of Bengali food, of banana flowers or *shorshe mach* – fish in mustard sauce. Then she pulls up the skirts of her pastel chiffon sari, sits next to me delicately arranging the pleats and explains the traditional properties of each dish. 'This one heats up the body, so shouldn't be taken too often in the hot summer season. It should always be followed by curds to cool down the system.' Her round sparkling face lightly brushed with make-up, long black wavy hair and dark brown eyes make her look like an image of the goddess Lakshmi grown a little thin and weary from twenty-five years of household duties. She makes this comparison often, laughing and saying, 'I'm one of those puja-time Lakshmis, a perfect wife and bride, but my worshippers forgot to throw me into the Hooghly at the end of the festival and I haven't been repainted recently.' Then she gossips for hours, asking questions about my life with Maurice. Taking me to Bengali plays and Indian classical music recitals in the city, she lends me her jewellery and saris. Our daily Bengali lessons always turn away from the declensions of verbs to discussions of traditional culture and stories of her life. While absorbing the rich vowel sounds and thickened consonants of her accent, I can't help but mimic her immaculate posture and elegant hand-movements straight out of a Tagore dance-drama. She has made it clear that this is exactly her intention: she wants to tutor me in proper deportment as she does her other young charges sent by their parents for Hindi and Bengali lessons. Mrs Gupta is offering me a guiding friendship that has revived my teenage dreams of dressing up as someone else. This time my fantasy is not an eighteenth-century gentleman. Mrs Gupta wants to teach me how to be a traditional Bengali lady. Out of curiosity and the sheer pleasure of wrapping myself in yards of sumptuous silk, I'm more than willing to play along. Especially because each morn-ing, after dressing, I don't recognize myself in the mirror. There is a joy in this because the fair-skinned woman staring back could be Victoria Skinner before she was sent to Simla for a proper Christian education.

But what is making me anxious in this autorick-shaw, leading me to fidget and pull my clothes back into place, is something Mrs Gupta told me during a lesson yesterday. Throughout the city taxi drivers and shopkeepers call me *memsaheb*, so I had asked Mrs Gupta what this meant. Her eyes had lit up at the question. She explained that as a result of our conversations about my marriage, she had just been writing a poem about *memsahebs* or foreign women. In it she criticized Bengali husbands who don't help their wives with their household duties and make it difficult for them to feel romantic because they are always so tired. She wished that all Bengali husbands could be trained by *memsahebs* like me. Sighing with resignation she added, 'But then, what to do? No-one but me knows how to cook the dishes properly. My son, daughter and husband can't eat outside, they're so used to the way my food tastes.'

Touched by Mrs Gupta's admission that it is not always so wonderful being like Lakshmi, and glad that she trusted our friendship enough to confide in me, I had let her continue.

'I was so young when I married and I had to learn so much. I was excited by all the preparations, finery, jewellery and I was at the centre of it all. See, Laura, I didn't even know what would happen on the third night, the night of flowers when the bride and groom are left alone. I was so upset, I ran all the way to my mother's house and told her what my husband had done. I thought he was a monster. She said that's just what men do. My husband was patient, I was lucky. He hardly scolded me when the rice was overcooked or I didn't understand his needs.'

Startled by the intimacy of this admission, I drew my chair closer to her and asked if she had ever wanted to be a *memsaheb*. Her soft face had hardened with shock.

'No, "*memsaheb*" is used to describe those ladies you see in the old British Clubs, smoking, drinking, wearing short skirts or low-back sari blouses. My mother-in-law had a friend who married a railway officer and whose children studied in a convent school. She went to Kharagpur to visit them with my husband when he was small and was horrified by the children's free manners, foul language and fighting, and her friend's *memsaheb* deportment. It was all due to the railway colony, she said, which had made them westernized and she didn't dare take her son there again. Its influence would have spoilt his future. So, no, I wouldn't have liked really to be a *memsaheb*, then my deportment would have spoilt my husband's future also. It is good that I am innocent of such things.'

Suddenly there was a distance between us, which I wanted to dissolve. So I asked her how I could make sure that I wasn't mistaken for an immoral, badly behaved *memsaheb*.

Mrs Gupta enthusiastically advised, 'Maybe it would help if you wore a *shakha pola* bracelet and *sindoor* in your hair. These are the signs of a Bengali married woman. Then people are less likely to bother you with unwanted attentions. Have I taught you the word *lojja* yet, Laura? Write this down: *lojja kora*, to feel shy; *lojja hoya*, to feel ashamed; *lojja dewa*, to make somebody embarrassed. *Lojja* is a feminine emotion. When I first married my mother-in-law corrected me about this, telling me when to cover my head with my sari fall, scolding me for laughing and staring. I was so young then and finally understood why mothers-in-law were called *tiktikki* – lizards. She was always there watching from the corner of the room.'

Now, in public, I try as hard as possible to behave with appropriate *lojja*. The last thing I want to be seen as is a *memsaheb*. Hence my frantic efforts in this autorickshaw to wrap my *dupatta* back around me.

As the autorickshaw slows, trapped by a belching truck, I look up at the hoardings and shop signs that litter the roadside with hopeful claims. A notice reading 'Society for the Scientific Study of Astrology, computer horoscopes provided' is tied to the branches of a tree whose trunk is festooned with flower-offerings to Siva. 'Jack and Jill's Nursery School, English speaking teachers' stands above the grand arches of a crumbling mansion, once a home where traditional musicians gathered to entertain the extended family. 'Rapunzel Beauty Home, bridal makeup, *chandan* experts, women only', promises the smoked-glass window of a beauty parlour, which is guarded by a *durwan* in a red turban and the photograph of Miss World, Sushmita Sen. As the traffic speeds up again a rusted bus careers past painted with the words 'Kiss me quick' and 'pilot' above an aeroplane on the driver's door. The remains of last year's puja celebrations, an image of the goddess Durga slaying a lion, sponsored by the neighbourhood Marxist unit, lies dumped under a tree. All around fragments of Europe and India jostle against one another, making the familiar strange and the strange familiar. This cacophony exhilarates me; it is so unlike what I had expected, given my Sussex family's silence about the colonial past and my grandfather's dreams of exotic worlds. These streets speak of the past and refuse to remain exotic. In Calcutta, with the help of Mrs Gupta's transforming lessons, I am hopeful that I will be able to shake off all the conventions I've been served up.

But I'm heading for St James, a school that was founded in the 1890s to make such conventions stick. Raj officials and charitable societies had built many schools like this one for Eurasians. They were concerned by the scandal of white-skinned children running wild and going native in the bazaars. The only solution for their rootlessness, which threatened British prestige, was to scrub them down, teach them

41

about the Pennines, the robin redbreast, technical draughtsmanship, moral decency and the Norman Conquest. These children, the bastard sons of army officers or the offspring of temporary paper marriages contracted between Chinese tanners or Manila sailors and Eurasian women, were taken from their parents and placed within the walls of St James. As they entered the school they passed through a gateway of forgetting into a dream of Britain.

A few days ago in the National Library, the old Lieutenant Governor's mansion that is now filled with scholars rewriting the history of India, I had read the memos and reports of the pauperism commissions which led to the founding of St James. Lingering on the few words from Eurasians that appeared in the documents, I was shocked to discover that they were attributed only initials; they were anonymous, their lives transformed into mere case studies of the degeneration produced by cross-breeding. The fragments offered by the official documents seemed quite callously to reduce Anglo-Indians to a type. Rather than revealing rich details of their lives, they speculated lavishly on the causes of their meandering and wasted existence. Their 'type' was created, it was thought, by everything from early marriages and the consumption of spicy food, which made Eurasians licentious, to the degenerating influences of the Indian climate which turned the rosy cheeks of children into the sallow, hungry look of drunken footpath beggars.

Turning to Indian nationalist documents, I wondered if I would find a more sympathetic attitude. Leafing through a journal from 1920s Calcutta that was filled with accounts of constitutional reforms and progress in science, I could find only one article that gave a Bengali nationalist view of Anglo-Indians. The writer argued that Anglo-Indians corrupted the great heritages of India and Britain. Each culture had much to offer the world, but when they were confused in

Eurasian families only the worst qualities of both civilizations came out. Therefore such families should not be encouraged and could not contribute to the future of independent India. To prove his point he quoted Gandhi, who argued that Eurasians lived a 'false mode' of European existence in India. The nationalist and Raj documents simply mirrored each other. Looking around the elegant hall that once hosted the Lieutenant Governors' lavish recreations of London society events peppered with rajahs and attendants in traditional dress, I knew that I would find few clues to the real life of Anglo-Indians in the National Library.

This is why I am heading for the Founder's Day Service at St James; here there are many Anglo-Indian teachers. A friend, Annindita, who is married to an Anglo-Indian and works at the school, has promised to introduce me to them. Perhaps they can tell me more.

As Calcutta's hybrid street signs catch my eye again, I smile at the irony of that old Bengali nationalist's vision of an independent India untouched by Western pollutions. The autorickshaw draws up at the twin turmeric-yellow towers of St James's Church and groups of uniformed boys cluster around its gates chattering and buying *kathi* rolls. These Indian middle-class boys are now standing where Anglo-Indians had stood a century ago. Their parents have sent them here so that they can learn the class credentials, inflections of English and discipline they need to equip themselves for careers in the Indian Administrative Service or multinational companies. It is becoming clear to me that in looking for the meanings of British history in Anglo-Indian lives, I will also find out something about contemporary India.

Annindita waves at me from the gates. As usual her brusque schoolmarm manner, quick movements and clipped bob seem at odds with her ethnic cotton sari and the huge red *bindi* on her forehead. She hurries me through the Norman-arched doorway. Inside it is damp and musty, like an English parish church. The mahogany pews are filled with the sons of Bengal scrubbed down and uncomfortable in their starched uniforms. The assembled congregation sings the school song:

Ecclesia et Patria
We vow again our loyalty
To Mother-Church and to our land
We Jacobeans proudly stand
Knit by this bond of fealty
Our Church comes first – Ecclesia
God's brotherhood of every race
We'll raise the Cross in every place
Our land comes next – our Patria
This land of Ind where God had cast
Our lot, that we with service true
May bring to her some treasures new
Hail Alma Mater, hail, all hail
Unsullied will we bear abroad
The honour of the school we love.

I close my eyes and for a second I could be back in an assembly at St Paul's. But opening them again I'm not so sure. The walls of the church are Krishna blue, the robes of the Reverend Andrew Simick deep purple. Proud mothers wear chiffon saris and have their hair parted and marked with red *sindoor*. Sikh boys adjust their turbans in the heat. The boy sitting next to me seems to be murmuring the Koran under the Lord's prayer. But still pupils march like foot soldiers of the Raj to the altar to receive the honour of medals for achievements in their final examinations. The procession is accompanied by the singing of the senior choir conducted by Mr Gomes. They are joined with gusto by the voices of Anglo-Indian teachers among the congregation, recognizable from their Western clothes. They all seem to have been tailored from

44

illustrations in an Enid Blyton adventure: frocks and pearls, perfectly knotted ties, severely starched shirts and neatly ironed trousers. Their singing rises above the rote learning of the pupils and reluctant tones of their parents.

The congregation disperses for the rest of the day's events: a past-versus-present cricket match; performances of Aristophanes' *The Frogs*; and to view the history and science exhibitions in the classrooms. Annindita is rushing me from my seat to meet the other Anglo-Indian teachers. She points out a group of them, saying, 'The official constitutional definition of an Anglo-Indian is someone with a British ancestor somewhere in the male line of inheritance. But all the features get mixed up together, the worst of the Indian and the worst of the British. Still, you can always tell the Anglo ladies from their seductive walk and their frocks, of course – down south they are called frock people.' We make our way towards the small huddle of Western clothes among the saris, and Annindita introduces Gavin and Gary, who are brothers, Francis Gomes and Susannah Johnson. Despite their formal clothes, Gavin and Gary have identical clipped short-back-and-sides haircuts straight from *Rebel Without a Cause*. The only difference between them is Gavin's manicured moustache. Although they are both in their forties, they have the thin, muscular frames of a young James Dean. Yet their precisely ironed clothes and broad grins are very different from his teenage sulkiness. Francis sports an extravagant, long, pointed moustache, which may even be waxed, and a fluorescent tie covered in lime-green polo players. Susannah has the wavy bob, string of knotted pearls and pink flapper dress of a 'thirties socialite, though she is probably only a few years older than I am.

Everyone's welcoming smiles suggest that formalities are unnecessary, but Annindita introduces me: 'Laura's come here to study you and the railways.'

'You better write a spicy tale so it's just like us. We're hot and spicy like our food,' jokes Francis, turning the disapproving words of Raj officials into a tempting promise.

'You better tell me all the gossip then.'

'Oh, we're much too hot for you to handle,' flirts Gavin.

Growing nervous about the turn the conversation is taking, Annindita demurely arranges her sari.

Gary seems hesitant to speak and is standing back from the conversation, but suddenly asks, 'Are you sure you've not come just to prove that we are all British and get us passports?'

I feel embarrassed by his association of me with officials sitting in judgement on his identity, but before I can answer Francis teases, 'No chance of that for me, Gary. Where would I have a passport for? My mother was Anglo, my father's father West Indian, my wife's Chinese, regular United Nations I am.'

Susannah looks angry and fiddles with her long string of pearls. She can't resist making her statement of affiliations: 'Some of us know where we belong. My father was a British soldier and we are all moving to Australia as soon as the papers come through. There's a future for our children there, nothing here for them, even the Indians are leaving their own country.'

Everyone ignores her, apart from Annindita who nods in approval that there will be one less Anglo-Indian in India.

'Me and my brothers and sisters, all seven of us, grew up on the railways,' Gary says. 'We can help you with your research.'

'Yeah and it's made us full of steam. Should see us all when we get together for a drink, even Annindita because she's married an Anglo-Indian takes a nip now and then. What about that drink we had the other night, eh Mrs Annindita? Are you married, Laura? Even if you are, you better watch out for us,' Gavin flirts again, making Annindita search around in the crowd of sari-clad mothers for an excuse to end the conversation.

'Yes I am, actually.'

'Is he British or American?' Gavin enquires.

'He's from the Ivory Coast in Africa.'

Susannah looks shocked and there is a moment's silence before Francis smiles and chortles, 'Oh, you better come and talk to me then to get tips on all those United Nations peace negotiations you'll have to get into at home.'

Gary, who has been lost in thought for a while, begins to reminisce: 'That upcountry life on the railways was beautiful. When Anglos had to move from the railway colonies to Cal, they used to call it immigration. Those colonies were the proper Britain and all. Some of the old railway folk couldn't cope and threw themselves on the nearest railway track rather than live in the slums at Tangra. Only other place like it is this school, decent like.'

Gavin immediately dispels his brother's dream: 'Gary fancies himself as the last *saheb* turned a little brown in the sun. Don't pay any attention to him. Why don't you come over to have typical Anglo-Indian food just so we can get you all spiced up as well? Come to Gary's house this weekend, though you'll have to find your way through the Muharram crowds and all.'

'We'll introduce you to the whole jing bang family,' Gary promises. 'We've even got some foreign liquor. My uncle Leslie's staying too, he worked as a driver on the railways all his life.'

'You'll get some masala from him. Want to come too, Mrs Annindita?' adds Gavin cheekily.

'I'll definitely come,' I reply.

Annindita declines the invitation and is now desperate for a distraction. I am enjoying the restless movement of the conversation. If anyone starts to wax lyrical about Britain they are jumped on and teased mercilessly. As I note down the directions to Gary's house, right by the ice-skating rink, left past the *mishti* stall, Annindita finds her escape route: 'There's the son of a friend of mine. He was head boy in St James. Now he's an undergraduate studying sociology in Presidency College. He can be a great help to you. Take you to all the bookshops on College Street, introduce you to professors. He's a brilliant student.'

Before I have a chance to say goodbye, Annindita pulls me over to the brilliant student, who makes an eccentric introduction.

'Hello, my Bengali nickname – *dak nam* – is Bunty, but my given name is Subhrasheel. You can call me whatever you like.'

Feeling as though I have stumbled on to the set of some Indian version of *Tom Brown's Schooldays*, I say, 'I'll call you Subhrasheel, if that's OK?'

'Bunty's too Anglicized for someone as tribal Bengali looking as me?'

Ruffled, I try to explain: 'No, it's just Bunty makes me think of girls' hockey teams.'

'Well, maybe that's the only name that suits me after years in this school. Presidency College was a shock after all of this. My mentor now is a professor who wears a dhoti and whose life work is to apply Marxist theories to the countryside of Bengal. My classmates protest the introduction of Coke machines into the canteen as a symbol of multinational domination, but it makes a change from all of this! Annindita tells me you are studying Anglo-Indians. Have you heard the joke about the Anglo-Indian National Library? They lost the book.'

I smile, as Subhrasheel's joke captures exactly my experience so far. Although it's not really that the book has been lost, rather that it has never been written or, if it has, it hasn't made it through the doors of any national library.

Annindita laughs loudly: 'Yes, that's the problem

exactly, no heritage, no tradition, no culture. That's why Freddie and I make sure our daughter does her *kathakali* dance lessons regularly. We don't want her to end up like Gavin and Gary. Bunty will be able to teach you more about the real Calcutta than any of these types. You should spend some time with him. Then maybe you'll realize that you should choose a different subject from Anglo-Indians. There's really nothing to write about there of any value. Anyway, all the real ones have left long ago for Britain and Australia. The ones left here really aren't Anglo at all, just Indian Christians who have put on airs.'

Subhrasheel seems to agree with Annindita and offers his help in guiding me through a Bengali Calcutta: 'You should come over to my house next month. We're having a friend, a Baul singer, to visit. He lives with my aunt in Paris. You can taste some typical dishes and listen to some real traditions, ye olde folk music.'

I notice his voice has thickened with a Bengali accent as he says this, but he seems to want to share another joke as his tone turns into a parody of BBC English at the end. But I'm not sure if he's making fun of Annindita or me with this invitation. Annindita is now eager to show me the exhibition she and her students have assembled on the discovery of America by Christopher Columbus. We pass through the long corridors of the Upper School designed to reproduce the damp gloom of my homeland. There is no sign of Calcutta's burning sun inside these halls.

And there on the Upper School classroom walls is Columbus on his quest. Twin brothers stand by the display, which takes us from Spanish kings to the skyscrapers of New York. They are dressed in matching costumes of Columbus's cape, hat and gold cross of conquest. They take it in turns to give an account of the statistics of provisions, men and arms necessary for the journey and the fabulous fortunes heaped up after the arrival in America. As I congratulate them on their knowledge, one of the twins starts to ask me how he can get a scholarship to study at an American university. Annindita abruptly pulls me away to introduce me to Mr Lawrence-Penn, a governor of the school.

She whispers, 'He's another Anglo-Indian, he can help you too. Be polite.'

The governor pulls his broad shoulders into a military posture and pats his white hair, which is as stiff as a judge's wig. As I am now coming to expect, he announces his family heredity: 'I'm descended from the Penn family that founded Pennsylvania. That's why I'm so interested in this display, learning about the country my ancestors created. Never been there myself, must have more relatives there than here though by now. I've always wanted to go there.'

I am struck at this moment by an uncomfortable irony. Columbus set out with a dream of discovering a shorter route to the riches of India. When he stepped on to America's shores he thought he had realized his dream and was on Indian soil. Now for the Bengali twins dressed as Columbus and for Mr Lawrence-Penn, America, not India, is the promised land.

That old Bengali nationalist whose words I had read in the journal in the National Library would have been profoundly shocked by this Founder's Day. Everyone here seems to long for a future that has nothing to do with India, taught to dream of it inside the walls of this school as Eurasians were generations ago. But these Bengali schoolboys and their proud parents would refuse to admit their kinship to this Eurasian experience. Annindita, although she teaches here and has an Anglo-Indian husband, still speaks the nationalist's words of rejection. Perhaps these judgements are all about middle-class Bengali fears of admitting the relevance of the colonial past to their

50

present. Glancing at my watch, I make an excuse to leave: I have an errand to run before this evening's Bengali lesson.

Climbing down from a bus heaving with office workers returning home, I struggle to find a foothold on the cramped pavement. Rash Behari Avenue is filled with crowds either stalled in their tracks by an India-versus-Pakistan cricket match playing in the window of the Videocon shop or involved in the serious business of bargain-hunting among the make-shift stalls. Everything is for sale here, from cotton saris to willow-pattern china, from spicy pickles to the latest in sunglasses. Heading for Gariahat Market to buy *shakha pola* bracelets as Mrs Gupta advised, I enjoy the tumult, the unexpected collisions with passers-by and the overpowering noise of generators fuelling the lights of *paan* stalls. It is impossible to remain self-absorbed. The crowds constantly remind you that you are not alone, nor can you pretend to be invisible behind a book or newspaper as everyone does in London. There is no neutrality. Each journey takes you somewhere unexpected, as if the city had a plan of its own for you, formed from the multiple desires of all its inhabitants.

Reaching the entrance to Gariahat Market, I head for Babul's religious goods stall, where he sells conch shells, images of baby Krishna, small brass vessels for offerings and wedding regalia. But religious goods are rumoured not to be his main source of income, for he is a black marketeer and volunteer traffic officer. A commanding presence with a bristling moustache and eyes that are constantly weighing you up, he directs the traffic in, to say the least, an unorthodox manner which bears little resemblance to the city's official regulations. Some say he supplies illegal liquor to the traffic police when they are on their long weekend duties during *bandhs*, the political strikes that hit Calcutta every other week. I know he can procure cooking gas for me without the official ration card. He lives with his sister and her son, although there are those who speculate whether they are brother and sister at all. Somehow I relish the idea that it is from his stall that Bengali families buy tradition. Their daily pujas and marriage ceremonies are performed with accessories supplied by someone who doesn't even live up to simple ideas of decency and, what is more, is at the very centre of the black market that caters for South Calcutta's everyday needs. Much as I think that I should follow Mrs Gupta's advice and try to avoid traditional judgements of my *memsaheb* character by wearing *lojja* on my wrists, I'm secretly happy that I'm buying my *shakha pola* from Babul.

Babul greets me and to my delight insists on speaking Bengali and introducing me to the neighbouring stallholders. Purchasing the bracelets will be a lengthy transaction, more about christening a relationship than handing over money. As we sip from our clay cups of tea and munch on *moori*, puffed rice spiced with the pungent flavour of mustard oil, an old man shuffles up to us. Treading heavily on the squashed tuberoses and discarded vegetables, he is dishevelled and carrying a long wooden stick. Babul introduces him as the Professor. The Professor changes abruptly when he sees me.

'You're British?' he asks enthusiastically. I admit my origins and he launches into a speech: 'I wrote to Mrs Thatcher, a letter that held all my ideas for world peace. Get rid of the governments is what I said, none of this state business. I told her I admired all her measures to set people free from their tortures and machinations and intrusions. Privacy, private enterprise, I told her. Then we can be alone. Then we can follow our hearts. She's going to make me the head of her world government. She told me. I got her letter five years ago. She's just waiting for when all her pieces are lined up, then I'll get the call. You can join me in my scheme. Just make sure when you see her to mention my name, the Professor, Gariahat.'

Then, suddenly distracted, he says a courtly goodbye and disappears again into the crowd. Babul quietly tells me not to worry about the Professor. He is just harmlessly mad, a permanent fixture in the bustling market. No-one is quite sure what happened to the Professor. One rumour is that he was involved in the Naxalite Movement in the 1970s. As a student at Presidency College he was inspired by its promise of a Maoist peasant-led revolution, left his studies and took to the streets. With his comrades he hatched schemes to disrupt the status quo by planting bombs and preaching the cause in rural areas. He was arrested, tortured and imprisoned and, when he was finally released ten years later, he had gone mad. Others say he fell in love with an upper-caste woman at college. They met secretly in the Lakes, until her father found out. When she was married off to some-one else, he lost his mind.

As Babul opens the packets of red plastic and delicately carved shell bangles, I think about the Professor's tragedy. He had been sent mad by daring to break the rules of Bengali society, and here I am trying to conform to them. Now that I have seen the dark side of these rules, I'm not sure that I'm right to be so attracted by Mrs Gupta's offers of transformation into a traditional Bengali lady. Why has the Professor become obsessed with Margaret Thatcher? Is there some obscure link between Bengali tradition and her trumpeting of a return to Victorian values? As I make my way back to my flat, the newly purchased *shakha pola* feel heavy on my wrist and I have painful marks on my hand from forcing them there.

In my flat, Mrs Gupta's round face lights up with delight when she sees my *shakha pola*. She pulls up a low, intricate Rajasthani stool for me to sit on, watching to see whether I cross my legs like a *memsaheb*.

Arranged on the table ready for the lesson are a Bengali cartoon-book of the Jallianwallah Bagh massacre and a collection of Sukumar Rai's caustic nonsense rhymes.

Sighing with appreciation, she says, 'How wonderful, no-one could mistake you for *Tash* now. *Tash* is slang word for Anglo-Indians and Indian Christians. It means someone low class and of easy virtue. Sukumar Rai wrote a poem about this – here, see.'

She opens the book and points to a comic rhyme about a Eurasian clerk in ill-fitting Western clothes with a weak constitution and wavering values.

'We Bengalis fear such *jater dosh*, a mistake in the line, a cross-breeding with Anglos or foreigners that pollutes our cultural and family inheritance. It corrupts our blue blood and produces weak-willed types such as Sukumar writes about. You will understand now, having met those teachers in St James.'

She hesitates and then explains how she knows that such things are true: 'We had something like this in our family. My father's uncle went to Glasgow to study to be a doctor. He returned with a British wife with whom he had three children. Nobody liked him in the family, he was too Anglicized, almost like *Tash* himself. He was a very high aristocratic type always talking of clubs in Glasgow and his experiences in Europe. But he mentally tortured his wife and she ended up in Woodlands Nursing Home, dead. Poor thing, she just couldn't live up to the standards required of a proper Bengali wife. He married again, a Bengali woman this time.'

Curious about the three children and what had happened to them, I ask her about their fate.

'Oh, the family would have nothing to do with them. I first met one of his children at his funeral in Nimtollah burning ghat. Everyone was ignoring Shila, his daughter, as we watched her father's body burning in the flames. No-one had told her he had died even. She had read some announcement in the newspaper.

She looked so coarse, with heavy build and white pock-marked skin, with none of the sweetness of a Bengali face or the freshness of her pure European mother. I felt sorry for her. She was so alone and lost. I started to talk to her. She told me the whole story of that part of the family, which I'd never heard before.'

I sit up in expectation of hearing the story, pleased that Mrs Gupta had felt sympathetic enough towards Shila to ask her about her life.

'Her eldest brother had been tyrannized by his father and he ran away from home. They never heard from him again, but they think he went to Europe to serve in Second World War and died as an enlisted man. Her younger brother married a Bengali woman, but divorced her. Shila, just like an Anglo-Indian, didn't like studies much and left home at eighteen to be a nurse and got married to a Bengali and had a son. But she left him and her son for another man. The father sent the son to a boarding school in the hills, but he was like Shila, somehow restless and couldn't study. He came back to Calcutta during the 1970s Naxalite Movement, all that terrible violence in the name of Marxist revolution, and his father couldn't keep him at home. He was still so restless. He became involved with the Naxalites and went to live with Shila again.'

I'm intrigued that Shila's son, like Victoria Skinner, had chosen to run away from the hill school he had been sent to, back to his mother's home. But he, unlike her, had the option of joining a political movement that sought to undermine the elite society that wouldn't accept him. Perhaps he had been a comrade of the Professor. I ask Mrs Gupta what had happened to him, thinking that maybe I could talk to him about his experiences.

'One day Shila came back to her house to find the door locked. She took a ladder up to open the window and get in and found him with a noose around his neck hanging dead. When Shila told me this story at the burning ghat with all the other relatives looking on with disapproving stares, she began to cry. I felt so sorry that her father had started all this mess by marrying a British woman. It made all these rootless, cross-breed, low-moral types. This is what happens with *jater dosh*.'

Mrs Gupta is smiling in satisfaction at having proved her point. Abruptly she turns towards me taking my hand in hers and urgently advises, 'There's something I've been meaning to tell you, Laura. You mustn't have children with your husband, he's a different *jati* from you after all – something tragic like this will happen because of the *jater dosh*.'

All of Mrs Gupta's gestures of friendship seem to have been leading up to this. Her personal confessions and careful attentions were not gifts freely given. Instead she wanted to take charge of my wayward life and avert its inevitable tragedies. Drawing away my hand, I wince at the *shakha pola* bracelets. Mrs Gupta is a mistress of boundaries rather than of transformations. Victorian ideas of respectability and race, the same as I had read in the National Library, are embodied in the woman sitting beside me dressed in a chiffon sari. How could I have fallen for her offer of turning me into a traditional Bengali woman?

Turning my eyes away from Mrs Gupta out of embarrassment, I stare at a reproduction of a nineteenth-century Khalighat print on the wall above us. Before, I loved its thick brush-strokes, earth hues and exotic flavour, but now it looks different. It shows a beautiful, lascivious sari-clad woman, who sits insolently astride the shoulders of her husband and leads her mother-in-law on a chain. She is the new breed of modern wife, the *memsaheb*, produced by the *Kali yug*, the age of darkness and degeneration that British rule has brought to India. This moral tale that has circulated in cheap copies throughout the city for a hundred years epitomizes all of Mrs Gupta's desires and fears. She can never allow herself to become polluted like this *memsaheb* or like me. Mrs Gupta's notion of tradition is as misleading as that map of the British Empire which hung on the walls of my grandfather's classroom, and is only as old as that map too. She composes herself as a pure Bengali woman, without seeing that this image has its origins in Raj history. Looking down at the cartoon-book account of British brutality on the table, I know she has good reasons for rejecting the Raj, but I can't share her path.

Ironically, in trying to conform to the role of Lakshmi she displays all the genteel pleasures and habits of a Victorian lady. Her house, blood-red concrete floors scrubbed and window grilles dusted daily, is barred from the market commerce of Rash Behari Avenue one street away. Unlocking the four padlocks to the outside, she sends her maid there, so she doesn't have to experience the conspiracy of Marwari traders and Bihari day-labourers to transform South Calcutta back into the den of thieves it was before the land was reclaimed by the British in the 1920s. A famous dacoit in the older days of highway robbery built a Kali temple just a few steps from where the market now is and his thieving ways seemed to Mrs Gupta to be returning through the broken concrete and in the chaos of hawkers and impolite stares.

She prefers the polite bargaining of the Good Companions Shop where she volunteers once a week, taken by her driver who since her childhood has safely deposited her wherever she needed to go so that she could avoid using the city's footpaths. Here she comes every week to sell needlepoint cushion covers, strawberry-embroidered tablecloths and daffodil-edged handkerchiefs made by poor *adivasi* women for wedding trousseaux, even though she knows that the other upper-caste ladies there sneer at her darker skin. Mrs Gupta continues the work of the British missionaries who set up the charity shop to generate income for the *adivasi* women they thought they were reforming from their wandering ways. Her siege mentality is an old tradition in her family. Through these same barred windows her mother-in-law silently watched drunken British Second World War troops molest a young Bengali woman, dragging her off into a gully. From these windows Mrs Gupta told me she also watches as the rickshaw pullers fresh from the village – 'so handsome, with muscles gleaming' – turn old after two monsoons. When her husband dies and her son has married she plans to live in the two-room flat I occupy. All you can see from its window is the jackfruit tree and the daily routine of her eighty-year-old gardener who looks like a sketch from a yellowing Bengali memoir. Suddenly the flat doesn't feel like a peaceful haven and I don't think I can be at home here. This house feels too much like a Victorian castle fit for a princess. The vassals, the impure and the immoral are kept outside its gates in a British fairy tale of Bengali purity. Remembering the irreverent conversation of Gary, Gavin and Francis at St James, I know that they challenge not only the notions of British identity that I came here to dispel, but also Mrs Gupta's ideas of traditional purity.

I walk to Gary's flat through the narrow streets of Beck Bagan as Muslim families ready themselves for Muharram celebrations. Hindi film music blares from neighbourhood stages and children pull at the green and gold tinsel streamers on models of mosques that will be carried through the streets. This used to be a purely Anglo-Indian neighbourhood, its limits mapped by Park Circus and the Church of Christ the King. Older Bengali friends have told me of the infamous delights of Anglo-Indian prostitutes who used to ply their trade on these streets. Now Muslims have moved in, pushed here by Hindu families refusing to rent out their properties to them. I ask directions to the flat from a group of boys playing street-cricket, and once they hear the address, they are no longer so curious about what I'm doing here. I must be some Anglo relative of the Jones family retracing old connections. Climbing a narrow, grimy staircase to Gary and Carol's top-floor flat I pass a crumpled old man who is sleeping next to a scrawny street-dog and a woman who bends over a kerosene stove, shielding her sari from the flames.

Inside the three-room flat crowded with furniture and people, lessons are being recited. Gary is presiding over a group of schoolboys gathered around a heavy dining table. Pink and white chintz curtains barely shelter the room from the burning sun that streams through the windows. The peeling avocado-green walls are hot to the touch, a disadvantage of living on the top floor, but then this is the only accommodation the family can afford. The heat of the living room increases as Carol, Gary's wife, cooks on three roaring gas stoves hidden behind a thin wooden partition with a giant dresser wedged against it. The pungent scent of frying garlic and ginger paste makes the assembled boys cough. Gary continues to tell them a story about how Atul was a good boy who saved up all his pennies to help his mother buy *subjhi* and *rotis*. The lace tablecloth is littered with exercise books. Gary is wearing shorts and a T-shirt that proclaims, 'I love Australia'. Yet he is giving a history lesson that weaves between Gandhi and St Francis of Assisi as models of courage and good works. Enjoying the eclectic sources of his moral tales, so unlike Mrs Gupta's lessons, I wait for the tuition to end. Occasionally Gary's wife, Carol, slips into the room to retrieve something from the refrigerator crawling with cockroaches, which hums violently in an attempt to counteract the heat.

The schoolboys scramble for the door, relieved to

escape the stifling room. Carol covers the table with what Gary calls a typical Anglo-Indian feast. Her long black hair is matted to her forehead with sweat from cooking and her skimpy black blouse and Chinese silk skirt stick to her body.

Gary winks at me and says, 'Look how beautiful my wife is. Even though she's an Anglo, she is so fair like a foreigner. Her face is my fortune, or perhaps my misfortune.'

Carol flirts back, 'Stop admiring then and start helping or I'll go and seek my fortune with someone else.'

Smiling happily from the affectionate scolding, he scurries into the kitchen to help her carry in the dishes. Carol obviously hasn't ever had to restrain herself under the watchful eyes of a *tiktikki*. The smell of chillies and coriander steams from plates of yellow rice and ball curry, roast beef spiced with masalas, Knorr's thick chicken noodle soup and potato chops.

Once the rest of the family arrives we settle down for the meal, heaping it up on steel *thalis*. Gary and Carol's children, Isolde, Lorissa and Theodore, squabble companionably over the food. Isolde is stunningly beautiful in a miniskirt and platform shoes. Gary proudly teases her, saying that she is sweet sixteen but he's not sure that she has never been kissed. Mrs Gupta and Shakuntala would be outraged by such a direct reference to affairs of the heart. Lorissa has all the self-consciousness of a thirteen-year-old and is uncomfortable in her flowery lace frock, which is bursting at its seams. Theodore, at seven, is a miniature Gary in shorts and T-shirt emblazoned with an American flag. Lila, Gary's sister, is delighted by the dish of roast beef, explaining that now she is married to a Hindu she rarely has an opportunity to eat it. Despite her Anglo-Indian appetites, she looks very much a demure Bengali wife in her emerald-green cotton sari and a glinting nosering. Arjun, her eight-year-old son, stares disapprovingly at his mother as she takes another helping. Gavin flirts occasionally with any woman in range. Leslie, Gavin and Gary's uncle, hovers in a corner nursing a glass of rum, showing no interest in the food. He is shrunken and lined from years of work as a railway driver, his hands knotted and calloused from hard labour. Once he must have been very good-looking and his neatly slicked-back hair and red check shirt show that he still takes pride in his appearance. The conversation that randomly shifts between English, Hindi and Bengali is almost as exhilarating as the hybrid, spicy food.

As we eat, our fingers stain with turmeric and oil. Photographs of the family's ancestors watch us. Above the dining table Carol's father and Gary's parents stare down, their clothes and the scenery retouched with pinks and blues to make them more vivid as time passes. Carol's father stands over the body of a now lurid lemon-yellow panther, rifle in hand. Gary's mother in a stylish 1940s suit and his father, wearing a tie which sports a cricketer in mid stroke, look improbably fashionable in front of a small red-brick railway driver's quarters. The neat frames, the strings of tuberoses draped around them and the intense colours of the photographs show that these are treasured possessions. In other places Sharukh Khan and Monisha Koirala film posters hang next to images of the Sacred Heart.

The meal over, Carol and I go into the bedroom. Presiding over it is a wooden shrine to Mary and Jesus. Bedecked with candles and incense, it is very similar to Mrs Gupta's puja shrine to Lakshmi. We swap Christmas cake recipes. Carol's contains *suji*, ghee, cardamoms and orange marmalade. As we turn the pages of her recipe book, I glimpse instructions for making *kul kul*, rose biscuits, monaco rolls and potato mash and prawns. Carol proudly shows me a rose sari in luminous nylon and huge costume-jewellery earrings, which she will wear later that day to a friend's Hindu wedding. She explains, 'Sometimes we have to change out of our national dress into that of Indians. They always tell us that we should wear it all the time, but why should we? We have a right to our traditions too.' Mrs Gupta would still be scandalized by Carol's showy taste, even if she was wearing a sari.

After gossiping with Carol some more, we rejoin the rest of the family in the other room. Carol and I sit next to Lila and Isolde, sinking into a huge lace-covered settee that is uncomfortable in the sweltering heat. Lorissa, curled in a corner, is lost in the pages of a detective novel, *The Cheshire Cat Murders*. At our feet Theodore and Arjun, Lila's son, are playing World Wrestling Federation snap. Leslie fidgets, perched on one of the dining-room chairs, sipping on another rum. Conscious of my Britishness, he snaps at Theodore, telling him to sit properly on a chair in my presence. Theodore ignores him and Gavin teases Leslie, 'Don't mind him, Laura, he's the only one around here who thinks he's true-blue, can't get all that boarding school education out of his system.' Leslie sinks into lonely silence again.

Undisturbed by our conversation, Isolde watches her idol Sharukh Khan on television in a Hindi film, *Kabhi Ha Kabhi Na*, set in Goa. She breaks her concentration to explain that it is an Anglo-Indian story in which the Christian heroine doesn't end up with the Hindu hero, but in a white wedding dress marrying a fellow Christian. Isolde has seen the film many times before and says that she would choose Sharukh Khan any day rather than the Christian fellow. Relishing this disregard for the niceties of caste and community, I ask her what other Hindi movies she likes. She watches any of them, but her heroine is Rekha as Madam X, who takes revenge on men who have mistreated her. But then, drawing herself up with the self-possession and strength of her heroine, she has a furious outburst:

'But I hate that movie, *Julie*, the one about the Anglo-Indian railway colony girl. Even though it's so old, from the 1970s, all the boys on the streets bring it up when they try their dirtiness on me. Do you know the story? Julie is taken advantage of by the Indian railway engineer's son, she gets pregnant and has a bastard child. It was the first time they showed unmarried sex in a Hindi movie. The actress couldn't get any work again after that. It ruined her career to play an Anglo girl and do such things on screen. She couldn't escape the scandal and now us Anglo-Indian girls have to suffer the shame of it as well.'

She is distracted from her outrage by a song sequence in which Sharukh Khan shocks a group of nuns on a Goan beach by proclaiming his love for the Christian heroine. Every day on the streets of Calcutta, Isolde reaps the salacious glances inspired by *Julie* and *Kabhi Ha Kabhi Na*. Yet she doesn't believe in these celluloid lessons. Instead she imagines herself as a formidable Madam X and dreams of Sharukh Khan as her boyfriend, ignoring the happy ending of *Kabhi Ha Kabhi Na*, which prescribes that communities should marry only within their boundaries. I wish I could introduce her to Shakuntala.

Praising the roast beef again, Lila explains that the only parts of her old life she hasn't given up are Jesus and an enthusiasm for this dish. Her Bengali husband refuses to sleep in the same bed as her when she has eaten it, but she still can't give it up. Jesus she also keeps in her life. Her mother-in-law has let her put an image of Jesus in the family puja room ever since she gave birth to a son. Laughing, she remembers her father-in-law's horror when she ate with the family the first time and she used her left hand. He stood up and walked out of the room. She learnt her lesson and has converted from a 'lefty'.

I ask her where she met her husband. Smiling with the romance of her memory, she says that he started

63

chatting to her in a nightclub and bought a motorcycle just so he could take her for rides on the outskirts of Calcutta, well out of the range of his relatives' prying eyes. They convinced his parents to let them marry by an act of subterfuge. Worried by their son's bachelorhood, his parents had advertised for brides in the newspaper. Lila sent her biodata and a photograph of herself dressed up in a sari to the post office box number. After perusing the candidates, her husband insisted that he wouldn't marry anybody but her. Lila's fair skin, demure outfit, convent education and impressive salary captivated his parents, so they agreed. Remembering Helen Skinner and Thomas John's conversion to Islam, I realize that Lila and her husband are not the first lovers to find a way round Mrs Gupta's rules of appropriate matrimony.

Gavin and Gary return from clearing up in the kitchen and I ask them about the photographs staring down from the walls. They produce a family photo album and start reminiscing. Curious, I ask about their ancestry, especially how or when their British relatives came out to India. The silence is palpable and uncomfortable. Everyone shifts in their seats and looks awkward as if I had said the most shocking thing imaginable. This is strange: Lila, Carol and Isolde had not hesitated to tell me intimate details of their lives earlier. Every Bengali I have met so far is quite happy to list generations of ancestors.

'Well, I'm not too sure about my mother, though she's from an old South Indian Anglo family,' Gary bravely volunteers. 'My father was from Rangoon, but his grandfather came out from Britain in the army or navy or on business. We know the certificates are in London, but we can't afford to get them. My uncle, who married my mother's sister, was British and worked on the European scale of wages on the railways all his life. My father always said his oldest ancestor was a relative of Sir William Jones. He ran away from

Britain to India after some family scandal. I've got relatives all over now, Australia, New Zealand, Croydon, San José.'

I realize I have blundered into a sensitive area and it may seem as though I too am challenging the family's whole sense of identity. But I'm still not sure exactly why my question is so threatening.

As Gary points to the photographs on the wall, I understand that they are some of the rare pieces of evidence of their family heritage actually in their possession.

'That picture of my parents on the wall was taken in the railway colony at Addra,' says Gary. 'That's where we grew up, all of my brothers and sisters.'

'Is this a picture of you when you were young?' I ask, pointing to two young boys festooned in racecourse tickets, playing cards and holding an empty whisky bottle.

'Yes, we were all dressed up for a pagal gymkhana in the railway colony,' Gary replies. 'We went as Daddy's pastimes. You know the joke? In this family now, we'd have to call it Mummy's pastimes, eh Carol?'

Carol pretends to be annoyed by this slur on her character and a flirtatious glance passes between them. Gavin laughs at the affectionate tension between his brother and sister-in-law. I relish this open display of love, unhindered by *lojja*.

'What's a pagal gymkhana?' I ask.

'It's a fancy dress, organized in the railway colonies by the Anglo-Indian Association,' Gavin explains. 'But you had to dress up in something totally different, like a man had to dress up like a woman and imitate a woman, something like that, or you had to imitate some type of actor. It was really fun and they were giving good prizes. Once I went dressed as yellow rice and ball curry with a yellow turban on my head and naked apart from a lungi, the brown of the curry was my skin. The name "pagal gymkhana" means "the club gone mad".'

I want to linger in this moment, which seems to capture this family's attitude to their identity, which is something shifting, malleable, a momentary dressing up that isn't limited by the past and doesn't predict the future. Maybe this pagal gymkhana can be my new home in Calcutta. Perhaps I can even rent a room in the same building as Gary and Carol. It is much more attractive than the sombre, judgemental atmosphere of Mrs Gupta's house. But as I am turning these ideas over in my mind, Leslie unexpectedly sits up in his chair and begins to speak.

'That railway life wasn't all good. Us Anglos are always restless, can't find a home anywhere. I've felt like that since a child. I was sent off to boarding school from Addra to Woodcot in Bangalore. Couldn't stand the place, so still and quiet and routine. I used to run away all the time, took to the tracks until I was back in Addra. I thought working on the railways would suit my nature. Used to love rushing from station to station, smart clothes packed in my driver's box ready to take out for the dance in the next colony. Stopped the train wherever I liked and went and hunted deer in the jungle. Could make my home on any platform, just lay my bundle down in the drivers' restroom.'

His spirit of nostalgia slips away, and grabbing the arm of his chair he continues, 'But that restlessness feels different now. I can't ever sit still. Always have to be on the move, walking round the house even. When I think about the past all I can see is every detail of the track I used to drive between Asansol and Addra. I tried to settle in the village outside Addra. When I woke up each morning in my railway quarters, I used to watch the villagers in the paddy fields and the rice growing. I wanted to live there. It looked so peaceful and Indian. Even tried it for a while. Took up with a village woman after I retired from the railways. But I got sick and had to go to Valliankarni church for a pilgrimage cure. When I got back to the village my girlfriend had married someone else. So I had to move on again. Never could find a home anywhere.'

Carol adds sadly, 'It's true what you say, Leslie, but it's other people who make us feel we don't have a home. On the streets of Calcutta taxi drivers never believe I live here. Always try to overcharge me like a tourist and all. That's why my fair face is a misfortune. Then I set them right in Bengali. And all that dirtiness, molestation and what they call eve-teasing me and my children get on the streets here. One man tried to grab Isolde the other day, taking advantage in the cover of the crowd. When I made a fuss, the crowd took the man's side, saying I shouldn't use such bad language and that my children and I weren't respectable. One proper-looking Bengali man picked up a shoe to hit me with. We know we belong here, but no-one else does. I've even got one Anglo friend who says he won't have any children, he doesn't want to continue a mixed-up race that nobody here will accept.'

Lila nods in agreement. 'Even though my Bengali mother-in-law is proud of my fair skin and convent education she has given me a Hindu name. She pretends I'm an Indian Christian rather than admit that her son has married an Anglo-Indian.'

Is it these hostile reactions to their mixed roots that are responsible for their ashamed silence at my question earlier? Not wanting to risk offending them again, I ask if these experiences have ever made them feel they want to move somewhere else, to Britain perhaps?

There is a pause and then Carol replies: 'Maybe my children would have a better future there, but I don't know if we would be light-skinned, white enough so that people would let us fit in there either. We'd never be allowed to be proper British like you can be.'

Trying to lighten the mood, Gary starts to sing and

within a line or two Carol, Gavin and Leslie are joining in. Laughing, Gary breaks off for a moment to whisper, 'It's Uncle Bert's version of "Oh to be in England" by Harry Belafonte!'

'Oh to be in England now the spring is here
Oh to be in England, drinking English beer
Boiled potatoes, roast beef and Yorkshire
   pudding too
That is what you always find upon a set menu
They don't know that I could work an Anglo
   English Fry
Tell me have you ever heard of snake and
   kidney pie
British people watching television every day
When the kiddies go to sleep they show the sexy
   play
They don't know that washing powder selling
   on the screen
Changes garments, clothings, skin into white like
   you've never seen.'

As they sing I stare at my hands, which look whiter than they ever have before. And I feel the privilege, the passport, they provide to indulge myself with ideas about transforming my identity. Mrs Gupta had welcomed my attempts to become like a Bengali woman because she thought that I, like her, had pure blue blood. This is a luxury that this family doesn't have. They are not allowed to belong anywhere, so experiments with their identity are forced on them, producing a restlessness not of their own making.

At the end of the song Leslie, a little drunker now, asks me about my husband back in America: 'Since the age of seventeen I've tried all sorts of women on my runs round the country, Oriya women, Bihari women, Bengali women and I know all about life from this. This kind of life is only natural, you know. No man or woman can stay without company for more than six months at a time. Don't take offence, but this isn't possible. Your husband and you are fretting about each other and if someone else comes to comfort then how could you or him resist? Even those Bengalis are the same, though they pretend they're holier than thou. Mrs Basu who lives upstairs to me was throwing her sari and blouse from the balcony the other day and asking me to pick them up. I offered to climb up to her on her sari blowing in the wind, just like Romeo and Juliet I said. She didn't look offended, looked quite pleased and all despite her proper airs. See, Laura, you also have to ask yourself, why did your husband let you leave him so easily and why did you go?'

Amused by Leslie's puncturing of Mrs Gupta's version of Bengali women's *lojja*, I'm nonetheless uncomfortable that he has turned the tables and is asking me about my private life. He is sowing seeds of doubt about my motives for being here.

'We trust each other. There's nothing to worry about there, we're very faithful,' I protest. But I am wondering why this question has never arisen before. Maurice had willingly let me go, proud of my academic ambitions, and I had not thought twice about it because I was so caught up in my subject. Feeling oddly guilty that I am here on a personal quest that doesn't include Maurice and is a luxury the Joneses will never have, I make an excuse to leave.

To clear my head I walk towards Gariahat junction, losing myself in the sheer pleasure of being part of the heaving crowd. A scruffy tourist is gripping a leaflet from a local ayurvedic store and a vial of homeopathic pills in his sweating hands. A patriarch passes by clutching a shopping bag overflowing with *ilish* fish, *karela* gourds and Cadbury's chocolate. Housewives are carrying cheap cooking oil stamped United States Government Aid, not for sale, bought on the way home from a stall outside Mother Theresa's mission.

Pulling my *dupatta* lower on my chest, I check to see if my *bindi* has slipped. A clerk, pens in pocket, trousers still neatly creased, leaps from a moving bus in front of me. He veers towards me. Hand reaching for my breast he says, ' "Real thing, baby, aha," ' and disappears. Suddenly I know that these streets do not promise liberation from conventions. Standing here making my choices of left or right, picking my way through the crowd, I stir up a series of old associations for Calcutta's inhabitants. For Mrs Gupta, I'm the hope and fear of freedom from Bengali tradition. For the Professor I am an emissary from Margaret Thatcher. For Gavin, Gary, Carol and Leslie by virtue of my white skin I am someone who, unlike them, could find a home in Britain. For this office-going clerk I'm part of an ad for Pepsi or Coke and easy game for eve-teasing because I am, after all, a *memsaheb*. Smiling bitterly at my earlier innocence, I realize that the layers of Raj history all around make personal transformations impossible. I become even more determined to expose them.

3

A Seance of Scandals

A cycle-rickshaw rattles past the railway inspectors' guest house and a breeze disturbs the velvet curtains, displaying their stained lining. They flutter quickly back to the floor like ruffled petticoats ashamed of being revealed. I wait for Subhrasheel to speak in the eerie green half-light still cast by the signal lamp. The rats are now scurrying boldly around the top of the mosquito nets. Subhrasheel is too lost in thought to notice them, the scar above his right eye twitching as it seems to do when he is disturbed. But then he comes to and, with a sadness in his voice, admits that he had discovered the secret of St James himself but had kept quiet about it.

'I was doing some research for the school magazine on St James' history. We wanted to do a special issue to celebrate its hundred and fortieth anniversary. I was shocked when I read that it was founded for Eurasian orphans and bastards. All my classmates' parents were so proud that their children were being taught in such a true-blue school and they would have been devastated to learn its origins. I lost all faith in the place. When our headmaster or teachers were scolding us about our muddy shoes, lack of sportsmanship or bad English accents, I had a secret weapon against them.'

Subhrasheel, like myself so long ago in St Paul's, had felt distant from the collective hallucination that was his school.

'Even though I kept my discovery a secret I often wondered about all those generations of Anglo-Indian boys who passed through St James. Tell me what you have found out about them.'

I wish that I could describe the lives of his predecessors in St James, but the documents in the National Library have given me so little to go on.

'I've only managed to uncover the barest details,' I explain. 'It's so frustrating. I want to give them back a character and a voice, but I can't.' I tell him what I know from the National Library about one of them. He was called as a witness before a pauperism commission in 1890. He had made a statement, listed under the anonymous initials AB:

I'm thirty-two years old, a bachelor. My father was a European soldier and my mother a Eurasian. I was educated at Moorgehatta orphanage and then at St James School. The school got me into the fitting shop of the East Bengal Railway. After three months the workshop was abolished. I then obtained work in the Entally workshops, stayed three months after which I resigned as I received no pay. During these six months my mother supplied me with clothes. I fell in among the troupe of the Attorney General, a retired circus performer who led a band of beggars and drafted petitions for us. I had a pitch for begging outside the United Services Club. After this I was a barman at a native liquor shop in Chowringhee. Then joined Wilson's Circus for eighteen months. I left the Circus at Allahabad. Then I was appointed on Tirhoot State Railway as a second guard and was discharged on reduction of establishment. I then came down to Calcutta. Since then I have had no regular work. I support myself by selling cigars on commission and by playing in a Foo Foo band. The pay does not include food, at all times plenty of drink is to be had at the weddings. The bands play chiefly at native weddings. I am not of intemperate habits and I have been strictly temperate for six or seven years. I get my food from the tiffin ground where gentlemen's servants bring leavings of their master's tiffins.

Reading between the lines, it is easy to imagine AB standing stiffly in front of disapproving Raj officials, desperate to prove that he is not intemperate, feckless or degenerate. But as for providing a picture of what his life was actually like, there is very little here.

Subhrasheel is not satisfied by my reluctance to speculate: 'But, Laura, you're not trying hard enough.'

Suddenly Subhrasheel folds his legs, consciously parodying a poster of Siva meditating, and calls forth a creaking groan from the mattress. Reaching his hands across the space separating our two beds, with the fake drama of a fairground master of ceremonies he proclaims, 'Let's try to bring AB's voice back! Put your palms in mine and let the seance begin.'

A soft regular thudding makes its way down the tarmac road past the crenellated red-brick church. Echoing in the colonnade of Billimoria's liquor shop at the end of the street, it draws closer. Laughing with half-scared relief, we realize it is not an uninvited spirit attracted by our game, but only the railway police nightwatchman's lathi striking the ground. He is checking for drunks, lovers and villagers hunting for scraps of railway property to pilfer. Yet the sound jars because it revives the long history of Raj regulations that still patrol Kharagpur. Subhrasheel ignores the insistent thuds and begins to imagine himself as AB.

'I stood stock still before St James School after a day's train ride from Moorgehatta, hungry and dusty from the journey, wondering how I would take the school's boiled cabbage and beef running red with blood that my ma said my father, just like a Blighty *saheb*, loved to eat. I tried to forget my Hindi and all. English had to be my mother tongue now. What stories would I tell the other boys about my father I'd never seen? I practised a lie about how my pa was a descendant of Sir William Jones. I remembered the name from a book that was on the shelf above the desk of the vice president of the orphanage. It had looked so pure in its shiny gold leaf. I looked at it long and hard to forget the pain while the *saheb* gave me a tight slap for eating Indian style with my hands. I wondered who St James was and what a Jacobean is. A Jacobean must be something like the sons of Jacob. Or something to do with my Sunday School lessons from the St James Bible, lessons I fidgeted through, longing to play in the shameless bushes outside, whose shady cover meant fun, games and wickedness. I thought maybe once I joined the school I wouldn't be asked any more about my ancestors. I could just tell everyone I was the son of the Bible, a Jacobean. God whose voice boomed through the daily sermons in the orphanage could be my father. If God was my pa then no-one could ever taunt me into bazaar fights by calling me a bastard son of a prostitute.

'Then I held myself back, suddenly fearful of the school's iron gate. What of my ma who had come every weekend to the orphanage calling me *beta* and bringing spicy *aloo* chops? She had rocked me to sleep so sweetly as I lay across her stomach singing, "Jack and Jill went up the hill to fetch a pail of *pani*, but Jack fell down and broke his topi and Jill came tumbling after." It was her that I must forget, and tell lies instead about a father I had never seen. But still I stepped across the threshold to my new kin and country.

'And look at my descendants, those Anglo-Indian schoolteachers like Gavin, Gary and Susannah. The only place they have found a home in this city is in the school that teaches them to forget they are Indian as much as they are British. Nothing will ever change for us. The British *saheb* told us to keep on the red, white and blue side of the world and now the Bengali *sahebs* only give us jobs here in the part of India that will be forever Britain where they think we belong.

'We should all have listened to the Attorney General. I met him in a gully beside a photographer's in New Market. He was renting out ladies' hats flush with red feathers, silver-topped canes, fancy watch-chains and army uniforms to the families from Dhurrumtollah who were waiting for their turn to sit in front of the lens and the country house backdrops inside. I was just fresh turned out from the railway, still wearing the uniform jacket the company had made me purchase before my first wages. He called out to me, "Hey, *chokra*, I'll give you fifteen rupees for that jacket." That was more than I'd made in a whole month before, so I took him up on his offer. But then we got to talking. I liked the look of his flashing green-grey eyes and strong build like a West Indian sailor. He looked like he knew things about the docks and highfalutin clubs of the city that I would never know. I asked him about his business:

' "Oh I'm a fixer, an arranger, a ringmaster for this circus all around. I used to be in the circus, but I left it because the wider world was a bigger, better show to manage. There's real prospects here. See these *kintal* folk lining up for my wares, I'm selling them back the self that they never had. They can make-believe they are true-blue lords and ladies for a few minutes. They're not the only ones putting on the greasepaint. Inside that *palki* over there is the wife of one of those North Calcutta Zemindar bigwigs. Two generations back his grandfather had no land. He hung around the East India factories arranging nautch girl displays and teaching Bengali and Sanskrit to the Company's officers, had an enthusiasm for raunchy *kobi gaan* songs as well, staying up all hours. Then he got himself into spying on Suraj just before Palassey. There he was after the battle was over suddenly with a grant of land from the Company and putting on airs. Then he set about collecting together a crowd of pandits to research and write down a perfect pedigree with some Rajput princes thrown in way back. Ever since then his sons and grandsons recite it at their weddings and lecture their wives to only travel in *palkis*, hidden from view. Suddenly the Bengalis became true-blue as well. See, it's all greasepaint, I could take you and make you into anything with the fancy stuff on my stall here. After a while even you would believe it too, but don't ever make that mistake, my lad. All those fancy hill schools and the plains varieties, St James, La Martinère and those pandits and Arya Samaj missions and those priests reciting catechism, they all try their best to make you think everyone can only be one thing, Indian or British, but me and my wares know there's no such thing. That's the secret of us Eurasians. That makes the *sahebs* of all colours so nervous about us, always wanting to put us back in some place."

'The Attorney General was right and all. I took instruction in the arts of begging and petition writing from him for a while, sitting over good beer and noodles in one of those Chinese joss houses full of gambling and opium smoke late into the night, learning the arts of pleading and disguise. But after all, I realized, however many times he called himself the Attorney General, he wasn't on the Queen's service in India with a cushy pension and furlough back home every year and I was still a beggar worrying my ma in her old age. He might have found out the secret of us Eurasians, but the world wasn't ready to hear about this kind of invention. It wasn't like one of those patents turning him a pretty penny. And still the world isn't ready to hear it. I fell out with him and left with

Wilson's Circus. There all the make-believe could earn you a living, not just put you back in your place with a cold look or a tight slap of a teacher's cane or policeman's lathi. And look at all my descendants here in Calcutta singing their praises to the Lord and Crown and Country. At least I knew I was working in a circus. None of those in Calcutta – Sikh, Hindu, Anglo-Indian, Muslim – have a clue they're in one.

'Oh and those long corridors that shut out Calcutta from St James. I couldn't forget them even after I had left. Just arrived in the school I thought all of Britain was these long, cavernous, windowless spaces, neat and ordered for columns of identical boys to march through on some efficient journey into the future, the heads of teachers appearing round doors to check on their progress. When I got my place as an apprentice on the railway, I used to wander after hours through the European first-class coaches when they were stationary in the shunting yard, just to get a taste of those corridors again. The coaches were so like the corridors, always travelling through India at night, window grilles battened according to the regulations for the heat, but more likely just so the colonial dignitaries inside could keep their minds straight on course for Britain, not even knowing India was outside. Guards appearing to check their rights to be there, stamping their tickets, clearing the footplates of stray beggars and curio sellers. I don't know why I wanted to be inside them again. I hated the corridors and the carriages, but I always dreamed of them. Climbed inside them whenever I could. Even years later when I was travelling with the circus. They somehow gave my loafing a direction, a destination other than just keeping body and soul together and following the annas wherever they could be made. I felt for a moment like that Columbus pasted to the walls of the school, a man with a mission. But to tell the truth he didn't really know where he was going

77

either. Just thought he did. Probably just after money too. Then he reached his goal, the shores of India, to find something very different from what he expected. Everyone in this city, they've all forgotten me, disowned me on their corridor journeys from a glorious national past into a national future. That's my British Bengali lesson to you.'

Subhrasheel lets the imaginary voice of AB die away and I start to wonder how much of the story he has conjured up and how much the attitudes and experiences are actually his own. I look puzzled and he knows what I am about to ask him. Before I can utter a word he smiles wickedly and says, 'But that's the point of seances and mediums. It becomes impossible to separate yourself from the long dead speaking through you.'

Relaxing, I smile back at him, sensing the deep understanding he has of the confusions that are at the very heart of Anglo-India and which I had found distilled in the halls of the Eastern Railway headquarters, a grand architectural replica of a Moghul palace, built by the British. It was a chance encounter at Subhrasheel's house that had persuaded me to go there.

4

The Moghul Palace

Wincing at the sound of Mrs Gupta fulfilling her duty by pounding spices on the *shilnora* upstairs, I dress carefully for the evening of Baul music that Subhrasheel promised a month ago at St James. Since then he has often turned up at my door, offering tickets for a rock show, book-buying expeditions to College Street or *dosas* at a South Indian restaurant. As we ride to our destinations he jokes in the breathless tones of a tour guide, 'On our left we have the Victoria Memorial, a white elephant built with stone exported from Wales'; 'On our right we have the Tourist Board of India-approved snake charmer, must be a few tigers around the corner too'; 'Straight ahead is where you can take your obligatory photograph of a beggar,' until we giggle into silence. Everywhere we end up in the city he meets one of his friends, whom he greets as appropriate with rough Bihari Hindi, chaste Bengali or clipped English. They vary from pigtailed schoolgirls and Anglo-Indian clerks to drug addicts he used to gamble with and neighbourhood *goondas* who handle vote-rigging and black market activities. He ignores the street railings separating him from them and leaps over the barriers before I know he is gone. Intensely curious, he gossips with autorickshaw and taxi drivers just to hear about their lives. He is equally keen to know the details of my life, throwing questions into the air and watching for the effect they will have, and I enjoy being part of his collection of unlikely friends.

I'm not sure what to wear tonight. Although Bengali tradition has been promised, Sharmila, Subhrasheel's aunt, and Pobon, the Baul singer, who live together in Paris, hardly conform to Mrs Gupta's codes. I've done my homework and found out that Bauls are members of an itinerant sect that combines Hindu and Muslim images in devotional songs. Their poetic verses often perplex respectable Bengalis with their sexual metaphors for religious emotion. But I don't want to shock Subhrasheel's parents so I decide on a very demure embroidered Lucknawi *salwar kameez*. No doubt Subhrasheel will tease me about the pale pink matronliness of my disguise and call me 'Auntie'. As an afterthought, I put on my *shakha pola* to complete the effect.

Safely over the railway crossing from the Lakes, an area that after dark is a haunt for courting couples and men seeking assignations with each other, I find the Roys' flat is identical to the other co-operative housing units. Here in the narrow winding streets the middle classes of the city live, watching their neighbours through the filigree bars that screen the balconies. The monotonous concrete façades are broken by terracotta paint and by the occasional glittering marble extravaganza of an eccentric, wealthy resident who has built their home to look like a ship or a temple. Rickshaw pullers wait by *biri* stalls gossiping and street-dogs hunt for the rich pickings that are available here. During the pujas, when Subhrasheel was a child, he took great delight in disturbing the peace by planting home-made fireworks in his neighbours' letter boxes. There is little trace of this anarchic spirit tonight. I barely recognize him as he mixes drinks for the guests and lets his exuberant teenage sisters and dignified mother dominate the conversation. In keeping with a night of tradition he is behaving like a good Bengali son.

Mrs Roy's long fingernails shimmer with silver polish and gold flowers carefully crafted by her family jeweller cast a warm light on her strong nose, ears and neck. She looks like Cleopatra just risen from a bath of milk, but her cropped hair suggests all these preparations are for an affair of state rather than of the heart. Her pupils at St James, where she teaches biology, must quake in their seats when she enters the room. She guides her guests through a Bengali meal in which the dishes progress from sour green-mango *daal* to the surprising sweetness of *roshogollas*. Sohag and Sohini, Subhrasheel's twin sisters, one in jeans and short hair, the other with flowing locks and wearing a *salwar kameez* which has fashionably flared sleeves, chatter away, finishing off each other's sentences. Mr Roy gazes with affection at his family from the sidelines, jumping up from his seat at the least excuse, like a small, nervous, greying bird. Probir, an old friend of Mr Roy's, in a showy kurta daubed with Bengali letters, keeps telling him to relax and take another drink. Sharmila sprawls in her chair, losing the thread of the conversation, pulling at her heavy Tibetan necklace in a happy reverie of her own. Pobon, self-conscious about his long, wild hair and faltering English, treats everybody with studied, gracious respect.

Once the meal is finished we shift into the living room. It is decorated with Belgian crystal vases and a print of Westminster Bridge, souvenirs of a long trip Mr and Mrs Roy made to Europe instead of buying a home. Scattered among them are clay miniatures of Ganesh. This is where guests are entertained, a place of elegance in the tiny four-room flat. At night the twins sleep on the floor here on a thin cotton mattress. Sharmila gets busy rolling a joint, much to the embarrassment of Mrs Roy. Pobon watches her and relaxes, his sleek hair springing to life with his dramatic gestures. Mr Roy flicks through an art book on the Impressionists, trying to ignore the disreputable goings-on and wrinkling his nose at the heady cannabis smoke. His friend Probir is gulping his fifth rum and Coke and wants everyone to listen to his slightly risqué jokes. This may be a night of tradition, but so far it shows no signs of turning into a scene from Mrs Gupta's repertoire. Mrs Roy continues to preside with the demeanour of a queen trying to hold all the contradictions together. Perhaps Subhrasheel's irreverence towards the rules of the city and eclectic choice of friends have come from spending many nights watching such confusions. Mrs Roy is trying to make me her ally in politesse and I am very willing to help her, not sure whether I should reveal that I am enjoying the chaos.

Mrs Roy chatters to me as Probir listens: 'We have relatives who live in London. They moved there when their son was six years old. It was for the child's benefit. When he lived in Calcutta he had memories of the city before Independence. He talked of cemeteries and gravestones, normal for a Christian child but very strange for a Hindu boy. His parents realized they were memories of a past life and so, to take him away from the sights and sounds of Calcutta that caused his remembrances, to preserve his sanity, they emigrated to Britain.'

I think how strange it is that London was chosen for this small boy to erase his dissonant older self. Like the medal that Mr Ghosh had returned to the British Museum, he was sent to Britain. And yet, ironically, it was Calcutta that had held all sorts of dangerous sensual memories of the boy's foreign, Christian past. This is exactly why I have come here, to revive this past that the boy was made to forget. Mrs Roy gets up to go and gossip with her daughters in the other room and I wonder if she has given up on her balancing act.

Probir seems very keen to get my attention as he knocks back his drink.

'Anglo-Indians, I could tell you a thing or two about them for your research,' he slurs. 'I used to have an Anglo-Indian girlfriend. We had nothing in common really, used to quarrel about everything except when we were in bed or when I used to recite Shakespeare to her. We used to spend hours together. I'd practically get through the complete works in one sitting. She would lie at my feet, looking up at me as I ran through *Julius Caesar, Midsummer Night's Dream* and all the rest. I came to my senses eventually. I realized that I was just alienated from my Bengali roots by all my education. But I still haven't forgotten all those speeches. Would you like to hear one?'

He leans over, touching my arm in an entreaty that I will say yes. I don't want to tell him that I may not be as fascinated as his Anglo-Indian girlfriend was by this skill. It's an eccentric idea that Shakespeare had provided the seduction routines for a man wearing a kurta covered in Bengali letters. If these are the stories that Subhrasheel has heard all his life, then it is not surprising he is equally sceptical about British and Bengali high culture. His cryptic comment at St James about a night of Bengali tradition suddenly makes sense: he is laughing at both of the traditions.

Probir's imminent recital is interrupted by Subhrasheel, who wants me to talk to Pobon: 'Pobon's had an interesting life, Laura. Do you know what Bauls are?'

I wonder if he is pretending to be a tour guide again, but I say, 'A little, but tell me.'

'They are the ragamuffin Rastafarians of Bengal much beloved of Tagore, Peter Gabriel and now the global commerce of world music. A common theme of their music is the cage of the body and the six vices that control its actions.'

'I'm just a singer trying to make a living,' shrugs

Pobon. 'Don't ask me about Baul tradition. But I know a thing or two about the railways. That's part of your research, isn't it? I've travelled on them since I ran away from my village as a boy. I'd sing to the commuters on the local trains to make a little money. I've written a song about the railways that I could sing to you.' He sits on the floor and sings in rough Bengali, his eyes fixed on me. His thick sweet voice soars above the bitter rhythmic plucking on the *dotara*.

Mr Roy puts down his book and Probir, now sentimental and drunk, throws an arm around his friend's shoulders. Sharmila closes her eyes, nodding her head to the music.

Subhrasheel watches to see what effect the song has on me. He is nervous, as if this is an experiment that is gradually escaping his control. The only other time I've heard such powerful music was in Spain when a group of gypsies took over a village square for one night, sending the regular inhabitants scurrying behind shut doors. A shrivelled eighty-year-old man had drawn up his frail body to fill a flamenco song with a life's suffering. But it is the words of Pobon's song that catch my attention:

'The Engine is the source of fire
How much strength the carriage has!
This carriage has six *sahebs*, two who shovel filth
Two carriages push up against each other
How many men fall under the influence of lust!
A woman climbs from the carriage at the station,
Running running rushing rushing,
The train stops its rhythm, panting she says
Help me, please give me water
How much strength the carriage has!'

This is a different take on the railways from the triumphant histories written about its contribution to India's progress. Governor-generals, civil servants and

railway officials were convinced that they were bringing a benevolent technology to India, which would
modernize its economy and dissolve the prejudices of
caste. They were proud that when Sikhs, Muslims
and Hindus sat together in carriages they were united
under the simple law of whether they could afford
the same class of ticket. Endless books have been
published that confirm these social and economic
achievements. The only dissenting voices just quibbled
about the extent to which they occurred. But from the
experience of years spent leaping on and off carriages
as they rattled to their destinations, Pobon sees this
history differently. For him the railway causes chaos
and takes control of human desires. The engine is a
source of evil. The *sahebs*, the British, who drive it,
stoke the fires of lust. And within the carriage, a
woman becomes a victim, escaping only by stepping
off the train. If economics was the sole point of the
railways in India, then why did Raj officials worry so
much about the moral education of their employees
and spend money so lavishly on reproducing English
villages in the Indian countryside? Pobon's song
suggests that the railways were more concerned with
taking over people's bodies and souls than with profit
and loss.

Still sweating from the effort of singing, Pobon
confirms my thoughts, explaining the meaning: 'It's the
usual song of a Baul changed round a bit. Instead of
the cage of the body with its six vices, I've made it a
railway carriage driven by six white men, six *sahebs*.
These wicked ones take over. Happens all the time on
those local trains, men taking advantage of women
crammed together in close quarters. We have the
British to thank for this. They brought the railways
here, didn't they?'

This scepticism reminds me of the disdain my
grandfather had for his father's gift of technology to
Ethiopia. Pobon writes down the song for me. Taking

the piece of paper, I know that I will treasure it as much as my grandfather did those small, delicate Nigerian boxes and replicas of Benin bronzes that filled his home. Pobon's song and Mrs Roy's story about the Hindu boy encourage me to think that underneath the official histories in national archives I may be able to uncover more of these wished-away pasts. What would I discover in the day-to-day records mouldering out of sight in the old headquarters of the railways? Unlike the official histories, they won't be able to hide the past. My only fear is that these documents may no longer exist. Then Pobon's song will remain only a visionary, mysterious fragment – the single piece of a long-lost jigsaw puzzle.

Subhrasheel is still agitated. Maybe the strain of subduing his spirit for the family gathering is becoming too much for him. He makes an excuse to show me his room. School sports and debating trophies are filled with cigarette butts, the remains of late-night discussions with college friends. Books on Greek and Roman mythology lean against second-hand sociology textbooks. Cuttings from magazine ads are randomly pasted over each other on the walls so that their slogans no longer make sense. Subhrasheel sits stiffly on the bed and I draw up a rigid wooden chair, wondering why he has brought me here. After some hesitation, he asks if I've heard of Bhai Phota. I shrug and ask him to explain.

'We've known each other for a little while now,' he says, 'and I really enjoy spending time with you. I think we get on very well. I'd like you to be my *didi*, my sister.'

Seeing my enthusiastic smile, he warns, 'Don't say yes too fast. It's a very serious thing in my family. I can only choose one non-blood sister in my life. You'd have to agree to help me with anything in the future. In the ceremony that would make me your brother you have to lay three thorns in the path of Yama, the god of death, to stop him. When I get married you'd have to come all the way from wherever you are. I'll also come to you whenever you need help. It's a lifetime's commitment, as serious as marriage. Are you ready for it? The time for the ceremony isn't until the end of October, so you have a while to make up your mind.'

This is turning back into a night of tradition; Subhrasheel is the last person I would have expected to subscribe to such a ceremony. He is usually so scornful of rituals, advancing some sociological explanation for their existence. What startles me more is that I feel ridiculously happy and flattered. Subhrasheel is offering me a kinship to Calcutta that contains no compromise. And it is a kinship to Subhrasheel who slips over all the boundaries of the city.

Trying not to sound too eager, I promise, 'I'll think about it, but I'm almost certain the answer will be yes.'

Subhrasheel laughs, his taut body becoming fluid again. 'Good, I thought after tonight seeing you dressed like that I was going to have to treat you respectfully and call you "Auntie" for ever. Now you can be my elder sister.'

Back at my flat, I call up Maurice to share this good news. The line crackles, making his voice hard to hear, but through the transcontinental static his anger is audible. 'What are you doing? Have you gone mad?' he says. 'It's almost our wedding anniversary and you are talking about binding brotherhood ceremonies with another man.'

I try to explain that it just means I'll have a brother, that I won't be an only child any more and that I'll have a good friend here whom I can trust. But it's obvious he thinks there's more to it, and nothing I say seems to convince him otherwise.

Lying on the bed and listening to the sounds of Calcutta fall away as it gets later into the night, I wonder about Maurice's strong reaction to Subhrasheel's offer. The last crescendo of a song from a

Hindi film in the nearby cinema disappears, leaving the rumble of a bus heading for the terminus. A rickshaw driver strikes his bell to attract a final customer. Eventually the barking and scuffles of street-dogs take over from the noises of the human population and I am alone with sweat outlining my body on the sheets. Maurice must fear that all of these sounds will become more familiar to me than our life back in Michigan. In his anger he was reminding me to think about us. In a rush of guilt, I understand his concern. How could I have resented his suspicions when he was thinking only of the preciousness of our marriage, to both of us? I drift off into peaceful sleep with thoughts of Maurice echoing like a sweet lullaby.

The next morning the sounds build again: sweepers' brushes, quarrels from the slum, conch shells heralding pujas. Shaking off the worries of the night before, I return to the task at hand, my search for the other pieces of Pobon's puzzle at the Eastern Railway headquarters. When I have found them, I will be a step closer to returning to Maurice.

Dalhousie Square was the administrative heart of colonial Calcutta. Its corners are still mapped by the pillars of the Raj: the Writers' Building, from where civil servants issued decisions; the dome of the General Post Office; the whitewashed tower of St Mary's Church and the Eastern Railway headquarters. Only St Mary's has fallen into disuse after Independence. Clouds of black fumes belch from careering buses and linger in the Moghul filigree of the Eastern Railway's red-brick façade, not quite reaching its frost-white Islamic dome but hovering around a tarnished frieze that trumpets the progress of technology from the discoveries of the ancient Greeks to the Industrial Revolution. The verandas and keyhole windows stacked up towards the dome reveal glimpses of white-shirted officers and kurta-clad peons rushing about their tasks, coughing occasionally from the acrid dust. The crowds outside are kept at bay by huge, sharp cast-iron railings. Emissaries from petty businessmen waiting for tender forms, market traders queuing for train tickets and hopeful supplicants for employment cluster around its brooding solemnity, looking up at its façade for an answer. The makeshift stalls built against the perimeter fence offer those not privileged enough to be part of its commercial grandeur the hope of gaining admittance. Hawkers are selling old railway-service exam papers, which they promise will provide aspirants the key to employment within its halls. Other stalls trade in refreshments for the expectant crowds, tempting them with the smells of cut cucumbers, *kathi* rolls and *nimbu pani*, lemon water. Today a union-led sit-in blocks the central gate. The protesters are lobbying for the recruitment and promotion of scheduled castes and tribes, who by law are supposed to have equal access to jobs but in practice rarely do. The urgent tones of an agitator blare through a megaphone, barely audible above the brawling traffic, yet the protesters' faces are hopeful of the financial security of a future spent within the walls of the Eastern Railway headquarters. They hand out leaflets to those fortunate enough to be admitted through its gates. These cheaply printed scraps of paper cry for justice. A sympathetic railway clerk takes a sheaf of them and carries them past the gate into the central courtyard. Curious to know what he will do with them and distracted from my search for the office of the Deputy General Manager, I follow him inside.

In the courtyard business continues undisturbed by the leaflets that the clerk tries to pass to others. Designed by a London architect who never went to India, the courtyard is surrounded by architectural follies. On the left is a turmeric-coloured mosque against which a group of Railway Protection Force guards in khaki uniforms lounge with guns strung over their shoulders. The clerk gives a leaflet to each of them, but they hand them back with a look of disdain as if to indicate that this petty turmoil is beneath them. On the right, low green box hedges wind along the length of the main building, which is a strange mixture of a red-brick Greek temple and a Victorian fantasy of a harem. Cooks in dhotis skirt the hedges carrying *thalis* to the canteen. They are much too busy to be interrupted by the fluttering sheets of paper. The clerk posts one of the leaflets on the wall of the main building next to an icon of Ramakrishna on which Hindu workers are smearing sandalwood paste, adding ochre to its lime green, golden yellow and peacock blue. A steel-grey air-conditioned Ambassador car marked 'Vigilance Department' waits inside the classical portal that frames the main entrance, the car door held open by a *durwan* in a red turban as charcoal-suited officers climb in. He waves away the clerk who is trying to hand the leaflets to the officials. Rising from the portal a grand central staircase covered in a maroon carpet is filled with peons, a class of employees considered even lower than humble clerks, carrying tea in flowery bone-china cups to railway officers. They, also, are much too busy to read the plaintive requests of unemployed workers.

I follow the clerk through windowless corridors and stairways. Their darkness seems designed for conspiracies and lost hopes. Dust and *biri* smoke swirl in the hazy gloom. At last, the clerk finds an audience for the leaflets among his fellow workers clustered around *paan* sellers, who are murmuring injustices outside the scrutiny of officers. Cascading files stained black from dust and red from betel-nut juice are dumped haphazardly on the stairs. Some of the clerks grow bored with the familiar story told in the pamphlets and drop them on to the piles of discarded official correspondence, broken clay teacups and leaf plates. Another clerk passes and picks one up, shaking off the dust and reddened spit that has already collected on it. He carries it up a spiral staircase that ends abruptly in front of a jet-black door marked in white letters simply 'Secret Cell', through which he disappears.

Retracing my steps, looking for a route out of this maze, suddenly I'm blinking in the light of the verandas, open to the view of the streets. The sunlight pours down on an endless vista of weary faces waiting on benches below signs leading to the air-conditioned offices of the Deputy Personnel Officer, Additional Personnel Officer and Assistant Additional Personnel Officer. By the doors peons distribute slips of paper hanging from strings to the waiting people, on which they can write their requests. To relieve their boredom, some of them are reading the union pamphlets. Climbing higher I resume my search for the office of the Deputy General Manager in grand corridors where the sunlight streams on to faded photographs of steam engines. Finally I find it. Taking my own slip of paper, I sit on a bench beside flustered officers with sheaves of letters for the Deputy General Manager to sign. My neighbour is holding one of the union leaflets.

I don't have to wait long. The red light above the door turns green and I'm ushered inside. Shivering in the air-conditioned atmosphere, I remember the sharpness of frosty British mornings. Here the clamouring crowds are inaudible, muffled by the thick walls; only the metallic ring of one of the three telephones on the Deputy Manager's desk and the clink of a teacup break the expectant silence. My neighbour follows me in and places the leaflet on the desk. The Deputy General Manager shifts his huge bulk slightly, picks it up, glances at it, writes something and orders a clerk, 'Please file this somewhere out of my sight.'

His giant frame wrapped in the best of bespoke pigeon-grey suits is planted under a list of his ancestors, the names of previous officers painted in gold leaf below the heraldic shield of the Eastern Railway. Aside from the progression from English to Indian names, little has changed in this room full of people waiting for the attention of their superior officer. Sitting down on the couch next to the wall furthest from his desk, I realize that everyone else is standing, so I get up. The Deputy General Manager interrupts his telephone conversation with a nod to indicate I can sit down again. He snaps into the telephone and his anger is amplified by the unnatural silence around. His Hindi is cracked by the repetition of the English phrase, 'It's bloody well not good enough.' Replacing the receiver, he interrogates me about my reasons for being here. Presenting my research visa, I explain my need for pre-Independence records of the railways. Smiling, he enjoys the sensation of the authority he is exercising over a foreigner. He says they have no records anywhere, that my search will be fruitless, besides he can't just let me see any documents I choose as they have many secret maps and other information stored away that could be used by foreign agents. Then in the space of a few seconds he makes calls to Dhanbad, Howrah, Jamalpur and the Personnel Librarian, juggling between his three phones. He informs me I will have to return here many times to find out anything, then launches into a speech about how I should tell the story of the railways.

'The British gave us a great gift in building the railways, housing facilities and these offices here.' He looks with pride at the ancestral board above him and waves his hand at the clerks who are hanging on his every word. 'The railways are a nation-building lifeline. They have many social effects apart from the movement of raw materials. They help societies to intermingle. Everyone had to travel across India's length and breadth, Muslims, Hindus, low caste, high caste all sitting together. The price of a ticket became the only distinction between our citizens. The railway colonies inspire a brotherly community. There are no caste distinctions there, only rank matters. We sort out work problems man to man, between ourselves, in the officers' clubs. The housing provision . . .' He picks up an official letter in mid-sentence and everyone waits for him to finish. 'The housing provision is good. When posted to Ondal I lived in the old Chief Mechanical Engineer's bungalow, wonderful place. I never wanted to leave it. It had a garden the size of four tennis courts and a fireplace which we never used. My *durwan* told me of Mr Timms, the old British engineer. He had a horse and car. He used to come home from work each day in the car and the horse would open the gate for him, it was so loyal and properly trained. One day the horse didn't open the gate. So he shot it.'

He laughs long and hard at this. I shiver again because the ghost of Mr Timms is presiding in this room. What hope have I of uncovering the other pieces of Pobon's puzzle, when one of the six *sahebs* from his song is still in control of the railway head-quarters?

A tall, lanky man as taut as the string wrapped around the bulging files on the desk walks in and the Deputy General Manager shouts at him for interrupting his joke, but he introduces him as Mr Bose, the Personnel Librarian. Hovering at the edge of the room, casting curious glances at me and nervously pulling at his pencil moustache, Mr Bose flinches as the Deputy General Manager issues his commands: 'You have many new books on the history of the railways and railway legal procedures in your Personnel Library, it is your duty to help this scholar.'

Annoyed by his posturing and determined that he shouldn't just brush aside my request, I look him in the eye and say quietly but firmly, 'I need pre-Independence original records, not new books.'

He pauses, then says, 'Come and talk to me again next Friday,' and he waves us out.

In the corridors once again, Mr Bose sprints ahead, watching out for the impressed expressions on the faces of his colleagues as we pass by. I follow two steps behind without a clue as to where we are heading. I ask him but he signals with his hand that we shouldn't speak here. He slows down in a grey room the size of a warehouse. Here, the commodities stacked up in storage are the clerks themselves. Hundreds of them sit in front of tiny wooden school desks, in attitudes of bored inactivity, occasionally turning over the two sheets of paper in front of them. Far above each of them a fan clatters. The current of air serves only to rustle black dust on the pages of files piled almost to the ceiling on top of steel *almirahs*. Their doors hang open, barely managing to restrain more files inside. One that has fallen out on to the floor reads, 'Appeal against dismissal, Mr Chowdhury, 1986'. The cover is signed by ten or so officers who seem to have considered his case and found it inconclusive. On the wall placards lecture the clerks with sayings from Vivekananda, 'Civilization is man's call to do his duty' and 'Cleanliness is next to Godliness'. Mr Bose unlocks the padlock on a small cabin built out from the wall marked 'Personnel Library: do not enter without permission'.

Inside the library are cabinets of new books and my hope of finding old documents evaporates. Behind Mr Bose's desk is a window opening on to a shaft of brick walls and a contraption that funnels water into the officers' air-conditioned rooms above. Here the heat is oppressive and the drops of water falling from the machine are painfully inviting. Mr Bose is talking about everything but the matter at hand.

'I am a great classical violinist,' he says, 'but I had to give it up because my fiancée's family thought all that performance would lead to bad morals. I also went to

Doon School, the place where the sons of politicians and our great families go, so I know about morals and public service. I had a chance for a scholarship for accountancy in London, but my fiancée couldn't live without me so I couldn't go.'

Trying to keep him to the point, I ask if he knows of any old documents. He is offended by this mundane question but nonetheless replies, 'There are definitely documents. I will help you, but it will take time and effort. And I can't talk about them here. After work tomorrow you must meet my fiancée and we'll go to Gol Park where I have a flat we plan to live in after we are married. It cost at least two lakhs of rupees.'

His crumpled and faded lavender shirt shows no evidence of the riches needed to buy such a flat. And then abruptly, as if remembering some unfinished business, he picks up the telephone and says, 'Is that Head of Personnel? Yes, hello, sir. I have a friend, a hardworking fellow. He is sitting the exam for promotion, please make sure he passes, you owe me a favour. Sir, yes, you know why, sir.'

I can't understand why he was speaking in English to the officer or why he suddenly called him in my presence.

Putting the receiver down, he addresses me again: 'First you must read all these books, then you can look at old documents. You must come back daily and study them. Give me your address so I can get information to you whenever I receive it.'

Dependent on his goodwill, I give him my address. Opening a book on regulations for railway drivers just to show my commitment, I sit for hours randomly taking notes as a succession of weary railway workers arrive from colonies all over Bihar and Bengal. Their faces lined and their bodies shrunken from years of labour, they all make the same request: 'Please help me look up the laws covering my case. I have a large family. I have to support them. Please help me before I lose my railway house and job.'

Mr Bose introduces each one to me, saying, 'I'm even helping foreigners now.'

Then they turn to the details of their despair and to finding ways to insert it into the legal language of the books around us. As the working day draws to a close I begin to fear that I'll spend the rest of my life pointlessly circulating like the union pamphlet through these corridors and offices. And yet I'm transfixed by this place. It's a vast waiting room, one where whole lives pass among dust and discarded papers in the expectation of the arrival of justice. I remember Pobon's words about the strength of the carriage and the woman who cried out for release from its power and I see how they capture the plight of the workers who come here, but I have yet to figure out why Pobon sang of lust and moral evils.

As I feared on the first day, weeks pass with no sign of any documents. The Divisional General Manager calls me into his office daily to check on my persistence. My only progress is into a relaxed friendship with Mr Bose, who keeps arriving at my flat to propose schemes for finding documents. He offered to travel to the Railway Board in New Delhi where he has very important contacts and do 2,000 rupees' worth of photocopying for me. I was thrilled by his gesture, but explained that I needed to see the papers myself to work out which ones would be relevant. He has promised to be my ally in the railway headquarters and to help trace Mr Ghosh, who sent the letter to the British Museum. And he has introduced me to his fiancée, Lolita. Her lavish curves wrapped in pastel chiffon saris and her lips carefully painted with frosted pink are oddly voluptuous next to Mr Bose's long, skinny frame. As our friendship develops, they begin to ask me for small favours. Lolita is studying part-time by correspondence course for a BA in English Literature, so that she can rise higher than her present job as a Mechanical Engineering Department clerk. She sits surrounded by Tennyson, Dickens and Chaucer in her room in the tiny ramshackle flat she shares with her parents. When she drops hints about how expensive her textbooks are I buy her one. Another time, feeling I can't refuse her request, I stay up into the small hours writing essays for her on 'Travel Broadens the Mind' and 'Duty is the Highest Calling'. These will help her prepare for the exams that will qualify her for promotion.

Mr Bose is careful to make sure that the three of us never meet up inside the railway offices and at first I don't understand why he is so worried about fellow workers knowing of his love for Lolita. But one day, as we sit eating noodles at a roadside stall in Gol Park, Mr Bose begins to pour out their troubles. He is scared of rumours flying around the office about their relationship. They would harm their chances of promotion and reach the ears of Lolita's father, a retired railway officer who does not approve of their love. He dislikes Mr Bose because he is not a proper railway officer, only a lowly clerk, and does not have good prospects. As Mr Bose bitterly lists the barriers to their match, I think of the weekly matrimonial ads in the *Statesman* newspaper. They proudly announce that a bride is wanted for a railway officer or a class III clerk. The judgements made in the halls of the Eastern Railway about character and promotion affect so much more than the salary of their inmates. Mr Bose continues to explain that one of Lolita's fellow workers, who was envious of their love, had warned her father that Mr Bose takes bribes so that he has money to visit prostitutes. Then pulling on his pencil moustache he mournfully adds, 'These rumours about my immorality could destroy everything, spoil my chances for marriage and a good career.' He asks if I have noticed the middle-aged man, who sits under a staircase in the railway headquarters pouring tea into clay cups from a huge white teapot held together with red string. This man had once been a fully fledged peon, until he was investigated by the Vigilance Department, the 'Secret Cell' I had seen a clerk bearing the union leaflet disappear into on my first visit. The department spies on railway workers, watching for sudden increases in income or immoral behaviour that are clues to corruption. Their suspicions had settled on this man and he had begged his superiors to allow him at least to have a business selling tea in the building.

Mr Bose confesses that he too had been a member of the Vigilance Department but, accused by a jealous fellow worker of taking bribes, he was punished by demotion to the Personnel Library. Even though we are far away from the headquarters and surrounded by bustling, indifferent crowds, he looks around fearfully and then whispers, 'I've been inside that Secret Cell and I know its true nature; even they will take a little money to suspend enquiries against individuals. Only the poor are prosecuted. Be careful what you do inside the office, they are watching us always. Last year a man committed suicide just outside the office, took a gun to his head. He had been falsely accused of immorality. After dark none of the clerks like to be near the door, they hear the shot ringing out again and again.'

What I hear ringing in Mr Bose's scared voice and the tale of his thwarted love for Lolita is Pobon's warning about the two *sahebs* who shovel filth. The railway bureaucrats seek out rumours of lust and immorality. If they don't find them, they invent them anyway, with tragic consequences. But I still don't know why the railway is mixed up in generating such rumours rather than profits and I never will unless I can uncover some original sources on its history.

In a last effort to find some documents, Mr Bose takes me to meet Mr Raffiq who presides over the Chief Mechanical Engineer's Library at the very top of the building, under the dome that graces the pinnacle of the palace. The stairway that leads to the dome and the Deputy General Manager's office would be a perfect stage-set for Flaubert's oriental travel writings. Clerks hover on the stairs waiting for *darshan* of the Emperor inside the office or for a violent death hatched from courtly intrigues. As we approach the library, the sunlight falls on plaster bosses and arches copied from seraglios and throne rooms. Mr Bose explains that this part of the building is all that remains of the Moghul Emperor's palace on which the British built the headquarters. It is obvious that this is untrue, but his claim has a poetic truth as forceful as Pobon's song.

He continues, 'There are ghosts here too. Near midnight the Railway Protection Force hear the sounds of laughter and *ghazals* coming from these arches, the spirits of the old Emperor, his courtiers and wives that live on throughout this building. They guard and keep this place. A few years before there were plans to break down these arches; the railway needed more room for offices. But accidents started to happen to the workmen and they said they saw things. Finally the *mistree* told the officer in charge that they couldn't change anything here otherwise the whole building would collapse. That's what the accidents and spirit voices meant.'

Mr Bose leaves me outside the imposing leather door of the Chief Mechanical Engineer's Library. On the left is a small cubby hole in which three stenographers sit bent over ancient, clattering typewriters. They look up curiously but, before they can speak, a *durwan* ceremoniously opens the library door.

Mr Raffiq, the librarian, greets me like an old courtier offering me tea and plates of *roshogollas* and *sandesh*. Neatly attired in a red-striped shirt, he repeatedly brushes flecks of dust from his crisp cuffs. A ribald selection of red, blue and green pens sprouts from his shirt pocket. He selects one or the other of them and carefully marks the spines of the shiny books which are piled in front of him. Oak bookcases, exported years ago from Britain, line two walls, but they are filled with new railway yearbooks and technical manuals on the stresses to concrete, wood and iron in the Indian environment. Two assistants circulate around the room with blackened rags, dusting and redusting the bookcases. The other walls are invisible behind piles of unsorted books and there seems to be no place in which they could be catalogued and stored. Mr Raffiq repeatedly orders the peons to bring more refreshments and begins a lecture on how a woman of good character wouldn't be wandering around Calcutta on her own, adding that I must drink a lot of liquor like all Britishers, it's the cold climate that makes it necessary. Confused as to which statement to object to first, I lose my chance to assert my respectability, as he tells me that he will teach me *ghazals*, songs of love and longing, and accompany me round the city to protect my virtue. Squirming in his seat, he explains that he has piles caused by the dusty environment in the library and that he can't get his body cleansed or running properly. No attempt to turn the conversation round to my search for old documents succeeds in steering him away from his own chosen topics.

The door opens and to my amazement in walks Leslie. He shuffles from foot to foot waiting for Mr Raffiq to acknowledge his presence, not daring to greet me. Mr Raffiq gives me a railway yearbook to read and then turns his attention to Leslie.

'Good, you've come again. Did you bring your papers?'

'*Saheb*, yes, the lot of them.' Leslie unfolds dog-eared history sheets of his service.

'Then I can help you to draft your pension dues petition. You may get a chance this time. In the afternoon I'm calling to see the Assistant Additional Personnel Officer. He's ordered technical manuals from the library. With them I'll slip the petition to him.'

They set to writing a laboriously polite letter which, if I'm not mistaken, begins with 'The great influence and mercy of the Assistant Additional Personnel Officer is known far and wide.' Finally satisfied with the phrases, Mr Raffiq makes a suggestion: 'You should talk to Mrs Laura too. She is known to the Deputy General Manager, she might be able to help you.'

'Yes, *saheb*, I know her already.'

'Good, good, then you have another influential person on your side.'

I am embarrassed by the false idea that I have any power to help him, but Leslie turns towards me and explains his case: 'That wandering I told you about at Gary's house, it's all mixed up with this place. They won't give me my full dues, something about black marks on my history sheet. I was fond of the liquor, took it on all my driving, helps to keep you awake and all. Kills the boredom and stops you getting noddy. I tried to disguise it from the inspectors, chewing *paan* to cover up the smell. Sometimes they caught me. And now I don't have my full pension and I have to stay with whatever kin will give me a home. But I can never stay long, they get tired of a useless, restless fellow hanging around. I'll end up in one of those charity homes, Little Sisters of the Poor, St Vincent's or Tolly Homes, but they're even worse than the streets, all those nuns and nurses guarding over you as you wait to die. Can you help me?'

'Leslie, I only wish I could but I have no influence

101

at all. I'm just here waiting to look at a few old documents.'

I wonder if Mr Raffiq really has any influence either or whether he just enjoys being addressed as *saheb*. Leslie leaves, only a little hope remaining.

Once he is gone Mr Raffiq starts to lecture me again: 'What are you doing with such Anglo friends? He's a drunken, hopeless case. I know those types well. I grew up in railway colonies. When I was young I envied their sportsmanship, singing and dancing, but later once in railway service I understood they were feckless and immoral. They never got promotions, their fortunes declined because their family life and morals declined also. Don't waste yourself with them.'

I decide to leave and never return to this library. Mr Raffiq seems to sense this and with affected casualness announces, 'But I do have some old documents. Wait here.'

He sends one of the peons up a rickety ladder into the attic of the library. He returns with a leather-bound volume from the 1870s full of the cramped handwriting of previous generations of clerks. Mr Raffiq instructs the peon to wipe it with one of the blackened cloths.

Turning the pages for hours, I am bitterly disappointed. There are lavish lists of indents for materials, copious minutes of board meetings and endless accounts of profits and losses. There is nothing here that throws any light on the vagaries of the railway bureaucracy or that records the lives affected by it. Nothing apart from the handwriting of the clerk who spent his life copying these orders at one of the wooden desks in this warehouse of suffering. Its elaborate whorls, as distinctive as a fingerprint, are the only clues to the millions of lives like those of Leslie and Mr Bose that have been taken over by the six *sahebs* of Pobon's song. They give way after ten years to a more staccato hand, but we will never know what this change means. Was the clerk dismissed, demoted on false charges like the man who sits pouring tea under the staircase, or did he honourably retire?

Mr Bose comes to pick me up at the end of the working day. As he, Lolita and I ride home in a bus that is so crowded its thin metal walls seem to sweat and heave, I tell them of my frustration. Mr Bose smiles and says, 'Don't worry, I can help you find out about railway culture. Come and talk to my mother and me about it this weekend. She's an expert after marrying my father, a railway officer, and living in railway colonies at Jamalpur and Kharagpur.' Then, narrowly missing the glistening, irritated face of a neighbouring passenger, he produces with a flourish a crumpled piece of paper: 'And look here, I've got the address of Mr Ghosh, he's attached to the South-Eastern Railwaymen's Union office. We can visit him also.'

The South-Eastern Railwaymen's Union office is a small concrete box tacked on as an afterthought to a sprawl of red-brick tenements from an earlier era, which still house railway drivers. Before Independence, unions led mass strikes against racial privileges and low wages, but since then many of them have come to arrangements with their employers. Their representatives are welcome visitors in the Deputy General Manager's office and many, like this one, have premises provided by the railway. Sometimes they arrange shows of strength, staging noisy protests and marching through the corridors of the headquarters. Perhaps the railway bureaucracy can maintain its hypnotic power only by making sure that there is a regular flow of protesting supplicants outside its gates. But other unions, like the one I saw on my first day, remain radical. After all, it was an alliance of such unions that helped to bring down Indira Gandhi with mass strike action during the state of emergency in 1979.

Under a portrait of Lenin, Mr Ghosh stares at Mr Bose and me with dignified scepticism. He is wearing a long white kurta and dhoti, an outfit that would be more suited for a visit to a temple than the fomenting of revolution. The smooth-flowing cloth contrasts with his face, which is pock-marked and lined from years spent in a railway workshop among the burning fumes from red-hot steel. But in his retirement he has acquired a leisurely air. The poise with which he waits to hear our reasons for being here is reminiscent of an ancient village landowner receiving the pleas of his tenants. Behind him are neatly stacked pamphlets and copies of a volume strangely named *Railwayman's Chivalry*. The title captures perfectly Mr Ghosh's odd combination of old-fashioned aristocracy and work-worn body. He asks me what I think of America. Looking up at the portrait for guidance, I tell him of my shock at the deep divide between poverty and plenty and the lack of union power there. Mr Ghosh relaxes a little and lights a *biri*. Explaining that I am writing a history on the exploitation of railway workers under the British, I ask him why he returned his ancestor's medal, which was awarded for loyal service during a railway strike in the 1890s. He replies that all the relevant history has already been written by himself and his comrades and hands me the book entitled *Railwayman's Chivalry*. Mr Ghosh adds with quiet anger that before Independence the Indian workers were scared to enter the railway colonies, where they'd get beaten up by gangs of Europeans. Every time they saw a European or Eurasian worker they'd warn each other, 'A Topi's coming, a Topi's coming, get out of the way.'

In the Eastern Railway headquarters the central

staircase was marked 'Europeans only' and all the native clerks had to use the hidden, windowless staircases. His grandfather was a stationmaster at Monghyr, his father a babu clerk in the Eastern Railway headquarters and he had joined the railways as an apprentice workshop foreman in 1940. In the workshops he was treated like a 'godman' and had picked up his lifelong philosophy of management from British foremen, using their slang and threats of violence to discipline his workmen. After Independence he moved into Lilloah railway colony from the village encampments outside. He saw how, once there, all the Indians began to lose their extended family values, ladies standing outside in the streets, men drinking liquor, becoming like Anglo-Indians.

Snorting with disgust he says, 'Hindus have their villages, but for Anglo-Indians, wherever they work is their *desh* – their village-home. That's why I sent back the medal. We are a good Hindu family, we know our roots in our village in Panaghar. The medal made me feel too much like an Anglo-Indian. It has nothing to do with our nation or us. My son, when he was young, used to pick it up and ask me about what his grandfather had done to get such a beautiful bright thing. I wanted him to be a decent Hindu boy, not some *Tash*, so I hid it away. But it kept bothering me. I don't know if I would vote for the BJP but now, seeing how polluted we have been by invaders from the Muslims to the British, I think they are right. I read an article about an exhibition the British Museum was having in Delhi of Imperial Treasures from Rome. I knew the museum was an important place, a centre for learning and it kept all the valuable things from empires, so I sent the medal there.'

Filled with mixed emotions, I understand Mr Ghosh's anger at the racial inequalities of the Raj, but his bitterness leads him to express harsh prejudices against Anglo-Indians and Muslims. In Britain his letter had shown me the historical links between the Raj and institutions such as the British Museum that created vivid, unreal dreams of the Orient. Yet here in India, listening to his words, I realize that he, too, dreams of an unreal Orient. For him India must be returned to its timeless Hindu essence, whatever the cost to its Muslim and Christian citizens. Trying to argue back against his assertion that the BJP has got everything right with its version of a pure Hindu past, I make no impression on Mr Ghosh. I am a foreigner whom he associates with the old violences of the railway colony. In his mind he is hearing the words again, 'A Topi is coming, a Topi is coming.'

Taking a steamer with Mr Bose across the Hooghly and watching boys dive from its prow into the shining river, I feel cleansed of Mr Ghosh's bitterness and relax in the wavering rhythm of the water. We walk from the pier through North Calcutta's narrow streets surrounded by towering extended-family houses with the odd Doric column decorating their façades. Mr Bose weaves through the detritus of these families' lives as it spills out on to the streets. Ignoring a rickshaw puller washing under the fountain from a water pump; a child playing with a clay doll; a maid delivering saris for pressing to the *istri-wallah*, who sweats as he lifts his heavy metal iron filled with glowing charcoal, Mr Bose is absorbed in hatching schemes for making his parents agree to his marriage to Lolita. He explains that his mother is in favour of the match and she is going to ask Lolita's mother to come and see all his educational certificates. He is excited and hopeful that this will bring an end to their four years of waiting, promising that I will be the guest of honour at their wedding when it happens. We arrive outside one of the huge houses, which is now haphazardly divided up into separate flats so that the quarrelling family members don't have to speak to each other. We squeeze into a narrow passageway

106

leading to his parents' three-room flat, formerly occupied by their landlord's younger brother who has disappeared. Inside we find Mrs Bose sitting on the floor, a plain cotton sari wrapped around her tiny, delicate frame. Streaks of white wind through her long curly black hair and a lacy pattern of wrinkles spreads across her face as she greets us. The family's possessions – clothes, books, *thalis* – are piled on top of steel trunks and the room looks like a railway platform taken over by refugees.

Mrs Bose is surrounded by the dolls of Ramakrishna and Vivekananda that she explains she makes to express her artistic spirit. Continuing to sew together with white thread a doll that is a miniature image of herself, she proudly boasts that she also writes Bengali poetry about nature, religion and middle-class family problems. She hides them from her husband. When he first found out about them he told her that if she continued he would send all of her children to an orphanage. She started to write when she married and began to live in railway colonies. She had no friends there. Her husband wouldn't let her go outside freely; he thought that women should not roam about, that she would lose her Bengali ways if she spent too much time on the railway colony roads. Once she was standing in the garden of their railway quarters and he scolded her, 'Why are you standing outside like this? Are you a prostitute that you do this?' Mrs Bose explains with bitterness, 'In this way he was like all the men in the railway colony. Before and after Independence the culture remained the same. Male candidates order to female candidates you have to do this and that for me. This is not the story of one person, it is the story of all railway officers. Inside offices they are officers and outside the office they are giants or so they think.'

Mr Bose adds, 'My father maintains the railway culture. His bad behaviour to his family is railway culture because it is a tyrannical culture. He is habituated to maintain this culture from the office. In the railway colony there is nothing but office culture. This is why it is such a bad place. We were never allowed to go to the Railway Institute. Our father told us that there morality was not good. If we went there then we would not maintain a good life in the future. I would have learnt slang words. If I could not maintain my life then I would be cruel to my parents and shame them. I would end up choosing my wife only as a bed partner.'

Mrs Bose's bitterness flows again and the doll falls from her hands: 'My husband wanted the house to be like a prison. He feared the effect of the railway colony buildings. Living in them is not really like being in India. After Independence we have maintained this insular British culture. It is a low-minded, not a high-minded place. The other railway wives behave like reporters, spreading rumours about everyone's behaviour to their husbands. It is like a crossword, everybody lined up and ordered in regiments.'

The weight of the culture in the railway colonies has pressed down with a painful reality on Mr Bose and his mother's life. Independence has not brought an irreverent Bengali version of these English villages. Instead it has repainted the scenery with fears of pollution. Mr Bose's father and Mr Ghosh have not dissolved its prescriptive power, just reused it for different ends, to reinforce a tyrannical version of Bengali culture. Listening to these stories of individual lives that have been profoundly affected by the rules of the colonies makes me even more determined to expose the untold history of the railways. But how can I do this, if I can't find any records? I make a vow to wait in the headquarters for as long as it takes to make it yield its secrets.

The Deputy General Manager rewards my perseverance with an official letter that permits me to enter the Agent's Record Room. This room, the secret heart of the building, is an unlit corridor that leads nowhere, full of shelves and shelves of blackened files. Its entrances are guarded by *dufteri*, who were taken on years ago on the sports quota, destined to win tournament cups in hockey, athletics and football for the railway. Recruited because of their strong physique, they are now old and injured from the matches in which they defended the honour of the railway against other regional teams. They guard the gloom, undisturbed for months on end. They are pleased to have my company and use it as an opportunity to talk politics or just to talk. One old man with a cough so rasping I fear for his life, tells me that he is a fan of Godard films and discusses their finer points with me for hours. They fetch me sugared toast and clay cups of tea. I bring them occasional boxes of sweets. A woman comes to pray to Mecca in the privacy of the corridor at the appointed hours, but she never acknowledges our presence. I have not yet been allowed beyond the first set of shelves, which contain minutes of railway board meetings from 1850 onwards. I hungrily snatch opportunities to read them between the avid conversations.

The crumbling, rat-chewed pages are full of the same rational accounting as the ledgers in the Mechanical Engineering Library. Yet armed with the insights of Pobon's song, Mr Bose's stories and my experience of weeks spent here, I find new resonances in these records of the curt decisions and bizarre procedures that were implemented. I begin to understand how the Moghul Palace came into being. British railway officials just could not believe that Indians were capable of running a modern, industrial enterprise or that they could operate with the simple relationships of employer and employee. For generations they kept control of the railways in the hands of British officers and Anglo-Indian subordinates who levied a strict discipline on the mass of lower-level Indian workers. Railway doctors invented complex techniques to identify the nationality, race and caste of employees, which they used to fix them at a certain level in the hierarchy. West Indians, Bengalis, Sikhs, iron-making castes, Parsis and Brahmins were all tested for their innate efficiency and placed in appropriate roles in the railway enterprise. From the beginning the hierarchy was suffused with moral rather than economic judgements. British officers were not only guardians of efficiency but of morality as well, especially of the morality of their more dubious relatives, Anglo-Indians. They were given autocratic powers to dismiss and spy on their inferiors, who had no possibility of redress once their character had been besmirched by a black mark on their history sheets, the detailed personnel records that were kept on every employee.

Railway colonies had developed out of these bureaucratic obsessions with race and morality. At first European and Anglo-Indian drivers, guards, railway inspectors and workshop supervisors were housed in local bazaars in Howrah, near the newly built station with its elegant Florentine façade. But railway officials were soon shocked by the behaviour of these subordinates. They would mix with Indians, drinking and eating in the same crowded hotels. More dangerously they developed relationships with Indian Christian and Eurasian women. Poor whites picked up the speech patterns, dress habits and demeanour of Indians. Their children, offspring of their illicit affairs, were even worse. The lines between the races that were so important to the railway hierarchy were blurring. The whole illusion that the British were superior in morality and efficiency was threatened. When they tried to enforce discipline, the workers often reneged on their contracts, disappearing off to lead their own lives in the Mofussil, the country regions far away from the influence of Raj officials, or answered back with a new-found insolence. Something had to be done to stop all this degeneration.

The answer was simple: colonies had to be built to house Eurasians and working-class Europeans so that they would stay on the path of moral rectitude in the corrupting environment of India. They would be isolated within the boundaries of the railway colonies and encouraged to forget that they were even in India. The first were constructed in Jamalpur and Jubbulpur in the 1860s. The locations were chosen because of their distance from local towns and villages. Entertainment would be provided by reading rooms, filled with magazines and newspapers fresh off the steam packets, sports fields and regular dances at the Institute. The architecture was designed with no reference to local traditions. The streets were laid out so watchmen and the newly formed railway volunteer force could easily patrol them. This would not only make sure that workers behaved themselves, but also that rebellious Indian mobs could be stopped in their tracks. Hostels for apprentice railwaymen overseen by a master and matron would curb their adolescent waywardness. English-medium schools would be provided for the children and a healthy smattering of churches would see to the moral welfare of the workers. Later railway hill schools were built so that children could be sent as boarders far away from their parents, who still sometimes betrayed too many Indian habits. By 1876 there were colonies stretching along all the railway lines across India and the head of the Indian railways congratulated himself that

On approaching these places they present quite an imposing appearance. Large square brick houses are seen placed in compounds or gardens bearing a resemblance to the villas and mansions occupied by the wealthy citizens of a London suburb . . . In connection with this colony there are generally Institutes, libraries, swimming baths, billiard rooms, churches, schools, co-operative stores, hospitals, recreation grounds – everything in fact that can be thought of to afford occupation for the mind and body. It is very desirable to attend to the health, comfort, and amusement of European mechanics in India as well as to the education of their children. There are great temptations to indulgence and excess and it is obviously expedient to secure well behaved, steady and intelligent European communities of this class in the heart of India.

Indian workers were cordoned off beyond the sanitary zone of the colonies, left to build their own ramshackle houses. No wonder Mr Bose's father and Mr Ghosh feared that their families would be taken over by British values when they moved into the colonies after Independence. They were designed to produce this effect on the souls of their inhabitants.

Kharagpur was a later, grander version of this model, built in the early 1890s. By then the techniques of control had been refined. Colony committees of railway officers oversaw the petty disputes and welfare of the workers. There was even a team of sanitary inspectors headed by an officer who stamped all the goods in the market that were fit for consumption. They made sure no Indians set up stalls within the boundaries of the colony. Gambling and country liquor were forbidden. Special railway police had a lock-up at the station in which they imprisoned drunken Europeans and Eurasians. When as a result of Indian nationalist campaigns against British rule local democratic self-government was introduced in the late 1890s, railway colonies were excluded from the new regulations. Indian businessmen and nationalist politicians could sit on municipal councils in Calcutta and elsewhere, but they were not permitted to govern railway colonies. These would remain in the hands of British officers.

As in the earlier incarnations at Jamalpur and Jubbulpur, Indians were kept firmly beyond the boundaries of Kharagpur. But because railway officials were now acutely aware of the growing union movement in the railways that protested against racial inequalities, they came up with a new plan. Each Indian community was allotted a separate plot of land well beyond the sanitary zone in a policy of divide and rule. Dangerous alliances between the workshop staff would be prevented by separating them into Sikhs, Muslims and Hindus with their own villages and gurdwaras, mosques and temples. This strategy didn't work. There were pitched battles in the streets of Kharagpur during the strike of 1926. The railway volunteer force fired on the strikers. The rallying cry that rose up from the maidan in Kharagpur was 'Jai Hind ' – 'victory to India'.

But once Indians started to demand equal treatment and pay, railway officials came up with a novel solution that brought about the convoluted procedures of the Moghul Palace. They would not allow Indians to be members of unions because they were perceived as too irrational, immature and superstitious to take part in collective bargaining. Instead they would be permitted to write petitions to the Agent, the head of the railway company, requesting redress, and every level of the hierarchy would vet these before they reached him. The formality of these procedures was fantastic. The ultimate authority on the cases rested with the King in Britain, but in practice decisions lay

113

with the Agent alone. Because British officials refused to cede their racial and moral authority to guide the progress of capitalism in India they constructed a Byzantine and arbitrary bureaucracy. Its business was not to turn profits, but to sit in judgement on individual character, to promote spying on its workers and to determine their racial propensities. It's not surprising that all the Indian railways made losses. The Agents felt their practices were in keeping with the old traditions of Moghul India, but they had invented something quite new. All around me I had been experiencing the legacy of their creation. I was now not surprised that at night in the Eastern Railway headquarters you could hear the sounds of *ghazals*, laughing courtiers and the voice of an old Moghul ruler all coming from the British version of an Islamic dome that still covers the Agent's office.

On one of the long afternoons spent noting the dates and details of this story, I am interrupted by a middle-aged man turning prematurely grey. He is talking in Bengali to the head *dufteri*, asking questions about me. Finally he turns in my direction: 'I hear that you are staying in Mr Bose's flat in Gol Park. You've helped him to get a better position in the Northern Railway. You used your influence for him, didn't you?'

I'm getting used to this misguided assumption that I have power, but I'm irritated by the suggestion that I have taken up residence in Mr Bose's flat.

'No, I have absolutely no influence at all. And no, I'm not staying with Mr Bose,' I reply rather curtly.

He looks at me with knowing disbelief and says, 'Well, if you ever need help from me after Mr Bose has left for his new position, just inform me. My name is Mr Basu.'

Troubled by this mysterious visit, I brush off my hands, which are dusty from the files, and head for Mr Bose's office to find out what is going on.

Mr Bose is unusually dishevelled and irritated, barely managing to smile as I enter the Personnel Library. His pencil moustache is losing its definition, hidden by five o'clock shadow. I ask him the meaning of Mr Basu's cryptic conversation.

He snaps, annoyed by my ignorance of the procedures of the Moghul Palace, 'I told Mr Basu and everyone I meet that you stay with me. It will mean that all those bad characters won't know where you really live. And, yes, I lied about your influence, it gives you power. It will make people help you. I really have got a transfer and promotion to New Delhi to the Railway Board. I'll be leaving very soon. Perhaps now Lolita's parents will let me marry her.'

But of course this charade is all to do with Mr Bose's desire to improve his own position; he is trying to use me to suggest to colleagues that he has important contacts. I remember Mr Bose's call in English, apparently to a superior officer, on the first day I met him and his claims about going to Doon School, owning a flat in Gol Park and being offered a scholarship to London and realize that these were probably ploys to impress me with his credentials. Sighing, Mr Bose sinks back in his seat and apologizes for his curt response. He explains why he is in a bad mood. Despite his promotion his attempts to convince Lolita's parents about their marriage have been going awry. Her colleague has again been telling tales to her father about his morals and how he was demoted from the Vigilance Department for corruption. Lolita's mother is now eager to see his certificates so as to be certain Mr Bose is really as educated as he claims to be. Then he says that to cap it all he had three thousand rupees stolen from his bag on the bus this morning just when he was supposed to be spending it on new books for the library. He is distressed because he may be dismissed for this: can I help him out? Uncomfortable about the turn our friendship is taking, I explain that I don't have that kind of money freely available and that I really can't help.

Lolita walks in and Mr Bose leaps from his chair, shouting, 'How dare you come to my office? You know people are gossiping already.'

Her frosted pink smile slips and, mustering as much dignity as she can, she sweeps out of the room. Mr Bose is on the verge of tears. Cradling his head in his hands, he moans, 'It's all getting completely out of control.'

But there is more to Mr Bose's story and it explains why he is unshaven and so tired. All last night he was in the police *thana* helping to beat up a man who owes him money. His friend in the police found his debtor in the prostitutes' quarter of Calcutta and they struck him with bamboos until he promised to repay all of it. I don't know what to think. I am appalled by this violent episode, but I can no longer tell which of Mr Bose's stories are lies and which truthful. Perhaps he's trying to frighten me, sensing that I'm withdrawing my friendship. He seems to be approaching some kind of crisis and suddenly I no longer feel safe in his company. And I feel oddly powerless, realizing that my reputation in the railway headquarters is dependent on the rumours he spreads. I resolve that I will ask Subhrasheel to come to the offices and help me in my research. Then I will have an ally here who may be better equipped to judge what is going on and how to handle it all.

Subhrasheel can't believe that I swallowed Mr Bose's extravagant claims about his education and career. As we wind our way up one of the windowless staircases to the Personnel Library, he practises some lies about how his uncle is the Chief of Police in Calcutta. He thinks that Mr Bose will back off a little if he believes I have influential people to guard me. So many plots and counterplots have been hatched down the years on these dusty *paan*-stained stairs. When I first climbed them I never imagined that I would become a conspirator too.

Mr Bose nervously paces to and fro behind his desk, even more flustered than yesterday. He casts a suspicious glance at Subhrasheel: 'I have some private business to discuss with you, alone, Laura.'

'Subhrasheel is a close friend, he can stay.'

'Very well. I am not going to take up my new position in New Delhi. My mother had a heart attack last night caused by the smoke from the funeral ceremonies of my landlord. Now Lolita's mother won't be able to come over to look at my certificates for a while, my ma is too ill. I had to go to office and borrow fifteen thousand rupees from the library account for her emergency treatment in a nursing home. Please can I ask you as a friend to lend me the money so I can show it to my officer today? I'll repay you from the bank tomorrow.'

Feeling the need for a little circumspection, I ask him about the details of his mother's condition. Brushing aside my concern, he stresses his lost job opportunity and his immediate need for money. Subhrasheel takes over, telling him that I don't have that kind of money to spare, slipping in his lie about his uncle, the Chief of Police. Mr Bose stiffens and abruptly asks us to leave the office for a few minutes because he has to make a private call to check on his mother.

Outside, under the curious eyes of hundreds of clerks tapping away disconsolately at their typewriters, Subhrasheel whispers, 'It's obvious, Laura, this story cures all his problems at once. No-one will ever find out he lied about his position in New Delhi. Lolita's mother will be delayed from finding out the truth about his educational certificates. And he gains some money in the process.'

Despite his trickery, I feel sympathetic to Mr Bose. In order to save his prospects of marriage to Lolita, he has had to invent elaborate, desperate lies to counteract the Eastern Railway's web of intrigue against him.

When he calls us back in he has regained his composure. He wishes to inform us that his mother is much better, it was all a false alarm.

Subhrasheel and I settle into our work in the Record Room. To my surprise the *dufteris* allow us to look through the files deep in its recesses. Perhaps they are finally tired of all the years spent preventing people from seeing them. As we turn over banal reports of expenditures on housing and railway institutes we find what I have been looking for all along: sheaves and sheaves of petitions from railway workers to the Agent detailing their despair and the realities of railway colony life. The files date from 1920 to 1947. Their voices rise from the pages joining in with Pobon's song, until the crescendo is overwhelming. They complain of how British officers humiliate them, set their lackeys on them to beat them up and demand bribes in return for jobs. Some of them report on the immorality of their superior officers, mixing the languages of race and morality that they have learnt from the British to expose their hypocrisy. They accuse them of falling under the influence of 'great temptation' and of taking 'bribes for fornication'. More graphically, one petitioner uses the language of the history sheets drawn up by the personnel departments to document the story of Mr Jones, a railway inspector. He complains, 'What to say of the character of Mr Jones? It can be proved from the syphilitic eruption of Mr Jones who always enjoys the sweet company of low sweeper women of Inward and makes amorous gestures with them.' He details this officer's economic misdemeanours, and asserts that the unfair promotion of one of his friends was due to the aid this friend gave him in getting treated secretly for the syphilis at the

Calcutta Hospital of Tropical Medicine. Some labourers from the Lucknow Locomotive Works report, 'Here are two bribe eaters one of them is the chief man i.e. Mr Hemming Production Engineer who remember who has got three lady typists, one was pregnant and Mr Hemming took her to Simla and tried through the Doctors and organised an abortion and brought her back.' The intense scrutiny of fellow workers' morals is revealed in other petitions that typically report on colleagues' nocturnal habits: 'Ganga bears a doubtful character. He used to bring outsiders in the night to his quarters on the pleas of singing and music.' Other petitioners call for pure European officers to replace Anglo-Indians who bribe, beat them and seduce their wives, crying in despair, 'What hellish creatures are they?' These monsters of compromised morals are the monsters that the railway bureaucracy itself invents. I begin to understand that Mr Bose's despair is a long, tragic tradition that has been bequeathed to him by British railway officials.

Many petitioners have been sent mad by a lifetime of demanding justice from the Agent to no effect. An Anglo-Indian woman, Mrs Packwood, the widow of a railway driver, sends rational and plaintive letters to the Agent for years. She asks for fair treatment for her sons, who have been dismissed from their positions as trainee drivers because of minor misdemeanours. Then her writing grows erratic and desperate, her expressions bizarre and disjointed. I read and reread the last letter she sent to the Agent in 1930, thinking of the woman in Pobon's song:

> Kindly take an interest in my fatherless young ones because they are the real crown princes. Our family can prove our identity as pure Europeans and as a family that has pedigree in the King of England.
>
> I am in holy agony about my own sons' welfare.

I find that the cursed low who are aiding and abetting in mischief and crafty low black denominations have been cruelly detaining my sons and myself in our welfare. We are surrounded by errors of creation. My husband is dead and now his spirit haunts me and my sons. His ghost leads my sons astray and I find them always on the trail of some damned wench or in the arms of sluts. But my sons are good at heart when the spirit is not around them.

Please help them. At every turn no matter what we may do the cursed superior officers have been intolerably educated to annoy and we have been incessantly disfigured and discoloured. Mr Brooks and Davies and several others here have arrowed us and burrowed into our flesh and we are driven by every blast of creation. The Divisional Superintendent Mr Hunter knows the truth, but he seems to be waiting for the Gods to act and has not acted himself. The issue of employment for my sons seems to be in God's hands and he is playing on us for death sentence the while. Even though I excel in going to communion and knowledge of Catholic and Protestant prayers my sons have not even got their rights from the cursed office. Please in your great mercy and omnipotence help my sons with your benevolence.

Mrs Packwood's faltering plea, like Mr Bose's dilemma, only mirrors the madness of the railway bureaucracy. The Agent has written in red on the top of this file, 'This woman is obviously insane.' Yet given that railway officers conjure up a palace in which race, caste, religion and morality decide each employee's prospects for advancement, she is quite sane in offering proof of her faith, respectability and impeccable ancestry. The Agent and the Divisional Superintendents with their tyrannical authority to determine the fate of people are similar to gods and kings. And most strikingly she sees that it is the spirit of her dead husband who introduced her to this world full of errors of creation. He was the one who first took employment in the railway and placed her family under the malignant influence of the six *sahebs*.

Deeper within the files are a series of letters from a dismissed store clerk, Harendra Krishna De. Telling the Agent about the pilferage of spare parts from the godowns, he is alarmed by the risk to passenger safety that this causes. His British superior tells the store clerks and workmen, instead of replacing broken parts, to patch them together and he then sells off the new parts to scrap-metal merchants. Krishna De says he has collected in his private notebooks detailed information of this conspiracy and of the accidents it may have caused. He will make these available to the Agent. He also suggests an elaborate system of procedures for preventing this pilferage. The Agent consults with Krishna De's superior who dismisses the clerk's claims. Krishna De is sacked without pension for immoral behaviour. But he keeps writing to the Agent for six years, still believing he should strive for justice. He rails against the charge that has been falsely laid against him that he took sweeper women to empty carriages and slept with them. Reduced to penury and living with his relatives, a year later he loses his sanity and writes:

To the Agent, Fairleigh Place
From: Prince Albert Francis Augastion Charles
Emanuel of Sax Coburg and Gotha
Consort of Queen Victoria, On Her Majesty's
Service in India appeared in the guise of Hindu
divinity by name of Harendra Krishna De, 23
Telepara Lane, Shambazar, Calcutta.

Sir,

It is with a profound and deep feeling of heart that I am going to approach you after an age of protesting i.e. six years with the following facts for your kind decision and justice, trusting fervently you will not hesitate to take up the matter into your own hand through the proper channel.

This age is a period of changes and alterations and the apparent impossibilities are turned into possibilities, one thing which was unknown to the world, has come to be known before our eyes. Insignificant creatures like me, who were found trifling at first, have risen to the highest position. Robert Clive from the position of a petty clerk rose to the eminence of a great hero, so my arrival and service in your Company will exhibit my real appearance to the world as the consort of Queen Victoria.

I deem it proper to place my grievance before you hoping that you will take up the case for disposal at your Old Fairleigh Place, a historical building, and will record this royal secret matter of my true personage in the pages of the History of the East India Company.

Further if the case had been decided earlier, I assure you that the crises of the world might not have occurred nor would the British Nation have had to become so busy or anxious for their futurity in India.

I have the honour to be, Sir, your most obedient servant:

Harendra Krishna De

To prove his identity he encloses poems that Queen Victoria has written to him in his disguise as Prince Albert.

As I read these letters Mr Bose appears in the Record

Room. He has come to retrieve some papers for a railway worker who has arrived from Moghalserai for advice on his case. Eager to be friendly with him again, understanding his position better and appreciating the service he is trying to render to this worker, I tell him about what I have found. He picks up Harendra Krishna De's letter and reads it. He laughs wildly and says, 'Soon I will be writing letters like this to the Deputy General Manager.'

The days spent in the Record Room reveal other secrets to Subhrasheel and me. Among the caches of documents are files marked 'nationality'. These contain plaintive requests from Anglo-Indians to be listed as British in the railway employment hierarchy. They provide the proof of family anecdotes, medical certificates from doctors and private correspondence sometimes going back as far as the eighteenth century to persuade the bureaucrats of the truth of their origins. Raj officials close the files, coldly demanding more rigorous proof. The railway bureaucrats jealously guard the right to be British and the passage back to Britain on retirement that this classification guarantees.

Despite the finality of the Agent's decisions on the identity of Anglo-Indians, all the railway officials are uncertain about how to tell the difference between Anglo-Indians and Europeans. Doctors argue that skin colour is misleading because people turn dark after years of exposure to the Indian sun. English habits and demeanour can be faked. The only thing that counts as real proof is evidence of property in Britain or birth certificates and records stretching back over generations. But whenever Anglo-Indians try to find these documents to prove that they are British in their male line, they are met with the callousness of other bureaucracies who have destroyed them years ago. They have no hope of claiming their birthright. Reading the rejected requests, I understand the stiff silence in Gary and Carol's flat when I enquired about their British ancestry. My question echoed the suspicion of all these Raj officials. Their silence reflected the impossibility of proving their origins.

Looking up from his reading, Subhrasheel remarks, 'Now I understand that joke about the Anglo-Indian national library – these people have well and truly lost the book, and it's through no fault of their own.'

But I am distracted by a case I have just turned up which stops me in my tracks. The Stanhope Jones brothers are writing to the Agent in the 1930s and among their ancestors they list an Edith Batten. Batten is my mother's maiden name, not a common one at all. My mother's cousin has spent years tracing the family history and she swears that all the Battens are related not that far back. But neither she nor my grandfather had ever mentioned anyone going to India. Despite being drawn into the intrigues of the Moghul Palace I had felt able to maintain a distance from it, but now I seemed to be on the verge of discovering a personal interest, a story from my own family.

Turning over the brittle pages, my fingers blacken as I follow Mr C. Stanhope Jones and Mr V. Stanhope Jones's attempts to claim their British origins. A medical officer at Lilloah inspected them in 1939 and the officer writes to the Agent that 'from personal appearance and from the examination of their maternal and paternal records I am convinced that both these brothers are Europeans. I am informed that one of their brothers, who is on the Burma railways, is under the European leave rules,' and the Controller of Stores altered their record accordingly. The Agent protests at this decision taken without his authority and refers the Jones brothers to an interview with the Chief Medical Officer in Dalhousie Square. The doctor decides that they are actually Anglo-Indian. Mr C. Stanhope Jones protests:

How can my full blood brother be classified as
European in Burma and myself and my other
brother Anglo-Indian in India? England and the
Allies, Sir, are at war today only because Germany
deprived Poland of her birth right. If we are to take
the action of England as sincere then, Sir, you as
British Officers, must admit that I have a right to
fight for my proper place. I will no longer support
the British cause at war if I am treated so shame-
fully. How can I continue to be a patriot? I am
classified as a European British subject in the
regulation for registration for national service. I
cannot be European for one purpose and Anglo-
Indian for another.

The Agent writes back to him that the 'onus of proof'
lies with him alone and that he must present further
documentary evidence of his claims. Stanhope Jones
sends back the following copious list of records, none
of the originals of which still exist in the file in front of
me.

Records Offered to Prove Nationality
1. Extract from parish register books of St Johns
Calcutta, Mr E J Stanhope Jones married Miss E
Batten on 5/1/1900
2. Burial certificate of Mrs E J Stanhope Jones
3. Letter no. 6 dated 29/9/26 from R J Twyford
and Co., solicitors to Mrs S Stanhope Jones
6. Chart dated 10/12/29 showing the antecedents
paternal and maternal of Mr Stanhope Jones'
mother, Edith Batten.
8. Letter dated 4/4/1813 from Mr G N Stanhope
Jones to Fanny Wyatt

The Agent replies that this evidence contains 'no
relevant facts at all' and that Mr C. Stanhope Jones's
claim that his father wrote in 1906 protesting his own

classification as Anglo-Indian cannot be proved because the railway authorities have destroyed the papers long ago. On the other hand the railway records show that his father, himself and his brother have all along been listed as Anglo-Indian. Mr C. Stanhope Jones then tries to prove his mother's nationality by producing a letter from the Senior United Board Chaplain in India, Kasauli, certifying that to the best of his knowledge she was the daughter of English parents. He adds to this a promise of a certificate from the doctor who attended his mother in her last illness, but says that this will take time because he does not know where the doctor is now stationed. This still does not convince the Agent and the Stanhope Jones brothers remain unvindicated.

My suspicions of forgotten kinship to them will also have to remain unresolved. If they could not find the requisite documents in the 1930s what hope do I have now of unearthing them? Their story will have to remain forever disconnected from my family's belief that it has had no part in the Raj. My relatives in Britain, although proud of our family's lower-middle-class life as publicans and horse traders, have concentrated all their efforts on hunting down links through a bastard child to the Earl of Huntingdon. Even my rebellious grandfather spun tales about this brush with nobility. They are not alone in this. Britain has jealously guarded its shores from the influx of Anglo-Indian histories. I may be imagining a connection to Edith Batten, the Stanhope Jones family's story of British nationality may be untrue. But what frustrates me most is that, despite the copious records, I will never be able to find out if it is true or false.

When I explain the reason for my silence to Subhrasheel, he laughs: 'I don't know if my parents will want me to have someone with connections to *Tash* as my sister. But I'm all right with it. My family claims to have ancestral connections with Rajput princes. They sent detailed descriptions of their immaculate caste pedigree to British census officials in the early twentieth century. We still use them as reference for family history today. But I know those Rajput princes just rode in here on their horses, raped a few local tribals and that made our illustrious true-blue Bengali family. There are rumours of West Indian slaves and Portuguese mistresses too, kept for all kinds of purposes by our great-great-grandfather. He had a few children probably by them also. I'm with you, this purity thing is just one huge dream. We're all some variety of *Tash*, if only we would admit it. That's why we're so hung up on telling everybody we're nothing like Anglo-Indians.'

Smiling at Subhrasheel, I know that our separate family histories have brought us to the same point of understanding. The ceremony of Bhai Phota would only seal a kinship that has already grown between us.

Subhrasheel slowly wipes the black dust from his long fingers and says, 'I'll come with you when you go to Kharagpur. I'm so curious about the place now.' He laughs and adds ironically, 'Maybe the *Tash* in my blood is beginning to come out too.'

I am making my way past the temple at Ballygunj Phari to visit Gary's mother, Marigold, in the three-room flat which she shares with her unmarried daughter and two of her sons, their wives and three grandchildren. She welcomes me, saying that she has heard a lot about me from her son. Her black hair is peppered with grey, but her mulberry and white chintz frock is carefully ironed and sits snugly on her wiry, tough body. Inside the flat is as grim and dark as a long corridor, yet its sharp lines are smoothed with homely pleasures and rose-pink paint. Green chillies in oil sit on a window sill, gathering just the right degree of burning heat. Jeans, *salwar kameezes*, miniskirts, kurtas, T-shirts and *dupattas* dry scattered over teak dining-room chairs. A *shilnora* and *boti*, the cutting knife mounted on a board always associated with Bengali housewives, wait for use by the kitchen door next to a maturing pot of home-made marmalade. On the wall a needlepoint cloth embroidered with jasmine and daffodils proclaims, 'Home is where the Heart is'. Marigold sits down on a huge rose-red sofa and rocks her two-year-old grandson Sim to sleep, singing, 'Here we go on a frosty morning,' in the sweltering heat of June. Scolding Sim, she points at the nativity picture on the wall: 'Baby Jesus is angry with you. Yes, he is crying, look how angry he is with you, don't be dirty.' Then she tries to soothe him again with a tale of the three bears who went for a walk in the jungle only to get back and find their porridge eaten and someone sleeping on their charpoys. Sitting next to her is a sober woman in a black frock edged with a lace collar, puffing and sweating heavily in the heat. Marigold introduces her as Antoinette Fantome, an old school-friend from Loretto Convent, Entally, on a visit from St Vincent's, a nursing home run by Catholic nuns in which she is spending her old age. Absorbed in reminiscing about Loretto Convent, they ignore me, so I curl up on a giant armchair beside them and listen.

They become girlish and giggle as their recollections flow. They remember the excitement and humiliation when the convent girls of marriageable age were lined up by the nuns in front of potential husbands, all Anglo-Indian or enlisted British men. But Marigold remembers that the girls dreaded being chosen by a British man. She says, 'They were all so rough and you couldn't make out their caste. Many of them were married already. I had one friend in the railway colony who took up with a British army man, was going to marry him. Then he wrote admitting he had a wife and child back home. Should have seen the state of her, spoiled her chances. She should have stuck to the fellow her parents were arranging for her to marry. All the Europeans we knew in the railway colonies were illiterate, could only sign with thumb prints for their salary. Used to play tricks on them. They had coloured flags on their engines to identify which one was theirs to drive. We used to switch them round after dark. What a mess it was the next morning!'

I can hardly keep up with the surprises of this conversation. This doesn't fit Indian or British ideas of Anglo-Indian girls' desperate desires to marry up into white pedigrees. Mr Bose and Mrs Gupta would also be amazed to hear that Anglos had arranged marriages and did not just seek out bed partners. Before I can ask any questions, Antoinette and Marigold are talking about how they used to dress up as Snow White and the Seven Dwarfs at Loretto Convent.

Marigold jokes, 'More like Snow Black I was. Just like those Guy Fawkes parties at the Rangers' Club at Diwali time, everybody thinks it is true British traditions, but I like to call it Guy Gomes night. Can't stand those Anglos that put on airs, forgetting their Indian roots and all.'

Antoinette Fantome adds, 'My father was Irish, but we weren't like those glorified Anglo-Indians in the railway colonies who were fair and looked European and tried to pass themselves off as Domiciled Europeans. Putting on English caps, *baba*, what you get by doing all of that when you haven't been there? Never wanted to go to Britain myself. My father was entitled to get assisted passages there from the railways. My parents sold their house three times planning to go to England. But I took fright each time and told them not to go. When we were in the railway colony at Waltair, I sold my grand piano to get the tickets for London, but I lost all of this because when it came to it I just couldn't leave India.'

Looking at me, she hesitates before continuing, 'In

England they treat coloured Anglo-Indians very badly and India was in my blood just as much. My family tree, all of it, is in the Lucknow library at Kaiser Bagh. Used to have a copy of it, but I tore it up because I am the last in my family. Independence came and what use would Indians or I have for it after that?'

The Agent's Record Room did not have any documents that recorded this rejection of British traditions. Nor did it record this acute awareness of the ill-treatment that the white boundaries to national identity created. But my delight in this is halted by the realization that Antoinette Fantome ripped up her family history at Independence, seeing it as irrelevant to India's new national myths. This was a capitulation to another purist mythology that didn't want to recognize the mixed origins that were part of India's present as much as its past.

My fears are confirmed as Marigold speaks again: 'But it's all right for you, Antoinette, you don't have children. My uncle who adopted me was pure British and if I had the adoption papers now I could help my family. And now because I only thought selfishly of myself and not my children's future I never managed to get any evidence of adoption. My father-in-law emigrated to London in 1948 and asked us to come along after they had settled down, but I selfishly didn't want to leave my people, my family. I could have had the chance to go to Britain when my uncle went on his six months' privilege leave as a domiciled European, but I always refused, saying, "Oh no, I'm too black, even you will look down on me and treat me differently there. I don't want to go." '

Taking Antoinette's hand, she adds sadly, 'Because I had no proof, all the property in Britain went to the brother when my uncle died. Now I can't come to the rescue of my children. The Indians don't want them here and now the British won't believe they are entitled because I don't have any proof, any documents to show them. I tried writing to the railways, but they didn't have any records left either. What to do?'

Despite her irreverence Marigold is still caught in the binds that the Railway Record Room created. Deeply enfolded in its logic of whiteness, she imagines she would not be accepted in Britain. She knows her family has legitimate links to Britain, but she can't prove it as her family does not appear in the railway files. She feels that she is part Indian, but she is not accepted and cannot imagine a future for her children here. I'm curious about Marigold's adoption and what took her away from her family.

'I was adopted when I was six years old, went to live in the railway colony at Addra with my mother's sister and her husband. I cried and cried when I first got there. My uncle was so strange with his British ways. To look at his food only we would get sick. His roast had to be uncooked – how dirty it was. He smoked cigars and he used to put them in the holes in his bed for putting his mosquito net up. I wanted to see what it was like, to be like a *saheb* and all, so I used to steal the cigar and try it. Nearly coughed all my lungs up at once.'

Pulling her frock over her knees, she remembers, 'As we got older he used to be very particular in company about our habits. He wanted us to sit properly at the dining table and use a knife and fork British style. He didn't like it when we wore short dresses and people could see our panties when we picked berries from the bushes. The only time he slapped me was when some boys were over and I started laughing hard. He let us go to dances, but he was very particular about etiquette. I suppose each caste has to have its customs. Although you know what they say about Anglo-Indians, *"Anglo-Indian ka gari, Muslim ka hari, Bengali ka bari* – Anglo-Indians are only moving around in cars and trains, showing off, Muslims are

131

for cooking, and Bengalis are always working and investing in their home." '

Antoinette and Marigold laugh at this proverb. Marigold continues to reminisce: 'We used to make saris and lungis into frocks and skirts, tailored from foreign catalogues, for dances in the Railway Institute. My uncle made sure that the army boys could be friends in the dance hall only. Some people thought I was a flirt and when I started with my husband people said to him, "Why do you want her? She has had a good time with everybody." But I said being familiar and being popular are two different things. I told my future husband's family they could go and ask the priest for a reference for my character if they wanted. There were rumours or gossip in the railway colony whatever you did, good or bad. But the colony and my uncle taught me how to have the habits of the British caste, that's why my parents sent me there. They thought I would have a better chance at marriage and life.'

She pauses and then admits mournfully, 'Later my parents thought different, but then it was too late. When I used to come home and they spoke Tamil to me, I'd almost forgotten it all with my English education and etiquette. They'd say to me, "Oh, look at Marigold, she's become such a *memsaheb* now, hardly recognize her." I felt bad when they said that and I lost contact with my sisters because of this difference. It's like the partition between India and Pakistan between us, almost a different nationality I am. Sometimes I let the cat out of the bag when I'm with Tamils. Then I start to remember my mother tongue, but all that training takes over and I don't let on. Real upcountry railway girl I am, but then that country doesn't exist any more, does it? I should just throw in the towel and call myself a citizen of the world, at home nowhere and everywhere. A new caste no-one wants to call their own, a Tamil mem.'

Marigold begins to tease me: 'Watch out, Laura, you're sitting there in your *salwar kameez* and *shakha pola* bracelets and all, you'll just end up as a Bengali mem. Then what will your husband think? What caste is he? My husband was Anglo-Burmese.'

I don't know how to reply to this question and Marigold reads my confusion: 'Oh I was just enquiring about his education and all. That's what makes a caste, isn't it?'

I like her definition of caste origin as something fluid and amorphous. If it is fluid then there is still some hope of its being remoulded by the present. This is so different from the rigid sense of the weight of antecedents that I have encountered in the railway archives and in Bengali ancestral lines. There is a sense of life as a passage here.

Before I can reply to Marigold's question, Antoinette begins to speak: 'My sister's daughter, Clara, has become a Muslim *memsaheb*. She married a Muslim fellow, one with first-class education, certificates. She was fated, so what to do? That's why I ended up in St Vincent's. She's my only living relative. She comes and asks me to live with her and her husband, but I tell her always I couldn't do that. It would only cause problems for her with her parents-in-law. It makes me sad sometimes that she's broken her caste. Sometimes I worry because our link would have been broken among us, like my mother, my father, my sister, my niece, we would like to be wherever we are going all together, whether we go to heaven or hell, that's the thing you see.'

Losing her solemn mood Antoinette sharply pulls up her heavy frame and says, 'I'm very proud of my niece, she's a very good actress. She took the part of Peter who denied Christ at a school play, and how funny she did it, it was all foretold to me, in that play, like she changed and became a Muslim, they all clapped, very attractive. Too good she is as an actress. But then

133

that skill is with me also, served me well at times, even saved lives with it. Near Independence there was all that rioting between Hindus and Muslims. Even came to Lilloah railway colony where we were living. At about ten o'clock in the night a Muslim family came to me. They turned and told me, "Whatever you do, save us." The rioters weren't touching us at that time. All the Anglos painted crosses on their doors. The family, Jesus, three children they had. I was scared my life would also go, but I locked them, the family, in the bathroom. A person came up, one of the Hindus came up and said, "You've got someone in your place." I said, "What nonsense you talking, what I'll keep, you think I'll keep?" He said, "You have got." Lucky the children didn't make a noise. I was feeling very frightened, darling. I took a very big risk. We took them with our own hands and kept them safely. What they were doing down the road and on the street. They were taking little five-month-old baby, three-month-old baby, had a knife like that, up like that, the baby on the knife. Sometimes it's good to be a good actress. Always good at bluffing when we need to, us Anglos.'

This was the acting skill that British railway officials and Bengalis so feared in Anglo-Indians. It made them untrustworthy and subject to the scrutiny of railway doctors and agents. For Mr Ghosh this rootlessness was a vice, profoundly different from the loyalty of Bengalis to their *desh* or village home. But now I realize from Antoinette's story that it also allowed them to make moral choices that did not rest on the bloody lines of caste, religion and nationality. However heavily these lines cross over their lives, they also dissolve into fictions in their family and personal histories. Sim's father arrives and the conversation drifts into catching up on family news. I leave, thanking Antoinette and Marigold.

On the way home I begin excitedly to plan my trip to Kharagpur with Subhrasheel. There I will encounter more stories like these. They may finally shake off the weight of the Moghul Palace.

Reaching my flat, I settle down with a cup of the sweet milky tea and *sandesh* I have now acquired a taste for. Opening my daily newspaper, the *Statesman*, I read an article entitled 'Love Letters in the Sand'. The author, Kali Bandyopadhyay, is reminiscing about an old friend of his. His friend was besotted with a girl, Gopa, who lived in his neighbourhood. He followed her around for months, finally getting up the courage to send her love letters that were passed to her by a family servant. Gopa sent him affectionate letters back. They would meet at bus stops and occasionally he would turn up at her house to make duty visits to her parents, which would lay the ground for their marriage. A year later, around Kali puja, he got up the courage to write an eight-page letter to his Gopa proposing marriage. He was thrilled when he met her by the puja *pandal* and she said that her mother wanted to speak to him. Inside his love's house, her mother greeted him with great joy, but he couldn't see his one and only girl anywhere. Her mother said, 'I've read your letter with great interest, but we can never agree to the match.' Overcome with embarrassment, he cursed the family servant he had trusted with his future. Carrying a huge plate of sweets, Gopa appeared dressed in an expensive sari. Her mother said, 'Today is Bhai Phota, so now is the chance for Gopa to become your sister.' Gopa placed sandalwood paste on his forehead. Before he could gather his wits to stop it he was her brother, his passion made impossible for all time.

I remember the moment Subhrasheel chose to make his offer of brotherhood to me. It was just after Pobon's song about the chaos caused by the six vices and lust between men and women. Was this just a coincidence, or was Subhrasheel's suggestion of Bhai Phota an attempt to remove the possibility of any other kind of relationship with a married, older, British woman? Had Pobon been trying to tell two stories to me that night? One of the chaos caused by the railway bureaucracy that I had witnessed in the Eastern Railway headquarters; the other of the dangerous consequences of the growing friendship between Subhrasheel and me?

Perhaps Subhrasheel's curiosity about Anglo-Indians reflects more than a general distrust of Bengali and British high culture. Does he want to know more because his feelings were leading him to imagine straying into their domain? But I am still uncertain of the answer. His offer may be just a gift of simple affection. I spend the evening reading Pobon's song over and over again to divine its other meanings.

5

Bazaar Spies

Another train stops at Kharagpur junction and in the street outside the railway guest house passengers call for coolies and cycle-rickshaws to help them in the last leg of their long evening journeys. Beyond the mulberry curtains through the window the shadowy figure of the *durwan* rises from his charpoy. He curses as he searches in the darkness for the keys to admit a late-night guest to the room next door. The muffled thud of a heavy suitcase and the creaking furniture give no clues to the identity of our new neighbour.

Subhrasheel starts to speculate about who it is: 'Perhaps it's a secret agent from the Vigilance Department coming to spy on the colony. Or maybe it's Mr Bose come to check up on whether you are hanging out with bad characters. He'd have plenty of rumours to spread if he could see us here together in the same room.'

I begin to think that now is the moment to ask Subhrasheel about the Bhai Phota ceremony, and to discover his reasons for making his offer. I try to think of a diplomatic way of broaching the subject, and decide to describe the article in the *Statesman*. As I tell him all about it, I find myself revealing Maurice's anger at the proposal and so have hinted at a fear that Subhrasheel may desire me. He stiffens and the silence is heavy. Now my suspicions are suspended in the air between us and I'm acutely self-conscious about sharing this room. Even though the heat has grown more oppressive, I draw the stiff starched sheet up to my chin. As the rigidly ironed creases unfold it crackles noisily, making plain my defensive move. I can't bear to look across at Subhrasheel.

Mosquitoes whine relentlessly on the other side of the net. Subhrasheel yanks the mosquito net from his mattress, climbs out from underneath it and strides over to the cane lawn chair, planting himself in it at a distance from me. Then his voice, spiked with anger, crosses the space between us.

'You've obviously spent too long in the Eastern Railway headquarters,' he snaps, 'and now you assume that a plain offer of friendship is covering up some immoral motive. It's completely ridiculous.'

I feel heat flushing into my face. All the stories I have been unearthing show how easy it is to fall into the habit of suspecting illicit desires to be at the root of everything. I know I need to make amends, and I desperately don't want to hurt Subhrasheel any more than I have done. To soothe his anger I need to show that I understand that my suspicions have grown from a long, infamous tradition. Taking a deep breath, I begin again.

'Long before I came to Calcutta and Kharagpur I read the story of Anna Bella Chakrabarty in the India Office Library. I was immediately fascinated by her name, its fusion of Victorian delicacy and Bengali high-caste demureness. Who were her parents? Was she Indian Christian, Anglo-Indian, Hindu or Muslim? Perhaps she named herself. If so it was an interesting choice, a name that couldn't be pigeon-holed into one or other of India's communities. We will never know the answers to these questions, because they weren't seen as relevant to her case in the official documents. What I do know is that she lived for a time with a man known as her husband, a clerk in the Engineers' Office at Arrah, before he sent her, or she went of her own accord, to the military cantonment and railway colony of Dinapore . . .'

At that time, in 1876, Dinapore was the biggest military station between Calcutta and Allahabad and was renowned for its bazaar full of cheap, bustling tenements. The bazaar was notorious among officials as a home for half-caste pensioners and railwaymen's families in reduced circumstances. Temporary contracts of marriage or Nika marriages were common. The local army surgeons and railway officers thought women used these as a cover for prostitution. They condemned them for transferring their affections with great ease to new men. It was the kind of place, far from the high society of civil servants, which gave birth to generations of Anglo-Indians who drifted in and out of employ in the nearby railway colony. Just the same as Kharagpur Bazaar was two decades later. Anna Bella settled down in Turhatoli Orderly Bazaar where all the kept women of the 109th Regiment lived. She shared a dingy tenement with a group of Christian women who were married to soldiers or railway-men without the blessing of their husband's superior officers. There was a local nickname used to describe women such as Anna Bella. They were called the Roses. Not quite English Roses, but fragrant all the same.

But then one night Anna Bella was discovered by the cantonment police sitting with a British soldier under a mango tree. They hauled her off to the lock-up and charged her under the Contagious Diseases Act of 1869. The act was a very odd rule designed to provide a regular supply of undiseased prostitutes for the soldiers. These official prostitutes were recorded in registers and sent monthly to lock-hospitals for medical check-ups. Under the law any woman unwary enough to dally at night with military lovers or friends could be prosecuted and forced to declare herself as a registered prostitute. Anna Bella was convicted by the cantonment magistrate of being a public woman, of receiving men of the infantry and artillery at all hours of the night, fined fifty rupees and placed on the register. But she was not happy with her new status as a public woman and took the case to the High Court at Fort William in Calcutta.

The High Court disposed of the case promptly, ruling in her favour that there was no proof she was a prostitute. They criticized her for a certain looseness of morals demonstrated by her willingness to welcome men into her tenement block for evening entertainments. But they couldn't prove that she had received money for this. Anna Bella had won a victory for herself. It was possible to feel love, friendship or lust without being declared a prostitute. But ironically her successful appeal led to a toughening of the law and made the authorities even more vigilant, ever on the lookout for what might be deemed lustful liaisons.

Back in Dinapore the case was a sensational scandal. Parties were thrown in Turhatoli Bazaar and all the pensioners, Eurasians and unofficial wives breathed a sigh of relief. But the cantonment magistrate, staff surgeon and various officers were worried. They sat up late into the night discussing its implications, convened meetings in their bungalows and penned memos on the affections of Anglo-India. The staff surgeon rushed off a disgusted letter to the Magistrate of Patna informing him of the rejoicing in the bazaar. He warned the Magistrate that the Roses would now ply their trade with impunity. The High Court ruling made it a tricky matter to prosecute them. And, he added, the cases of disease among the soldiers would increase. The problem was that it was so hard to prove that any of them were prostitutes – even though he personally knew they were – because very often they plied their trade for lust only and refused to accept money from their paramours. The Magistrate's response was swift. Spies were posted in the bazaar and the character of every resident female was enquired into and reported. This kind of paranoia allowed for no distinction between friendship or love or lust and so, no matter what the nature of the relationship, it was regarded as prostitution. Soldiers' wives were reported to their husband's superiors for consorting with railway officers while their husbands were away; picking up businessmen from Patna with the help of coolies in the local auction house; or smuggling in lovers disguised as natives. As the activities of the authorities became more and more obsessional, it was as though matters of the heart had become an affair of state. The outraged letters sent to superior officers by husbands defending the sanctity of their marriages went unanswered. Husbands were suspected of covering up the monetary gains they received from prostituting their own wives. Here is one such indignant plea:

It is over a month and Colonel Emerson has not produced any proof of his statement against the character of my wife. I feel the accusation against my wife just as keenly as if I were in a higher position in life. I know that the law is open to me, but I am a poor man and cannot afford to go to law. I think my case is a very hard one. I therefore, through you as my commanding officer, respectfully appeal to the protection of the Major-General commanding the division, and trust that Colonel Emerson may be called upon either to prove his statement or to withdraw his letter and make an apology.

'Are these words of lust or love, outraged honour or a cover for pecuniary gain?' I ask Subhrasheel. 'Who can tell in the sprawling tenements, military

141

cantonments and railway colonies of Anglo-India? How do we pick our way through the shades of meaning and motive that insinuate themselves into our minds when suspicion, desire and lust seem to be at the very heart of everything? Now do you see why I misunderstood you?'

Subhrasheel drums his fingertips in irritation against the long arms of the chair, but at least now his anger isn't directed towards me.

He says, 'There are so many tangled webs of suspicion around us. Probir warned my parents that I was too old to be travelling alone with a foreign, elder, married woman to Kharagpur. My parents are just as uneasy about my motives for coming as you were about the Bhai Phota ceremony. How can we unravel our friendship from all of these layers?'

I don't know if we can. Although Raj history had lingered around us in Calcutta, since we started our journey to Kharagpur it has crowded in closer. We had both been curious about Kharagpur's realities, yet once we confronted them they began to draw us in. Earlier this evening Subhrasheel had hated me as a symbol of the past and I had just judged him with the suspicious eyes of a bazaar spy. And the old stories we are telling of Anglo-India are no longer distant vignettes of another time; instead they are part of our lives. The fate of our friendship depends on them. When I first saw the photographs of Kharagpur in the university library I could never have predicted this. Surely when Subhrasheel made his decision to come with me he hadn't anticipated it either. Thinking over our first two days here, I try to pin down the moments when harmless curiosity changed into an intimate connection with the past.

6

The Shameless Bushes

Subhrasheel leans out of the local train to Kharagpur, braced against its metallic jarring only by his finger-tips around the doorframe. Cooled by the hazy morning air whistling past the train, he searches for signs of our destination. Anchored to the hard wooden seat by the heat and the pressure of fellow passengers, I see Subhrasheel now watching me from across the carriage. He is crushed against empty palm-leaf fish baskets, jute sacks bulging with Murshidabad mangoes, and vendors whose lives are spent on this route. The scent of jasmine strings swinging in the hands of a hawker rises through the air, mingling with the pungent aromas of onion, mustard oil and black salt from the red, blue and green tin cans rattling around the neck of a *moori*-seller. In the stifling atmosphere sweat lingers, pouring from salesmen in crumpled shirts clutching vinyl suitcases full of samples, pleaders with oiled hair rehearsing legal speeches under their breath, and cub reporters from Bengali dailies hunting for news. Next to me a vendor unfurls a plastic key chain, a magenta bird that lights up and chirps. My neighbour, pock-marked and soiled from years of being shunted around, lets the showman perform his tricks, gossiping with him and enjoying his act. Subhrasheel maintains his nonchalant stare, undisturbed by a packet of emerald-green *tulsi* sweets thrust into his face by another hopeful vendor who tells him that they are guaranteed to soothe throats stinging from the diesel fumes of the train. Pasted on the rusted carriage walls are flyers for patent ayurvedic medicines that claim to cure all sexual diseases and desires. Overlapping them are communist party leaflets urging the passengers to attend a protest on the maidan against the GATT treaty. They display a cartoon of Uncle Sam grasping the tail of Mother India, a cow who weeps in despair. Barely visible beneath the layers is a notice that orders, 'National Property: do not deface'.

My limbs demand release from the heat and Subhrasheel's gaze. The more he stares the heavier my body gets. The fans above the passengers' heads stopped working years ago and the barred window is far away. There are no views of the picturesque villages or elegant women half-draped in saris that Victorian *sahebs* and *memsahebs* loved to note in their memoirs. Travelling in the tropical grandeur of first-class carriages they turned India into Kipling country, influenced by his short stories which were sold on every platform. But this carriage, like pre-Independence third- and fourth-class rolling stock, offers no languid contemplation of the Indian national landscape. Instead the eye is caught by the details of tired faces carrying their life stories to another temporary destination. The books sold to passengers – astrological guides and palm-reading manuals – offer instructions on how to decipher these stories. In the hiatus between departure and arrival the passengers speculate about one another. An ancient freedom fighter, wearing a *khadi* shirt and dhoti, frowns at the Marwari businessman opposite him, who is loudly chewing *paan* and rifling for food through the steel boxes stashed under his seat. A Bengali matron adjusts her white and red cotton sari, checking that none of her rolling stomach is showing, and purses her lips at the giggling maidservants beside her, whose purple and turquoise nylon saris offend her taste. Two seats away an off-duty Railway Protection Force guard relates his life spent patrolling trains in Bihar for dacoits. The only time he failed in his duty was when confronted by a crowd of women protesting on the tracks. He asks his new friend, 'How could I point a gun at them and maintain my honour?'

Just below the rumble of the train are speculations about the young college student accompanying a *memsaheb*. These murmurs have a long history. British railway officials and Indian nationalists years ago debated how Indian women could be encouraged to travel on the railways. Between them they came up with elaborate arrangements of screens and folding doors leading from *palkis* to ladies' compartments. These would prevent respectable women from being soiled by the gaze of the raucous hoi polloi, preserving their honour. But any woman who couldn't afford such elaborate arrangements was perceived as fair game for unwanted attentions. Now scenes in Hindi movies play with the erotic charge of the railway carriage. Govinda, the actor known for cheeky double entendres, sings to a starlet dressed as a tribal woman about the sensuous rhythms of the train. Sharukh Khan breaks into a ladies' compartment to find a collection of insatiable dancing girls who tug at him, making their desires obvious. Subhrasheel and I are caught in this public intimacy. Yet I still can't decipher the question in Subhrasheel's eyes. Why am I so curious? Why did I want to leap inside his body and hang from the carriage suspended from his fingertips? Is it just because I want to know where this journey is heading?

As the train grinds to a halt at yet another red-brick station the vendors sprint to the next carriage, searching for more customers. Before a new crowd arrives Subhrasheel manoeuvres through the empty space between us and squeezes himself beside me on the bench. My pock-marked neighbour raises an eyebrow as he sees Subhrasheel's leg crushed next to mine. Self-conscious about this proximity, I stare fixedly at my *shakha pola* bracelets. Then I whisper, 'Do you think our fellow passengers take us for a married couple from my bracelets?'

He laughs with a trace of scorn: 'No, you're much too old and plump-looking for someone like me. More likely they think I'm some drug addict who has latched on to an easy source of money. People always take my skinniness and snake eyes for signs of a heroin user. Sometimes it's a nuisance – I get bothered late at night on Park Street by drug peddlers or stopped after dark by married men asking for sexual favours in the Lakes. Other times it's useful. Fastest route for you to get a ticket to the latest sold-out Hindi blockbuster is to take me with you. All the black marketeers approach me to do a deal with one of their brothers first. The brethren of thieves always works wonders. My girlfriends, usually the demurely seething type, love this aura of wickedness as long as I can reassure them about my career prospects as well. So I'll probably end up marrying one of them and trying to live up to their desire for a sensuous chartered accountant. Make sure you come to the wedding just to see the show.'

'What would your father say if he knew about all of this? He's always going on about how proud he is of his respectable, well-brought-up children. How you are the one thing he has done right in his life.'

'I'm not quite as good as he thinks and not quite as wicked as I look.'

I ask him what kind of person he would choose to marry, feeling certain that he will amuse himself by trying to shock me.

'If I really wanted to upset the family I'd choose some *Tash* or, even worse, a Muslim.'

I smile, but he continues quite seriously, 'The one

thing that binds my family together through our squabbles is the massacre of my great-grandfather's family by Muslim labourers at Noakhali in 1946. My grandfather left the place only three days before; none of our generation would have been born if he had stayed. These murders are what sparked off the Great Calcutta Killing and led to the partition of India and Pakistan. Gandhi even came to our village home afterwards to try and prevent further rioting. Our family were the local landlords. Their house was vast and you had to approach it by crossing a lake. The lake had been built when an ancestor – on one of his usual drunken binges – climbed on to his horse and ordered the Muslim peasants to dig out all the land he rode across. We had the statutory torture chambers below the accounts room in the grain storage shed. When the Muslim labourers failed to turn up with their tribute they would be taken to this room, and released only when they were battered and chastened.'

Subhrasheel breaks off from his story, conscious that he may be overheard. Lowering his voice, he continues, trying not to look too conspiratorial: 'Anyway it was Lakshmi puja and my great-grandfather invited in one of his old friends from the village and his family. Even though they were Muslims, they ate the *prasad* with my family on these religious occasions and lay down with them to sleep off the feast.'

I imagine the assembled worshippers stretching out contented on long, low couches, drowsy from the rich food and hours of Sanskrit prayers to the goddess of prosperity. The *thalis* of delicacies that had been laid out in front of the goddess among the white filigree patterns of *alpana* lie half empty around the room. As conversation falters, their heads drop on to the red bolsters and they breathe in the scent of incense and flowers. No-one would ever expect such festivities to be the prelude to anything but another bountiful year.

Subhrasheel's voice drops to a whisper: 'This time

147

something was different. My great-grandfather's Muslim friend and his family refused to rest with them after the meal. Everyone thought this was strange but settled into sleep. They woke up to see a crowd of villagers led by the family's old friend overrunning the house. The crowd rounded up all the male members of the family, twenty-six in all. They took the family puja plates, the ones used for generations to make offerings to Lakshmi, cut off the men's heads and placed them on the plates. They were handed to the women who were forced to parade round with them. We still have the bloodstained plates. Only one brother survived. He was on the roof of the house firing bullets from an old musket. Our bloodline seems always to come back to this story of bloodletting. Wouldn't go down too well to betray this link, would it, however beautiful, fair or well educated a Muslim bride might be?'

Remembering Antoinette Fantome's very different story of partition, I protest, 'But why does this have to be the family story? Surely the way to prevent a repetition of violence is to forget or look for other stories? Just as many Muslims died in rioting as did Hindus. If you keep calculating your losses nothing will change. Every family has some tale of loss during partition.'

'It's not that easy. From when I was young my grandmother told me about all of this. But I must admit it's tempting to fall in love with a Muslim girl for the shock value. Maybe I'm just testing the waters for some later rebellion by being here with you. I quite like it here with my Firinghee *didi*.'

As the sign 'National Property: do not deface' catches my eye again, I am struck by the idea that the personal choices Subhrasheel is trying to make – to be my friend or to select a bride – eventually return to this command. Sexual diseases and desires, ties of affection, Mother India at threat from multinationals are all pasted over this central message. This is especially true in the space of this carriage, where public intimacies are magnified. I want to see Subhrasheel hanging out of the train again, feeling nothing but movement and transition, but his family story has carried us all the way to Kharagpur station.

The train disgorges its passengers and they breathe in the morning air, panting with relief. The longest platform in the world begins to stir with activity. People who have slept the night here waiting for delayed trains roll up their blankets and become disheartened as they see that this is yet another local train. The replacement driver, on his first run, is garlanded by his proud family and a red-coated coolie lifts his black steel box, painted with the words 'Stephen Rozario. In God We Trust', into the driver's cabin. A consignment of fish in huge metal vessels is loaded. Hawkers swap news about their early morning takings, disturbed by ragged children looking for scraps. We struggle through the exit to find hundreds of cycle-rickshaws, their drivers chatting and smoking *biris*, relaxing before the day's rush begins. We climb on to one and the driver is impressed when we tell him our destination is the Divisional Headquarters. Subhrasheel chats to him, explaining our business. Pressed against Subhrasheel in the narrow seat, my *dupatta* flying into his face, I try to appear as demure as possible. I remember the warnings of Mrs Bose and Marigold about the gossiping in railway colonies.

Streams of railway workers cycle along the grid of broad avenues to start their duties at the Divisional Headquarters. Fifth avenue, fourth avenue, third avenue provide a countdown to its centre of command. The whirring of bicycle wheels is interrupted by the strident whistle of a train and then a siren announcing the next shift in the railway workshops. The houses, equally spaced along the roads, are meticulously labelled, Type II or Block IV, and linked by webs of humming railway telephone wires and regimented lanes so that anyone's location can be pinpointed by the central intelligence twenty-four hours a day. The grandeur or modesty of each house displays the rank of its occupants. Hidden behind hedges and guarded by *durwans* are vast whitewashed bungalows for railway officers. Red crenellated towers rise above the porticoes of locomotive inspectors' villas, the harsh lines soothed by gardens overflowing with bougainvillaea and roses. The balmy scent of the purple and dusky-pink flowers jars with the astringent smell of diesel that fills the colony. Brick paths wind to the doors of drivers' cottages, made homely by steep red-tiled roofs and false wooden beams. A grim water tower looms like a gothic castle above its moat, which serves as a tank that supplies drinking water through underground channels to the colony. A vermilion Protestant church, with its Norman arches picked out in white, offers three daily services in English. There are no Moghul Palaces here; this is more like a utilitarian Windsor Castle. Each building is stamped by the rule of numbers and medieval siege-technology changed into comfortable nostalgia. This is no accident. When the colonies were designed, their architects were instructed to make them defensible from attack by Indian workers or local villagers. The broad avenues and crenellations were constructed to prevent crowds setting up barricades and to provide sight lines for rifles. They allowed the streets to be patrolled by railway volunteers. Quaint details barely camouflage this paranoia, but they were meant to fool the inhabitants into thinking that they were living in Britain.

Subhrasheel, as bemused by this bizarre setting as I am, plays an Anglo-Indian tour guide: 'All around us you see Ye Olde Englande, built to keep those Indian blighters out. Princess Diana was a Kharagpur girl, got her training for all those balls in the Railway Institute. Just like that Merle Oberon and Cliff Richard, related to my family she is, but she'd never own up to it. Proper Britain, this colony is. My relatives wrote to me about London when they moved there from here. Disappointed, they were, that the real London wasn't half as authentic as this place.'

His voice is drowned out by political slogans and Hindi film songs blaring from the communist party shack on the road that approaches the Divisional Headquarters. Swerving into the courtyard of the headquarters, already filled with chained bicycles, we see a workman painting over graffiti that have crept during the night on to the ash-grey walls. The Bengali words he's about to obliterate are *'amar desh'* – 'our country or our village'. The low building is a grander, scrubbed-down version of the longest platform in the world and huddles of workers wait for the signals issued from it which will permit their arrival or departure.

Offering the letter of introduction from the Deputy Manager in Calcutta with its case number stamped at the top as our admission ticket, we hunt for the office of the Assistant Additional District Manager through corridors that are only too familiar from the Eastern Railway headquarters. Our credentials checked by a harried peon, we enter his office, stepping on to a lawn of green carpet. The Assistant Additional District Manager is leaning back in his chair, contemplating the silver sports trophies displayed behind his desk. His greying wavy hair is scraped back and he pats it with a manicured finger, checking to see if any locks are out of place. Ignoring Subhrasheel, with precise etiquette he shakes my hand, orders tea and explains that he will arrange accommodation in the railway inspectors' guest house.

As we wait for the guides he has deemed suitable to accompany me around Kharagpur and describe its history, he tells me of his literary enthusiasm for magical realism. Warming to his subject and the

151

prospect of an educated audience, he continues to his conclusion: 'All this socialist realism that our Indian authors have gone in for since Independence doesn't capture the extraordinary everyday.' Glancing around his workplace and remembering the medieval accountancy of the colony outside I'm not surprised by his taste in novels, spending his life as he does in a place that has lost its reference point with the passing of British rule. Maybe he has realized that Kharagpur never referred to a reality anyway, that its Britain never existed anywhere. But I'm disappointed as he passionately explains that the insularity of the railway colony preserves the Victorian values that Margaret Thatcher had tried to reintroduce into Britain. He laughs and says, 'Perhaps she should have come and picked up a few tips from Kharagpur and our Divisional Manager here. Your research may provide some useful information for revitalizing management policies back in Britain.'

His moment of glory is abruptly curtailed by the arrival of a petitioner whose lined face seems out of place with her schoolgirl floral frock and long, care-free, curly hair. Without a pause, she nervously rattles off her prepared speech as the Assistant Additional Divisional Manager boils with indignation at the inter-ruption.

'Sir, I'm Hope Dover, my husband used to be a driver, sir. Now I'm a widow and my sons aren't getting a chance. Please take them on, they must be entitled under your railway family quota. I've tried with the personnel officer, but he just keeps me wait-ing. I've got all my husband's certificates here. I can hold my head up because his service was so good, but now what about my sons Henry and Roger? Give them a future.'

It's as though here in front of me is Mrs Packwood still demanding justice, no longer just a name on a yellowing file in the Eastern Railway headquarters.

The Assistant Additional Divisional Manager is fuming. He rises from his chair and shouts, 'Get out. You're not permitted in here. I'm much too busy with this important British guest sent from railway headquarters.'

Subhrasheel, who has been trying to contain his own rage, can't stand the show any longer. His right eye is twitching in anger as he realizes that his jokes on the cycle-rickshaw, which he had told in an Anglo-Indian accent, are turning into a painful drama enacted by the Assistant Additional Divisional Manager. The shock of seeing an Indian reproducing the behaviour of the British Raj is too much for him. He leaps up and hurries after Hope Dover.

The office door thuds to and the Assistant Additional Divisional Manager strokes his pocket handkerchief to regain his composure. The silence is broken by a buzzing sound from beneath the desk and he announces grandly, 'That must be the Kharagpur Sports Club members. They've preserved the old sporting life here and they'll be gentlemen enough to look after you properly.'

A peon admits three men in identical blazers glinting with brass buttons. They cautiously cross the green carpet, looking down at their footprints to make sure they aren't leaving any marks, and stand stiffly to attention. The Assistant Additional Divisional Manager nods to them and they sit down, their old bones creaking with the effort. One of them is six foot tall with an extravagant pomaded quiff and he smiles at me whenever his senior officer isn't looking. He dwarfs his companions, one whose blazer bursts with the effort of restraining his no longer muscular stomach and the other who is still lean but has a weary, wrinkled face almost as craggy as the harsh cloth tied into a turban on his head. The Assistant Additional Divisional Manager introduces them as a Muslim, a Hindu and a Sikh, adding that 'This is the only thing

153

that has changed since the British left. Now we have different communities employed at all levels here. The colony is a cosmopolitan, secular mini-India.'

Mr Singh, the Sikh, having received his order to speak, proudly lists the three generations of his family that have worked in Kharagpur. He has come prepared and produces a photograph of his great-grandfather lined up next to his fellow workshop labourers in front of a European foreman. On the bottom of the stained, sepia-tinted print is written, 'A tribute to Mr Johnson on his retirement and return to Britain.' Forgetting the watchful eyes of the Assistant Additional Divisional Manager for a moment, Mr Singh recalls how his father never entered the railway colony before Independence because if he had done he would have been chased out by gangs of Anglo-Indians. Once when Mr Singh was a small boy he had wanted to run along the longest platform in the world to greet a train his father had helped to build, but his father had held him back, warning him, 'What happens if you accidentally brush against one of the railway police? Then they'll beat you with their lathis.'

The Assistant Additional Divisional Manager draws him back to the official line by loudly tapping his pen against a delicate porcelain cup on his desk. Mr Singh nervously fingers his moustache, thinking of a way to continue that won't offend.

'All communities were separate then,' he says. 'We didn't have much to do with the British railway bureaucracy. Sikhs and Hindus sent messages home to the Punjab or Madras for wives. We built our gurdwaras or *mandirs* on the northern outskirts of the colony. All of this has changed now. See, we are here talking like equals to you in the office of our superior.'

The Assistant Additional Divisional Manager beams with pride at the secular democracy he presides over and Mr Singh relaxes, relieved that he has finally said the right thing. But all I can see in this room is a strange echo of the old records in the Eastern Railway headquarters. Raj bureaucrats had laid out separate plots of land outside the limits of Kharagpur for Muslim, Sikh and Hindu labourers to settle on with their families. They, like the Assistant Additional Divisional Manager, labelled each worker according to caste and religion. Now the mini-India of divisions has moved into the mini-Britain of the railway colony, but as I can see from the lordly manner of this officer neither of them has disappeared with Independence.

The man with the quiff, who was labelled a Muslim, has been growing impatient with Mr Singh's stilted speech. To my surprise he winks at me and then makes his own introduction: 'Which one of my names shall I give you, Mrs Laura? Family name is Mr Ahmed, but I'm also known as Begum. You know what that means? It's Hindi for "Lady".'

His face melts into infectious laughter and his old companions in the sports club join in, much to the dismay of their senior officer. Begum explains that he was a brilliant sportsman, so beyond macho with his muscles that he had to be nicknamed after a woman, no man could equal him.

'I'm an oddity in other ways as well,' he boasts. 'Married an Anglo-Indian girl. She was a shot-putter and sprinter for the railways. Still I'm a Muslim, but spend a lot of time praying in her direction and that of the sports pitch as well as Mecca. Tough nut for the BJP to figure out, *hai-na*? I'll help you in your research, know about all the castes and creeds and the grey areas between them in this colony here. Surprising how big those areas are. I'll take you on a historic tour and mix you up a bit too.'

I'm sorry that Subhrasheel is missing this, especially as the Assistant Additional Divisional Manager is now looking down at the papers in front of him with shocked embarrassment. Begum seems to have slipped through all the pigeon-holing of communities and races that the railway colony produces. The Assistant Additional Divisional Manager wants to get rid of us and still fulfil his duty to his senior officer in Calcutta, so he says, 'Yes, yes, you look after her, Mr Ahmed. I'll put my car at your disposal so you can show them around.'

Outside in the corridor Subhrasheel is looking happier. He tells me that he spoke to Mrs Dover and we are invited over to her place tomorrow. A frown appears again on the bridge of his nose.

He whispers to me, conscious of the assembled sports club, 'I couldn't stand it in that office, Laura. I'd rather spend the time here talking to *Tash* like Mrs Dover.'

Subhrasheel has been my only ally so far. Not wanting to lose him in the history of this place, I suggest that we go off to the sea in a couple of days: 'I've taken you from all your college friends in Calcutta, your exam-end celebrations. It would do us good to have a break.'

Begum interrupts us before Subhrasheel can reply, asking, 'So, are you ready to meet my Anglo relations?'

The Assistant Additional District Manager's Ambassador car carries us in state towards Hidgely station on the outskirts of the railway colony. As Begum begins to tell us what really goes on in the red-brick bungalows and tree-lined avenues, they lose their stiff respectability. Kharagpur Sports Club was built to instruct workers in healthy sobriety, but has become the rendezvous for what Begum refers to as 'real sports' who get up to their tricks there after dark. He adds conspiratorially, 'I usually supply the liquor for the "games". My wife could tell you something about those. Used to meet up with her there before we were married.'

The ceremonial street lined by the top officers' bungalows is known as 'Lovers Lane'. Passing the old drilling ground for railway volunteers, now used to train the Railway Protection Force, Begum laughs and says, 'More like Racket Protection Force they are, drilled there in how to take bribes.' As the avenues give way to the narrow earth roads and mud houses near Hidgely station, Begum points out the huts that are the homes for tribal Christians and the ramshackle compound known as Santa Barbara. It got this name because the goings-on there are more outrageous than in American soaps. Here the infamous Hamish Thomas presides over a group of Anglo-Indian families. Begum jokes, 'Real tribals they are, dancing and singing all the time with their many wives. True British headman Hamish is.' Scattered among the mud huts is the occasional red-brick house uncannily reminiscent of Croydon: 'In that one, Dolly Villa, lives Colt Campbell. He's an old friend of mine. Took to wearing a cowboy hat years ago, thinks he's part of the Wild West or maybe Wild East.'

Begum's gossiping brings Kharagpur to life as a place seething with anarchic identities. I could never have imagined that it would still be possible to live the kind of life Anna Bella did a century ago in Dinapore bazaar. Subhrasheel and I are getting into the swing of Begum's banter when we arrive at a palatial three-storey daisy-white house complete with satellite dish, shacks for servants and a garden that is a cornucopia of coriander, carrots, spinach, aubergines and chickens.

'These are my rich relations,' Begum says. 'My in-laws live here. The son makes his living as a navigator on the ships. His father used to have a girl in every railway colony, now he has a girl in every port. Anglos have to branch out a bit, move with the times. Though he's sobered up now he's married.'

Just outside the gate shaded by a mango tree is the patriarch of the family, Mr Delijah. In one arm he is holding a tiny, delicate toddler who is pulling at the candy-stripe flounces on her lemon-yellow frock. His other hand grasps a chain that barely restrains a growl-ing coal-black Alsatian.

'Don't mind Dennis the Menace,' he says. 'His bark's worse than his bite.' The dog yanks on the lead, yapping at our feet. 'Not like me. I may look and sound like an old one, but my punch still sends them packing. Used to be a boxer for the railways. They took me on as a driver only for my fighting skills.'

His nose is blunted from the bouts but his blue eyes still glitter with teasing challenges. As the little girl hides her face in Mr Delijah's shoulder, he tries to overcome her shyness by offering her small pink arm for a handshake: 'Meet my baby-doll granddaughter. So fair she looks. Just like a foreign doll.' She scrambles out of his embrace and runs off to play with the chickens in the yard, calling out to them in Bengali, '*Murgi, murgi, murgi.*' Passing a fir tree that Mr Delijah festoons with streamers at Christmas, he leads us into his house. Photographs of his son in school shorts posing by a railway carriage and of a much younger Mr Delijah with his fellow drivers gaze down at heavy lilac settees and teak sideboards adorned with antimacassars and doilies. Esmarelda, Begum and Mr Delijah's sister-in-law, walks heavily from the kitchen carrying the scent of beef and chillies with her. A large, imposing figure, parts of her seem to be escaping from her black lace frock.

Begum introduces us: 'They are a top-drawer team of spies sent from MI6, come to find out all the scandals of Kharagpur. Better watch out what you tell them.'

Everyone laughs, though I feel like some kind of bazaar spy sent by the district commissioner.

But Esmarelda looks unperturbed. 'We had a Bengali girl here once from some high-class Calcutta univer-sity,' she says. 'She went over to Santa Barbara compound and started enquiring with her books and forms about their ancestors. The cheek of it, staring down her nose at them. All the Anglos were drunk on a mixture of country and foreign liquor. Once you give them this they get all mixed up like *kitchuri*, what you British call kedgeree, and they mixed her up right and proper too. She never came back after that.'

I imagine this must have been the fate of those bazaar spies and railway doctors who, long ago, tried to prise out the race and caste of workers. At the risk of Esmarelda making *kitchuri* out of me I ask if they have any scandals to tell us, hoping that they will understand the spirit of my question. Mr Delijah's teasing eyes glitter again as he is clearly dying to tell a story.

'There used to be this character called the Midnight Man prowling around the colony. He dressed in full black. He turned the lights off in the drivers' houses and sneaked in. It was a good joke on everybody. Once a driver went off to go on the Madras mail and the Midnight Man jumped down from the upper balcony and startled his wife. When the wives were in their nighties and dressing gowns he would pass remarks through the windows, "You're looking very nice." One driver's wife was getting her husband's tiffin box ready and he caught the wife and kissed her. She gave him a tight slap, but he ran off at the last minute. All the boys set out to get him, but he always disappeared. He would jump in front of people when they were making love, but no-one could ever catch him.'

I am intrigued by this Midnight Man who seems to satirize the railway bureaucrat's obsessions with preserving the morals of the inhabitants of the railway colony. And I enjoy the irony that instead of preventing sexual misdemeanours, he commits them.

Esmarelda laughs scornfully. 'He wasn't the only one having his fun. Most probably the men in the railway colony only wanted to catch up with him because he knew all their secrets, spying on them going into other men's houses and all, after their wives. The running staff, guards and drivers, were the worst, especially those from Asansol, terrible they were. And the women from there as well. Once I was at a dance here with my boyfriend and this terrible cattish woman from Asansol came and danced with him all night. Beautiful he was, first saw him on a horse when I was fourteen at school in Darjeeling. He looked just like something out of a foreign picture. Met him again years later at this dance in the Railway Institute. I wanted to be a nun until I met him. Holy type I was. He was a wicked fellow, every time I said goodbye to him, I would say, "The devil and the angel are going. Cheerio, devil." He'd reply, swapping the names, "Don't you talk," then "Cheerio, devil" to me. Sometimes we'd walk in the Kharagpur gardens and I'd say, "I'll be Eve and you be Adam. I'll teach you how to eat the apple." '

Esmarelda breaks off as a train rattles over the tracks at Hidgely station. 'That'll be the 56 Down to Puri,' she says as if by reflex and then continues: 'So, this woman wouldn't leave my boyfriend alone at this dance, *baba*. But we played a trick on her. My boyfriend arranged a meeting with her down by the graveyard for the next day. He said come with me to see the show. We went and watched her walking up and down waiting for him from behind the shameless bushes. We laughed to see the frock she was wearing. Those bushes were useful for other things too. Once I put on my father's uniform greatcoat to help my friend, a disguise like, and hid behind the bushes with my friend. She thought her husband was cheating on her and wanted proof. So we hid and saw him up to everything with another girl. Should have seen the fight they got into after that. Plenty of scandals here still if you keep your eyes and ears open. Better watch out with that young Bengali fellow you've brought with you here, he looks like Mithun Chakrabarty, that old Hindi movie star – which one of you is the devil and which one the angel? Give a man an inch and he'll take a *bigha*. Don't mind eh, I'm just joking, bluffing and all.'

Subhrasheel smiles, enjoying the joke, but I feel uncomfortable because Esmarelda seems to be echoing my suspicions about the Bhai Phota ceremony. Changing the subject, I ask Mr Delijah about his family history.

'I'm not really an Anglo. I'm a pure Iranian Armenian Christian. I was born in Iran on my parents' orchard and vineyard there. But my mother died when I was very young. I was sent with my three brothers when I was five years old to Armenian College in Calcutta as a boarder. My father only visited us in India three or four times in his life. Things became bad for him in Iran so he sold his property and returned to Armenia, but by then I'd been to St James to learn proper English and joined the railway and become more like a true-blue Anglo-Indian. Only thing left from Iranian days was a burn on my arm from water spilling from a samovar. That always got me into trouble at school. The principal, Mr Clark, was from England and very strict. He kept on telling me he would reward me if I stood up straight-shouldered like a proper Britisher, but I couldn't on account of the burn. I felt so ashamed from the humiliation. But I showed him, I still became a boxer and accepted as an Anglo driver on the railways. Almost a Britisher there I was as I moved up the ranks to a mail driver. I used to love the steam trains. The Garrett train was so big it would rattle the windows on the houses forty yards away when it went past. Then the coal started to run out, so they brought in diesel, then that started to go so they tried electric, now the power plants are not producing enough so what will they do next? The railways will soon come to a standstill.'

'Amazing they haven't stopped already,' Begum laughs cheekily, 'with the qualifications the drivers don't have. You know the joke about the Bengal

Nagpur Railway, BNR, that's the old British name for this railway company? One of their drivers goes into hospital for brain surgery. Halfway through the operation the doctor left because his wife needed him at home. The patient checked out without his brain. A few weeks later he visited the doctor again. The doctor asked him how he'd been managing all this time. He replied, "Oh it's all right, I work for the BNR, that's Brains Not Required." In British times they were just looking for English types. If you wore the dress, played sports and put on a topi, they'd accept anybody. Lots of Indians and Indian Christians and Armenians like Mr Delijah became British that way. Find some English name in the graveyard, put on a driver's or guard's uniform, get some plush salary and everybody thought you had British blood. That's what I was saying about the grey areas in this place, many more here than anybody would admit. Longer you spend here, the more you'll find, Mrs Laura. Maybe find a few in yourself as well.'

Turning to Subhrasheel, Esmarelda says, 'Mr Mithun Chakrabarty, you better watch out too, you know what they say about Kharagpur girls? "*Tikri pa tikri loha ka maidan, Kharagpur ki chokri bhooth se be Shaitan*," meaning, "Rail by rail wrapping you in a field of iron, the girl from Kharagpur is worse than the devil." Full of their own tricks to trap you, railway colony girls are. Making up stories, laying down rails that mix you up and take you to different destinations.'

'You can stay here with us any time you like, Mrs Laura,' Mr Delijah offers, 'and we'll help you out in your researches.'

Mr Delijah, Esmarelda and Begum have spun a web around us, drawing us into the shadowy areas they have lived in all their lives. But while they voice the complaints of the railway workers' petitions, they have chosen to make light of them. Perhaps this is all they can do to cope with the everyday predicaments that result from the Raj history that surrounds them. We leave for the railway inspectors' guest house. Just outside the house we can still hear Mr Delijah singing to his baby-doll granddaughter, 'Ring-a-ring-a-roses, pocket full of posies, *Aashoo*, *Bashoo* all fall down,' and calling her in Hindi, '*Buddhu*, *Buddhuma*,' our sweet little silly one. In the air is the scent of incense Esmarelda is lighting under a shrine to Mary, preparing for a dusk puja.

The long, low bungalow looks like a rusting Raj first-class railway carriage abandoned in a siding, each door from the veranda leading into an isolated sleeping compartment. The guest-house bearers hover around in stained khaki uniforms as we sign our names in an ancient account book. They set to turning down starched sheets, drawing heavy mulberry velvet curtains and fetching tiffin carriers of *daal*, rice and *subji* from the railway canteen. Despite their elaborate formality, Subhrasheel and I can't shake off the jesting atmosphere of Mr Delijah's house. The Assistant Additional Divisional Manager has arranged only one room for us to share.

I joke with Subhrasheel: 'Must be because he assumes that as with all foreign women everything has happened between us already.'

'No, it's just because he thinks Mrs Laura *Memsaheb* is too demure and proper-looking for anything to happen with her sleazy Bengali friend, what with your public school and Cambridge education.'

Escaping the dark mahogany and dank air of the room, we drag chairs on to the veranda through the heavy door that swings shut to hide the night-time activities of guests. Over the top of a hedge that is being chewed by a cow and serving as a washing-line for the bearers' uniforms, we watch Billimoria's across the street. This is the only licensed liquor shop in the colony and we laugh at the railway staff skulking around its door and emerging with beer bottles wrapped in brown paper bags. It's an elaborate performance for such an innocent vice. Subhrasheel pretends to lead me astray by teaching me to play poker. I'm better than he expects for a beginner, although perhaps he's flattering me by letting me win. We are interrupted by the arrival of a respectable middle-aged man, pinstripe shirt ironed into place.

'I'm Mr Chatterjee,' he says, 'an old friend of Subhrasheel's mother. I'm an engineer in the railway workshop. She phoned and told me to pay a visit to check you were all right.'

Looking with disapproval at the playing cards, he cranes his neck to check the sleeping arrangements inside the room. The two beds placed far from each other don't reassure him. Inviting him to join us, Subhrasheel offers him beer and he accepts, glancing towards me to see if I will drink. Self-conscious about Mr Chatterjee's inspection, I decline. Subhrasheel performs as a perfect Bengali boy, enquiring about Mr Chatterjee's family. Mr Chatterjee is enjoying himself, but as he grows more drunk he becomes maudlin about his marriage, advising Subhrasheel to make the best of his youth. My boredom is reflected in Subhrasheel's eyes.

Turning for the first time towards me, Mr Chatterjee asks, 'You're married to an African, aren't you?'

'Yes, he's an oceanographer with good qualifications,' I add quickly. Keen to divert Mr Chatterjee from probing any further, I know he will be satisfied if he is reassured about Maurice's education.

'So why are you here, and him there in the USA? What did you marry him for if you aren't sharing your life, having children together?'

The beer is making Mr Chatterjee more outspoken than I had expected. Perhaps he thinks he can get away with such questions because I am a *memsaheb*, not a Bengali lady.

'I know, you married him for that one thing, that one

164

large qualification that all African men have, didn't you?'

Quietly fuming at this outrageous comment dressed up in Bengali respectability, I decide the only way out is to be utterly demure and call his bluff.

'I married him because I love his academic abilities and the security a permanent relationship gives me. And as for your last question, could you please explain exactly what you mean?'

Confused by my apparent innocence of his meaning, he shuts up. But then he can't quite resist having a go at Africa itself.

'I worked in Zambia in mining settlement before returning to the railways. Africa and India have different problems of development. Africans were in the trees a generation back. They had no culture, no artistic works of merit, so they have enormous strides to make before they reach India's level. They're just a tribal society, like our tribals here too. We have a thousand-year-old civilization. Have you seen the Ashok pillar in Delhi? It is made of a metal that never rusts and it's exactly the same circumference from top to bottom. How did India have this technology so long ago? A team of American scientists came to analyse it with sophisticated machinery, but they couldn't work out its formula. Problem here is that we've declined in our civilization due to all the invasions since the glorious Gupta Kingdoms. Though I must say I can't fault the British with their railways, colonies and all, they helped us come out of our long decline after the Muslims.'

I want to challenge Mr Chatterjee's twisted version of Indian and African history. It is painful to have come so far from the Britain that spawned this version of the world only to find it preserved here in Kharagpur.

Before I can speak, Subhrasheel, tired of being respectful to Mr Chatterjee, leaps in: 'Wasn't the Ashok pillar preserved by Moghul rulers, placed at the centre of their Qutab Minar complex? I don't know how you can distinguish Hindu and Muslim Indians from each other, their histories are so connected. I would also say the British started our decline, not prevented it. And Africans seem to be doing better than you, if Laura's husband's career is anything to go by.'

Mr Chatterjee is silenced. He glances at his watch: 'Must get back home now. Let me know if you need anything, I owe it as a duty to Subhrasheel's mother.'

Once he has gone, I ask Subhrasheel who on earth Mr Chatterjee is. Subhrasheel explains that he is some old boyfriend of his mother's. She spurned him. He moped around for years after she got married, calling her up and probably trying to tempt her away from his father. Subhrasheel adds, suddenly quiet and thoughtful, 'But my mother must have been really worried about us here together. He's the last person she'd want to speak to under normal circumstances.'

For the first time I really understand what it is like to be checked up on and to have my own virtue called into question. Our playful mood broken by the suspicions crowding round us, we retire to the room and sit stiffly on opposite sides. Subhrasheel writes in his diary and I scribble down notes of the day's events. Intensely curious about what he is writing about Kharagpur, I wonder if I appear in his account. Later, the mosquito nets drawn down between us, I promise him again that we will take a trip away from this place to Digha. Train announcements from the station echo through the close night air, and I dream of their destinations, Delhi, Madras, Hyderabad. Now I know why Esmarelda recites the names of trains as they pass. They promise escape, yet this is just a wishful illusion. Far from opening up new possibilities, they link India with the old paths of the British Raj. For a moment I want to be like Esmarelda's Kharagpur girl, worse than the devil, but binding iron rails together in patterns of her own making.

☙

The next day Hope Dover's son, Roger, picks us up from the railway inspectors' bungalow. Introducing himself as Bunty, Subhrasheel slips into an Anglo accent and I wonder whether lying in our separate beds last night our thoughts were so different. Is he attracted by the thought of becoming a Kharagpur boy? Roger's small, muscular frame is wrapped in a shirt decorated with giant lime-green and orange playing cards. Puffing himself up with pride he tells us it is tailored according to the latest London fashion from fabric he bought in Calcutta. Combined with his extravagantly flared white jeans it makes him look like a gangster's comic sidekick in a 'seventies Hindi film. Subhrasheel admires his haircut.

'It's *Beverly Hills 90210* mixed with Sunil Shetty's latest,' Roger enthuses. 'You can get one too at my It-alian barber. You know, you have to sit on an *It*, that's Bengali for brick, Mrs Laura, while he trims you on the roadside. From my style I get called Raja by all my local friends at the cockfights.'

Avoiding the potholes filled with monsoon rain, Roger weaves on his bicycle beside our cycle-rickshaw. Subhrasheel and Roger skip from subject to subject, until Roger turns bitter about his attempts to get a job on the railway: 'I can't get a chance, you have to have backing to get any work there. I thought it would help being a card-carrying member of the communist party. My friend is the local secretary of the CPI (M) party so I hang out at the office doing things, but I haven't seen any benefit from it. I can't find any work at all, and it's up to me to support my ma. She's hardly got enough to scrape by on, her pension's nothing, a month's allowance gets eaten up by all of us in a week.'

Suddenly losing my carefree mood, I wonder what I am doing heading for their house in the hope of sucking stories out of them, when all they need is the chance of a job.

'Have you ever got into any scraps for the party?' Subhrasheel asks, sobered up by Roger's problem.

'I used to get into trouble for them, but I gave it all up after I saw what they are really up to. All of us members are paid to go to the railway headquarters when a tender goes out. We collect all the application forms from the office. Once the party has a monopoly of them they sell them off to the people interested in putting in tenders. But the people above me take all the money and none of the trouble, so I don't do it any more. I'm thinking up some other schemes of my own, how to become a *goonda* type, it's all that's left for me now. I've got some good plans, Bunty. I'll let you in on them later. You can help with your Calcutta contacts. Something like that *French Connection* film it will be and then I'll be flying all over, London, Paris, New York, just watch me go, like greased lightning, the Kharagpur connection.'

We swerve to a halt outside a shack by Hidgely station, where villagers are picking over discarded heaps of coal from the steam age. A rusted iron girder props up one of the leaning yellow walls and above the door – a sheet of metal salvaged from the railway workshop dump – is a nameplate that reads Mr Frank Dover, ex-railway driver. A chicken scratches around the roots of a rose bush that blossoms only with thorns. As we hammer on the door, our shoes sink into tarry mud. Perhaps Mrs Packwood sat in such a house penning her letters to the Agent. Inside, the magnolia plaster walls are tarnished with stains from the leaking roof and sooty marks from the kerosene stove. Pinned over them are a Bengali calendar advertising a local trader, a film poster of Kajol and a photo of Hope and her five children in front of a backdrop of the Swiss

Alps. Bolsters and cheap cloth printed with blue-bells are thrown over huge steel trunks that serve as furniture. Hope Dover welcomes us with cups of sweet tea tasting of diesel.

'Don't mind the taste, Mrs Laura,' she says. 'The local well is poisoned from all the trains they have refuelled here. The *bhisti* brings the rich ones water from outside, but we can't afford it so we get this spiked water. Makes us run as fast as engines, it does.'

She laughs, her long curly hair flying like a school-girl's, but her face is cracked with wrinkles from years spent eking out a life on the outskirts of the colony. Roger and Subhrasheel vanish outside to discuss get-rich-quick schemes. Once we're alone, Hope pulls at her fraying frock and starts telling me her life almost as if she were writing a petition.

'I wasn't always a Kharagpur girl. Married into the railways, I did, when I was only fourteen. I didn't want to marry my husband. He was a full twenty-two years older than me. He was a widower and gave up his children by the previous marriage to his parents. My brother was in favour of the match, he worked with my husband for the railways. Our family was living in Calcutta and my husband came round all the time haunting our house. He first went after my sister, but she married another man. He kept on coming for five years because he wanted to marry some good Irish blood. Our family was the McCoys. I wouldn't pay him any mind. I'd go and play with my *choto* Bengali girls as soon as I saw him coming. My parents wouldn't let me get off that easily and we got married in Iqbal church in Metiabruz. Straight in the middle of the wedding I threw the ring back at him and said, "I don't want to go with this fellow, let me go back to my father and mother." After that I wouldn't go to his house for a full six months. Finally I joined him in Waltair, a small colony down south. I felt I was in prison, serving a sentence there I was. I couldn't roam about without being watched like in Cal.'

'What happened after that? You stayed with him?'

'What do you think happened next? My family came – what a stupid question – learnt all about the birds and bees, I did. You're a married woman too, must be knowing about all that Kama Sutra stuff.'

Hope laughs at my blush: 'One of my aunts blushes just like that – all that Irishness coming through. My youngest son also, Tarzan, he's just like a foreigner, hardly looks like my son, more like my aunts and uncles that live in Canada and London or that Prince William. He never likes to eat rice, *daal* and *rotis*. He'll only eat bread. We tell him when he's naughty that he's not really our son, that I found him on the maidan in Cal and brought him home. Then we tell him if he's not good we'll send him abroad, away from us all. Then he starts to cry, but some day we will send him abroad if he continues in his foreign ways. My granddaughter's different though, when she's naughty we call her our black baby, meaning black sheep, but she says, "No, I'm not black, I'm fair." See, my daughter married an Indian Christian, but the little one, the granddaughter, thinks she's pure Irish, likes her grandmother best. But where did my Irish blood really get me after all? Had to marry a husband I didn't love just because he wanted to be part of our bloodline so much.'

'Did you get to like each other in the end?'

'After we moved to Kharagpur, I liked it better. Could go for trips to Cal again, only three hours away. There I could roam the streets and gullies and always have something to watch, even just the trams moving. My husband used to allow me a lot of freedom, never getting angry with me if I rode on someone else's bicycle and I never got angry with him either. We came to an understanding that riding on a bicycle doesn't mean I'm going to fall in love with that person.'

Subhrasheel and Roger tumble in through the door looking a little flushed with drink. Hope becomes flirtatious again in Subhrasheel's presence and starts to direct her story at him: 'Now even I like to escape to Cal. My friends ask me, "What do you go to Cal for, don't you like those upcountry railway boys?" I say, "No, I've tried all sorts now, Oriya, Tamil, Anglo and now I want some Bengali boys." Why don't you both come to lunch day after tomorrow and I'll tell you some more yarns?'

We accept the invitation and I make an excuse for us to go, mainly because I'm curious about what Roger and Subhrasheel have been up to. We leave Hope sorting through rice for weevils and stones and humming a tune from the Hindi film *Raja Hindustani*.

Back at the railway inspectors' guest house, Subhrasheel tells me that he and Roger had watched a cockfight and drunk country liquor by the village tank. Roger proposed a wild idea of smuggling drugs from Calcutta to London via Kharagpur. His plan was to hide them inside vintage model cars – Rolls-Royces, MG sports cars – which would appear as innocent toys to customs officials. Then one day he would be able to afford a real life-size Rolls-Royce to drive round Kharagpur and impress the girls. Subhrasheel had pretended to know the price of hash in Calcutta, enjoying the pleasure of hatching a scheme that both of them knew was unrealistic. Subhrasheel was having a good time until Roger started to pour out his worries. He told Subhrasheel that he was the eldest son, responsible for the family, his two brothers and one unmarried sister. What would he do if his mother died tomorrow and he couldn't do his duty by the family? 'My father always told me that the British used to rule so the Anglos should always behave like rulers. They shouldn't take any rubbish from Indians. Always see them as what they are, our inferiors. We are the real *sahebs*,' he'd said in angry frustration.

Subhrasheel looks tired and distracted thinking about his conversations with Roger. 'It's one thing to sit in a library and imagine this place,' he says, 'quite another to see the reality of these people's lives. Let's get out of here for one day to Digha as you suggested. And now let's try to forget *sahebs*, *memsahebs* and Bengali respectability. Destroy all of these visions of your original purity and tell me about some sexual adventures from your past. In return, I'll tell you what a respectable Bengali boy really does with his girl-friends.'

Veiled behind separate mosquito nets in the half-light, we recount stories of our past escapades. Soon Subhrasheel's voice softens and is carried towards me along with the soft damp smell of the monsoon rain soothing the earth outside. In the air his words strike my mind and body. I sweat, but I can't tell if the water running on my flesh is from heat, the impact of his words or the raindrops falling outside. We have chosen a time-honoured route for escaping this place, so well worn that I wonder if it really is an escape any more. For these moments we are like Esmarelda, Begum, Hope and Mr Delijah. Now we are a Kharagpur girl and boy hiding under the darkness of a shameless bush, whispering scandals and pleasures.

The fan clatters to a halt. Its mechanical clicks cease, no longer marking the seconds passing in the night as regularly as a clock. In the lull of the power cut the other rhythms of Kharagpur that were hidden by the whirring of the fan and the glare of the strip light rise from the corners of the old railway inspectors' guest house. The ghosts of the past take over the darkness and like a slap in the face after our intimate whisperings Subhrasheel says, 'I hate it here, Laura. I hate you in this place.'

7

The Colonial Ledger

Our conversation has continued until the low ebb of the small hours. Kharagpur is almost silent, the duties of the past day forgotten and the ones of tomorrow not yet started. It is stripped down to a skeleton of noises: a breeze humming in the telephone wires; the *durwan* snoring on the veranda outside; and railway fish-plates creaking as they contract in the cooling air. My tired body longs for the rest that has settled on the railway colony. Subhrasheel seems drowsy as well, but he finds the energy to ask jokingly, 'Has Kharagpur turned us into *Tash*, as Mrs Gupta and Mr Ghosh warned it would?'

His question echoes my memory of the moments when, veiled behind the mosquito nets, we recounted stories of old love affairs and pleasures. We would have looked like *Tash* to a Bengali audience then. Yet my understanding of the word is different from that of Mrs Gupta and Mr Ghosh.

'No, well at least not in the way they meant,' I answer. 'Kharagpur boys and girls have no choice but to be *Tash*. Shut out from the rules of Bengali and Raj respectability, they comfort themselves by revealing the secret scandals that show the hypocrisy of the rules. That's what we've been doing as well by swapping all these tales of the past.'

With the history of the railway colony weighing down our friendship, we've followed the route of Kharagpur boys and girls. But the difference between us and them is that we have chosen to follow this path, driven by our own distrust of the rules gleaned from our family histories. Anglo-Indians do not choose to be *Tash* and there are plenty of stories hidden away in the India Office library that show they are not the ones who are fickle, lustful and driven by a desire for money. One such was the tale of Mahkin, a faithful *Tash* concubine, an unfaithful British husband, Edward, and his wife, Charlotte. Their drama was played out around 1879 in Rangoon on the outer reaches of British India. Back then, before the borders closed after Independence, Rangoon was well known to good Bengali boys from middle-class families. Calcutta's traders had business houses in both places and a regular ferry plied down the Hooghly and up the coast.

Edward arrived in Burma as a small boy with his father who was a captain in Her Majesty's 63rd Foot. His father died soon after, leaving him, his two sisters and their mother in straitened circumstances. He grew up to be a loyal son, working as a clerk in the shipping offices, always giving part of the proceeds to his mother. He met Mahkin and they perhaps fell in love; certainly they formed what was called 'a connection'. Edward's love was apparently very close to indifference for when he had piled up enough money he left for Calais. There he married Charlotte, whose parents had known him as a young child. They had a daughter and lived well in Manchester where Edward picked up casual work with the Siamese Embassy. But soon their funds ran out. They returned to Rangoon, without their baby, in search of a fortune. Two years later they still hadn't found that fortune, so Charlotte returned to England, showing perhaps a greater love for comfort than for her husband. They sent letters back and forth.

Edward's were full of passion, suspicious reproaches and indelicate gossip. Charlotte's made no declarations of love, but were friendly, if a little lecturing. Meanwhile Edward sought out Mahkin again, lived with her and they had four children.

Sixteen years later Charlotte asked an acquaintance recently returned from Burma whether that woman Mahkin was about her husband's house. Hearing she was, Charlotte took the long trip to Rangoon and filed a petition for divorce on the grounds of adultery. The court was unimpressed by her plea. They were more inclined to believe Edward. Under cross-examination he said that if his wife had come out to rejoin him at any time during the sixteen years, as she entered at one door, Mahkin would have gone out at the other. The court found his indifference to Mahkin highly convincing. They concluded that his infidelity with her did not really count as desertion or adultery. It was merely a convenient arrangement and very common among his class in India. It was an infidelity that proved Edward's loyalty to his wife. After all, Mahkin was not a European woman and so she didn't count. All the judges could see was an image of Mahkin waiting by the side of a lawn chair to pull Edward's boots off. Perhaps this was all Edward could see as well, for he didn't seem very eager to get divorced and marry Mahkin. The judges' refusal to grant a divorce left a wife in a hollow marriage thousands of miles from her husband and a faithful partner, Mahkin, and her children with no hope of legitimacy. Mahkin would always remain a concubine and her children, bastards.

Mahkin had a different view of the matter. She told the judge that she was angry and rejected Edward's advances when they first met again after his marriage. She was furious with him for giving her up for a European wife. Finally she yielded out of compassion for his poverty and supported him with her own funds for sixteen years. She would never have consented to be dropped or taken up at Edward's convenience. Of the three, the faithful mistress, indifferent lover and his wife, which one seems the most driven by lust or desire for money? What hope was there for Mahkin, her children and their descendants of ever becoming more than *Tash* in the eyes of good Bengali boys?

I wonder what Subhrasheel would make of this, but when I've finished relating Mahkin's story he simply laughs. The sound startles the rats and they look down at him, distracted from their gnawing. Getting up from the cane lawn chair, he lifts the candle to stare at his reflection in the dressing-table mirror. The blank, dull surface begins to shimmer with feathered cracks and deepens with light and shade. Subhrasheel raises a finger to trace his arched cheekbones, which are outlined starkly by the flame.

'Mahkin seems very close now. I've always wondered where I got my flared nose and high cheekbones. My mother's family had a grand past as supervisors in the tea estates of Assam, where the migrant labourers of Burma and Bhutan sought work. Maybe one of my ancestors knew more of arrangements like Edward's with Mahkin than my family has ever let on. Long ago some *Tash* child may have slipped into our high-caste pedigree.'

But Subhrasheel has never had to feel the shame of illegitimacy, despite his ancestors' probable liaisons with Firinghees in Noakhali and Assam. Hope clings to the significance of her Irish blood, even though it just got her into a loveless marriage and into the prison of the railway colony. She is too ashamed to talk about her Indian ancestors, because then she would have to admit the 'convenient arrangements' with Indian women that were part of her history. When Roger told Subhrasheel about the British *sahebs*' greatness that he was supposed to have inherited, he was trying to deflect the shame bequeathed to him by Raj laws. Even in the scandalous world of Anglo-India there are some painful secrets that are too dangerous to tell.

Subhrasheel's voice is now thick with drowsiness as he mutters, half asleep: 'Let's sleep a little before you resume your mission of making Anglo-Indians tell you all their secrets.'

He switches off the signal lamp, blows out the candle and climbs under his mosquito net. Through the haze of the net his back rises and falls with deep, even breaths.

My eyes begin to lose focus, but on the edge of sleep I think I hear Subhrasheel whisper, 'And you, Laura, after choosing to be a Kharagpur girl, do you have secrets that are too dangerous to tell?'

I drift off into a dream. Lying naked on a desk in the Eastern Railway headquarters, I feel its vast hardwood surface pressing into my back. Maybe it is made of polished sleepers experimented on for years to make them resistant to termites and the Indian climate, and now they are being reused in a desk as a souvenir of all those scientific enquiries. Once these sleepers bound India together with their solidity. Splinters needle my skin and my limbs are mapped by pinpricks. Dust rises and falls, collecting between my fingers, outlining them with the chalk residue of a crime scene, or perhaps I'm just becoming like the mouldering files all around. My hair flutters like their pages under the fan. I can't move because I know that all of this is to do with some official procedure. Subhrasheel is there, taking a pen from the pocket of his old-fashioned suit. Two clerks appear from behind the screen that hides the natives' staircases from the grand central one that Raj officials walk up every morning. They are carrying a giant leather-bound ledger. Subhrasheel slits some fresh pages open and I can feel the cut in my body.

'Madam,' Subhrasheel says in clipped upper-class

English, 'we require a few statistics, which will be passed in triplicate to Moghalserai. We won't inconvenience you too much, just touch yourself and we'll observe and note breathing rhythms, heartbeat, etc. as a guide to your desire.'

I follow his orders, hating the sensations, which come mechanically as a function of rhythms and pressures. The nib of a pen scratches across the page, recording my reactions.

The dull click of the fan wakes me. On the opposite bed Subhrasheel still breathes peacefully in the interlude of rest that evades me. What am I doing having a dream like this about him? Why am I calculating exactly how far my hand would have to stretch out to touch his back? We have opened the colonial ledger, bringing it up from the foundations of the building through the maze of hidden staircases. And now even in the depths of sleep it invades my thoughts. Willing myself still, I vow that I will never act on this desire. It would be no different to the convenient arrangement that Edward struck up with Mahkin. I love Maurice. Any affair would be a short-term improvisation that would jeopardize our marriage. I allow a flood of wonderful experiences I have shared with Maurice into my mind: a night of pure wonder curled around each other, watching meteor showers cascade over a Michigan lake; hours walking through the coffee plantations he used to play in as a child, our mouths still sweet from eating fresh palm-sap; and years spent weaving our lives together with homespun threads of simple daily joys. My dream will remain a dangerous, shameful secret.

Soon, when my research is over, I can return to Maurice. To make him real in this place that he has never seen, I focus on all the stories of his life before he met me. When Maurice was small he lived in a village surrounded by his father's six wives and their ambitious children. He would follow his grandfather on drunken hunts for King-juice, rescuing him from roadsides, hoping that one day he'd reveal the secret of his powers to predict poisonings and deaths. Finally his grandfather gave him a potion that would reveal the future if he washed his eyes with it, but all it did was burn them. At the age of seven his mother had given him away to her brother, a schoolteacher, so he could get a better education in the large towns where his uncle was posted. Taking his uncle's hand he climbed into the Bacca, a rusted van weighed down with the disappointments of a bad market day – chickens and plantains – and his tears mingled with traces of the red earth of the village at his feet.

His first home after that was a diamond-mining town populated only by women and children. The men were rumoured to have been killed by government guards during unlicensed hunts for the precious stones. They only ever returned to their village in the form of newspaper lists of illicit mining statistics. Here Baoule replaced Yacouba on his tongue and it felt as harsh as the diamond dust that hung in the air. Disillusioned with his grandfather's knowledge, shifting from one alien place to another and shutting out his loss, he found that the classroom and later university provided an abstract space of learning, which became his home. The letters he received from his village – asking for money and affection – became increasingly strange and distracting. It had changed anyway, overrun by miners, refugees from the war in Liberia who had been drawn across the border by the opening of a Canadian gold-processing plant nearby. They had even dug into the sacred hillside beyond the coffee plantations, where the ancestral spirits of the village lived. He pursued his new dream all the way to a doctoral programme in oceanography in the United States, wanting to obliterate his personal losses in the white, fluorescent light of laboratories. Maurice had experienced too much of the wandering I craved. He had chosen to forge a new home with me. I had rewarded him by leaving to pursue my quest. Maurice loved me enough to let me go. Now I must continue to love him enough to return to him.

8

A Field of Iron

In the blistering morning sunlight we set out for Digha in a rented, ramshackle Ambassador car. As the rigid avenues of Kharagpur give way to potholed muddy roads, I shake off the weight of my guilty dream and our intimate storytelling. The driver has an assistant whose job is to keep him awake with jokes and sit with a screwdriver wedged into the tape deck to keep it playing. As they hum songs from *1942: A Love Story*, the latest Hindi blockbuster, Subhrasheel translates the chorus for me: ' "Don't say a word. Don't worry. Just be still in this small moment of time we have together." '

I am about to ask him the plot, but he's ahead of me and explains that the bad guy is a particularly brutal British officer, modelled on General Dyer who ordered the Jallianwalla Bagh massacre. At the end of the film he is not only shot and impaled on the flag of India, but also burnt and hung. Meanwhile Jackie Shroff appears as a Bengali terrorist and the hero and demure Indian heroine fall in love against picturesque hill-station backdrops. In this song apparently they're waltzing their way around a deserted theatre. Subhrasheel teases me that I wouldn't like that part because I'd prefer the hero to choose some *Tash* and for them never to stop telling dirty stories to each other. He jokes that he'd like to be the Bengali terrorist, mysterious and unattainable, just turning up to disturb the plot with carefully placed explosive devices. He mimes wrapping a huge scarf around his face and looking brooding and dangerous. We collapse into laughter. Then, rushing on to another topic, Subhrasheel spins a myth about the paddy fields stretching to the horizon all along the road, how they are so sacred to the typical Indian villager that they never walk on them with shoes on. I know he's lying, he knows that I know this, but neither of us cares. He swears he's telling the truth: 'This is an old tradition that only real Indian villagers like me, who preserve ancient Hindu truths in Calcutta's urban jungle, know.'

Another song plays, this time about the monsoon's wild abandon. On cue giant raindrops splash on to the windscreen and the car splutters to a halt. The driver's assistant readies his screwdriver and some wire to fix the engine with. Subhrasheel leaps out of the car singing the words of the song, 'Rhim-Jhim, Rhim-Jhim,' and I follow. My clothes soaked and heavy against my body, I protest and say I want to get back inside again. Subhrasheel places his finger against my lips and sings, ' "Don't do a thing, Don't say a word, We just have this one moment in time," ' then breaks into laughter, asking, 'Do I look like a terrorist, a hero or something else to you, my *didi*?'

Once we are back inside the repaired car I attempt to defuse the charged atmosphere by putting on a tape of the Zairian band that played at my wedding. Fearful that Subhrasheel has somehow detected my guilty dream or that his sleep wasn't as peaceful as it seemed last night, I'm desperate to remind myself of Maurice. Subhrasheel's mood shifts and he argues ferociously with me about British politics. He asks me why I would vote for Labour, what difference would it make, their policies are now so similar to a bleeding-heart version of Thatcherism. Just when I'm beginning to think he really does believe in a version of anti-state anarchism, he asks me: 'You almost thought you'd pinned me down, didn't you? Never make the mistake of believing anyone, especially me, when you seem to have reached their core. We're all making myths out of ourselves and each other.'

We pull into Digha. All the hotels are shuttered and boarded up against the monsoon rain and unseasonal visitors like us. The modest pleasures it offers to Calcutta clerks and their families are meagre and drab, but I can smell the salty expanse of the Indian Ocean. A lone vendor blows a conch shell in the vain hope of customers and crab-leg stalls offer their delicacies to nobody. The sky is overcast and I say to Subhrasheel, 'This could almost be a dirty weekend in 'fifties Brighton, if I wasn't here with my younger brother.'

'Sorry I didn't bring my salesman's briefcase and long dirty mac then.'

This impression is confirmed as we register at a beachfront hotel, the International Inn, whose motto encourages its customers to 'stay local, think global'. The desk clerk looks disapproving when we book a double room because it is cheaper than two separate rooms and write in the ledger, Subhrasheel Roy, 21, student, Indian and Mrs Laura Bear, 28, research scholar, British. We enjoy his dismay. He asks for Subhrasheel's father's address, and we imagine him trying to blackmail us later. Subhrasheel writes some near approximation just in case our impression is correct. We spend a few hours in the arid room sitting on its bland hotel furniture, inventing the stories the clerk will tell about us after we leave.

Subhrasheel jokes, 'This place's motto should be stay global, think local.' He grows restless, perching on the balustrade of the balcony, arm of a chair, edge of the bed. 'I'm hungry. Are you ready for dinner and the beach scene? The rain and wind machine are already running for our camera shot.'

My bare feet sink into the burnt-sienna sand and I watch dusk collecting on the distant grey horizon. The beach is deserted apart from an occasional fisherman, one of whom has warned us about the crabs which bury themselves under the sand, leaving only their breathing spikes like unicorn horns dangerously exposed. I look out for them as Subhrasheel tells me that any moment now a crowd of a hundred junior artistes in the ethnic costume of Bombay's fisherman caste will appear dancing to some filmi tune. I search for shells and find two perfectly formed spirals. Subhrasheel pretends to spoil the moment by telling me that their shape is mathematically explicable, 'just like the formulas your husband makes up to explain those waves over there'.

Then he runs off towards the peacock-blue waves, yelling, 'Follow me, let's shout at the sea.'

I reach the hissing waves just behind him, panting, and for no reason at all I shout, 'Ma Kali.'

Subhrasheel turns towards me: 'So now you're trying to turn this beach scene into a religious biopic, but don't forget which story you're invoking. I know quite a lot about my naughty Aunt Kali, patroness of fertility and destruction. Our family stopped worshipping Lakshmi after the Noakhali massacre and took up Kali. Lakshmi, the goddess of prosperity, brought them only disaster during her puja and they needed a less demure family goddess, powerful enough to protect them from further losses.' He explains that Kali came to earth to rid it of demons, but became much too enthusiastic and started to destroy everything and everyone in sight. The whole order of the world was threatened. Only one thing could stop her and that was her husband, Siva. He lay at her feet and she stepped on him by mistake. She was so ashamed, it brought her back to her senses, her tongue stuck out in *lojja* and the world became calm again. Then Subhrasheel's voice grows quiet and serious: 'Her power is now only restrained by her husband. Is this how you want it all to end with your feminist sensibilities?'

I don't know how to answer this, unable to tell whether I'm invoking Kali in her moment of wild abandon or in her moment of shame confronted by her husband. We walk away from the sea in silence, my thoughts anything but peaceful. Last night's dream and my desire hover around like the ash-grey clouds on the horizon. We linger in the safe neutrality of choosing a place to eat, deciding on a beachfront South Indian restaurant, where our only audience is two card-sharps in the corner gambling as night falls. As our throats burn with flame-orange *rasam* and our fingers are tickled by feathery *dosas*, the tide turns and soon we can hear huge waves crashing against concrete blocks outside, placed there to prevent the erosion of the resort's polite pleasures. Our conversation – heated by the masalas and rushing with the brawling rhythm of the sea – grows argumentative. Subhrasheel throws down stinging challenges that wash away reasoned composure, trying to undermine my positions on politics and history. Soon I'm flushed with the excitement of the battle, lingering in the resonances of his voice, losing track of everything but the rolling richness of the moment.

The meal over, Subhrasheel dares me to walk back to the hotel along the sea wall rather than through the desultory, muddy streets blinking with kerosene lamps. Leaving behind fishermen and tea-sellers huddled around cow-dung fires and staring sadly at the raging waves, we wind along the precipice of the sea wall. Here there is nothing but darkness, the rasping of pebbles dragged across rocks and spray from the waves splashing our faces. Sprinting ahead, turning towards the horizon, Subhrasheel curves his body to brace himself against the wind. Looming black against the waves, he is a thin question mark waiting for me. The salt water running into my mouth could be the taste of Subhrasheel's skin against my tongue. Hesitantly I pick my way along the narrow concrete towards him.

For an instant he is close to me, then he leaps over the sea wall, turns towards me in the dark and offers one last ridiculous wager: 'So, my true-blue *memsaheb*, you were a deputy head girl at your school. I'm just a Bengali boy, but I was made of sterling enough stuff to be head boy of St James. I'm the one who would have made it as an explorer to the source of the Nile – bet you wouldn't dare to go closer to the sea.'

His words are painfully close to my secret dream in which my desire was mapped in a colonial ledger. In a rush of anger, before I realize what's happening, my feet are slipping on slimy oyster-grey rocks and sinking into the traces of his footprints disappearing as the current pulls the sand back into the sea. Then there is the slap of cold water drenching my body. Reaching out for the heat of his arms to save me from the next wave, I shout above the roar: 'So what usually happens after the wet sari scene?'

'That's always left up to the imagination,' he replies and finally I taste his skin.

But we are not alone for long. Climbing over the sea wall towards us is an old man, dhoti blowing like the wings of an avenging angel in the wind. He's shouting at us and we can hardly hear him over the thundering waves. I think I can catch some of the words. He may be screaming *Tash* or something. We grab clothes and seaweed, unable to make out the difference in the damp slickness, and run for the International Inn. On the way I ask Subhrasheel what the old man was saying. He lies, 'He's our appreciative audience. He said, "I've always wanted to do something like that, but I missed out in my youth." ' At the hotel we wake up the desk clerk, who looks triumphant that all his suspicions are confirmed. Back in the room we mark the blank wall with sand and mud, leaving impressions of our passion.

'Are you sure you want to do this?' I ask.

'Everything is arranged for this to happen from the battle of Plassey onwards. We're just following the script of Hindi movies, colonial titillations, speculations about *Tash*, nationalist respectability. This isn't a seduction, it's just us following the traditional temptations,' he says, unwinding my stained purple *dupatta*. My tastefully embroidered *salwar kameez*, its small daisies worthy of a railway clerk's wife, soon lies crumpled under our feet on the floor. His darting hands remove my last defence, a pouch containing my damp passport and traveller's cheques. His fingertips linger on my *shakha pola* bracelets and he whispers, 'Why did you ever believe Mrs Gupta's version of morality? The more you became a Bengali princess, the more you changed into a Rapunzel longing to let down her hair for pleasures to come climbing up to her. Let's leave these on.'

In the half-light of the television turned on to protect us from prying ears, he talks to my body, calling it by Bengali names, *motu, gutu singh, choto gunda*, sweet plump one, little wrestler, little Mafioso until it is broken into so many parts and pleasures I can't put it back together. It appears outside of me, manipulated, used and fragmented until it is a myth between us, a toy, a dialogue, a counter in a game. What is he saying? What is he calling me? Who am I? I try to climb inside his body to catch a glimpse of what he sees and I'm pulled back by the rasping of sand and his tongue on my thigh. I assume that we both want this betrayal of Maurice to be over quickly but he says, 'Slow down, you're such an earnest girl following manifestos of sex, we have a long night ahead of us.' I stare at my hand and wrist now against the bedpost. The *shakha pola* bracelets rattle with our movements and he whispers, teasing, 'You're such a good girl, such a good wife.' Then he enfolds me with a tenderness that burns.

Hours later, the white noise of the television buzzing in the corner, pale dawn light settling on our flesh, I ask him: 'What happened to the respectable, virginal Bengali boy in all that passion?'

'What passion? That was technique. Others have tried to pass it off as love but, sister, technique is smart and just the moment it sees that you are trying to masquerade it with sentiments it gets wild. Like lust it is a loner but an honest and upright one. Let's just say that love would give its eyes to be like technique.'

Then he kisses me with a passion so faked it must be true. At least, I want it to be true.

After the long drive back to Kharagpur all we long for is sleep, but Begum is coming to collect us for a historic tour of the railway colony. Staring in the mirror, running my fingers around the bite marks on my neck, I don't recognize myself. Wrapping a *dupatta* around the bruises, I'm aware that no-one would be surprised to see them there. Maybe I'm trying to hide them from my own eyes. I have to stop this but, half-serious, I pray to Siva for a few more hours of vertigo. Subhrasheel comes up behind me, drapes himself around my shoulders. Striking a pose he says with irony, 'Don't we look like a Benetton ad, promising world integration by buying a T-shirt?' When Begum knocks at the door he darts away.

First on the itinerary is the Kali *mandir*, across the railway tracks on the north side of the colony. Nervous at my memory of the invocation on the beach at Digha, I hover in the temple offices among the inventories of incense and timetables for pujas, not wanting to enter her sanctuary. From behind his desk, the oldest pandit tells us about the *mandir*'s foundation in 1902 by an

Indian railway contractor in penance for building a butcher's shop that sold beef for the Europeans in the colony. This had brought a curse on him that made him sterile. After the construction he finally had a son, but his son had no children so the curse continued. Now the temple is purifying itself again, for in the recent renovations they painted over the European faces which had gazed down from its arches. Thinking of the calm after Siva brought Kali to a standstill, I understand this effort to recreate a Hindu purity. Longing for this peace away from Kharagpur's polluting field of iron, I also realize that if it ever returns it will feel like a desperate lie. Subhrasheel wanders off to visit the image of his aunt Kali. He walks back framed against the sand-yellow steps and sea-blue arches of the temple. Reaching my side and pulling at the locket around his neck, which his mother gave him so that Siva could protect him from illness and accidents, he whispers, scared, 'She's in her most frightening, abandoned form. Why did you have to mention her at Digha?'

Our historic tour continues with the Catholic graveyard. It rises among the concrete blocks built to house Indian railway workers. The memorials to private faiths, loves and griefs are crumbling and overgrown. I pull away grass and leaves to try to revive their inscriptions. Begum teases me and says, 'Now we've got you wondering, looking for your ancestors too.' Ignoring him, I continue to read the headstones. In the middle of the graveyard we come across a middle-aged man in his best clothes weeping while he washes his wife's grave. He has anointed it with flowers, incense and candles in earthen cups. Begum introduces us.

Distracted by his grief, Mr Vanjo starts to pour out his sorrow, just because we are here: 'I come to wash her memorial every day. I come here to talk to her. I might be mad, all my children tell me so, but I just have to do it. Look at the state of the graveyard, all the angels' faces smashed and all. They're all taken off with the iron crosses to build *paan* stalls. If I didn't come that would happen to my wife's grave too.'

Silenced by Mr Vanjo's grief, loyalty and loss, I don't know if my mourning is for him, for my inevitable renouncing of Subhrasheel, or for the old innocence of my marriage to Maurice. Making excuses to Begum, we cut short our tour and find a temporary release in sleep back at the railway inspectors' guest house.

Subhrasheel wakes me murmuring painfully tender names, *Kashmiri bou, tesu* – Kashmiri wife, little Anglo. We drink green coconut water, its salt-sweet taste refreshing memories of passion. He retraces the imprint of his teeth on my neck, willing it not to fade, wanting it to be permanent witness of last night.

'If I ever took someone else to Digha, I'd probably end up throwing them into the sea and catching the next bus out of there. They wouldn't be you.' And he adds, pinning me to the sheets, 'Have you ever done anything like this before, deceived your husband?'

'No. I've always thought of myself as a simple, loyal person. Perhaps I've just always been taken in by the masquerade of love. I much prefer your technique.'

He grows angry. 'Don't ever compare me to him, don't fool yourself you will never find anyone who loves you as much as your husband.'

'But I'm not sure I want that kind of love.'

Shutting out the pain of our spiralling mood, he reminds me that we have to go to Mrs Dover for lunch. Last time her stories led us on the path to Digha, turning us into a Kharagpur boy and girl. Maybe she will give us wicked courage again.

We arrive at her shack to find it bolted and no sign of the steaming rice, *daal* and conversation we need to revive ourselves. Subhrasheel bangs on the metal door, not expecting a response, to find it opened by Hope who looks more ragged than before, one arm swollen and in a sling. The injury unexplained, she smiles with strained politeness and asks us in. Once we are inside she loses all her reserve.

She tells us she was remembering her husband's death today, it almost seemed as if he was with her: 'He had gone into hospital, complaining of pains. A strange lump would appear on his foot and disappear again each time they called a doctor to look. He couldn't properly speak and remember things. But then, the day of his death, he started to talk. He said his mother was calling to him, "Son, son, it's your brother's birthday today, come home to celebrate it with us." Both his mother and brother were dead and then he was dead also. They say that when a dead person you love appears to you that means you will die also. We couldn't explain to the young ones where he was gone. We tell them he is in heaven with all the good things and if you pray for rain then he will throw some down. On very rainy days, my granddaughter tells us how naughty Grandpa is being today.'

A tear appears on Hope's wrinkled cheek, but she stops others falling by continuing her story: 'My husband left me with no papers for this house and left his bank account papers with his previous children, my stepchildren. They're trying to take this house from me. My son, Roger, he's a waster, a topper too. He beats me to get money. He was after all the certificates in my husband's railway box and he took the key string and almost strangled me, my eyes were popping out beside the house wall. He has all sorts of bad habits. He goes round to an eighty-year-old woman nearby, Clarice in her Palace, her Irish blood makes her alluring. She entertains all the young boys with music, liquor and cigarettes. She blackens her eyes and has a good full figure, bloated from drink. Says she's a hairdresser, but I think she's an old Calcutta madam the way she carries on. Roger will get his come-uppance. God will punish those who beat their mothers. If you hit them with your hands you get leprosy, if you swear at them he gives you cancer of the mouth. If I die all this will happen to my son.'

Subhrasheel goes off to make tea and I hold Hope's hand.

'Roger just wants to always call back the spirit of his dead father. My granddaughter can hear her grandfather calling her and my daughter sees him in dreams bringing sweets to their house. You know how he really died, he was murdered. Used to go over to that Santa Barbara compound. If Bunty went there young girls would force themselves on him for money. My husband caught his death from a blue stone they put in his drink one night. Now my son's following in his footsteps. He goes over to Clarice's house at all hours of the night. He'll catch leprosy from her son-in-law, who lives there with Clarice. Roger bathes him and all. If he got infected everyone would be thinking that it was something bad in his parents' blood. It would affect the standing of our whole family.'

Hope hesitates for a moment, pulls herself up and straightens her crumpled and stained frock. She takes the tea from Subhrasheel and continues: 'Still, apart from the troubles with my son, my husband's death wasn't so hard on me. We used to go our own way and do our own things in the evenings. We weren't like the De Souzas, they loved each other so much they died from it. One day this couple were at home and the wife dropped dead in the bathroom of a heart attack, the husband seeing this died also. It's good not to love someone too much, sentiments are not always a blessing in this world.'

Composed again, her mood shifts and she flirts with Subhrasheel. Looking for clues to my dilemma in Hope's tales, I can find only desolate images of an emotional detachment that renounces passion to avoid pain. Is this the sole route left for a Kharagpur girl? Roger and Henry, his younger brother, rush in through the door in their best-pressed jeans. Henry towers over his brother but follows his lead, hanging back as Roger explains that they want to take Subhrasheel to meet Clarice in her Palace. Henry seems to copy Roger's gangster fashion sense as well. Tied around his head and hanging down his back is a red nylon scarf which makes him look like a cross between a pirate, a Hindi film villain and a rap star. Hope draws me towards her and whispers, 'We better go with them just to make sure they don't get up to any wickedness.'

The Palace is guarded by a concrete keep and a gate with 'Casa Loma' emblazoned in gold lettering on it. Beside the house runs a chicken farm, a legitimate source of business now in disuse because the locals gradually stole all the chickens from it at night. Two howling charcoal dogs bare their teeth at us and we skirt around them, just out of reach of the length of their chains. At the front door are two giggling, glittering village girls in showy pink saris and fake gold jewellery, so over made up that Hope confides, 'They must be waiting to get their fare to Sonagachi from Clarice, that's the place in Calcutta where she keeps some of her houses of ill-repute. On route for a life of easy virtue, they are.'

Clarice herself appears, withered but handsome in a *Dallas*-style green *salwar kameez*, lurid and silver-encrusted, her deeply dyed black hair backcombed into a bouffant beehive and giant gold earrings competing for attention with her lavish wrinkles. Inside we sink into plush crimson-velvet settees and Mona Lisa stares down from the wall. Shakin' Stevens and Cliff Richard blare from a small tape deck. Clarice eyes Subhrasheel voraciously and he avoids her stare by going off into another room with Roger and Henry. Clarice pours out sweet plum wine into glasses decorated with semi-nude women in page three poses who become naked as the glasses are filled. She is barely civil to her female visitors, enjoying the shock her den of vice produces.

'Indians are not liberal enough. They are always criticizing and watching others and spreading rumours. It's not like this abroad in Australia and Britain. There married couples swap house keys and partners. Here in India they do the same, have you seen all those magazine small ads looking for broad-minded couples? But they pretend to be oh so respectable. And the looks I've got on the street ever since I was fourteen, so lusting they are, from all those well-dressed married men. I decided long ago to start trading in that lust. Stop all those pretences and make a little money. Turn a penny from all this dirtiness. It's made me well off and secure after all.'

She gestures at the opulent room. I want to leave this lair, to believe in faithfulness again. Each word she says reminds me of last night's illicit passion. Subhrasheel returns and I can tell he wants to leave as well.

As we ride back to the railway inspectors' guest house in a cycle-rickshaw, he reaches for my breast under the cover of my shawl. To distract me from his search for pleasure he directs my eyes to the stars: 'Up there, can't you see the railway-carriage constellation, next to the signal-light moon?' Although he is trying to entertain me, all our universe seems to be marked by Kharagpur's iron field.

Throwing open the heavy wooden door of the railway guest house, Subhrasheel tells me that while I was with Clarice and Hope, Roger and Henry were showing him a stash of porno pictures and telling him about visiting prostitutes in Sonagachi. Roger had said he didn't care about women any longer because there was one Indian girl he fell in love with but she left him for someone else.

'You won't do that to me, will you?' he asks, suddenly afraid.

'I don't know. Let's just be quiet.'

Picking up a textbook, packed into my luggage days

ago when I thought I was coming to Kharagpur only for research, I try to lose myself in the pages. But Subhrasheel won't be ignored: he takes it from my hands and pulls off my clothes.

He turns my head to face the mirror that has graced the railway inspectors' guest house for a hundred years. The reflection looks like a standard porno shot from a film entitled *Western Belles and Eastern Boys* or Duras's *The Lover* playing in some Calcutta cinema where all Western art films end their lives as titillation for college students and *paan*-sellers. And now we are in the frame, tinged an exotic green by the old railway signal light hanging in the corner of the room and with art-directed authenticity supplied by the cane lawn chair. All around us are traces of the past and present of Raj history. We are not alone in this room.

Then he's inside me, but I have no inside. My skin unfurls until I am as insubstantial as a chiffon *dupatta*, fluttering in the breeze of the fan and folded into shape by his touch. Subhrasheel's tongue caresses into being fingers, breasts, thighs, then the rhythm changes and they disappear. Reaching out for him in the darkness I try to anchor my body, placing it under the weight of his chest, but he moves and I am left quivering in the unpredictable flow of our passion. Clasping the rough cotton of the starched sheets, I breathe in the smells carried to me on the monsoon air: diesel fumes, sweat, damp mud and plaster.

Subhrasheel murmurs, 'True-blue *memsaheb*, Mrs Chatterjee, Kharagpur girl.' His hot breath sears my neck and each word cascades with contradictory allusions: British, Bengali, Anglo-Indian.

In the quiet of my mind, I spin my own story about Subhrasheel and me to explain how we got here. Thinking of an audience back home in London to whom I will have to justify this betrayal of Maurice, I blame it all on Subhrasheel's beauty. The list of metaphors for him stutters into my mind: green coconut body, *kathakali* hands, kohl-black eyes. Glancing around for help, I notice the imprints of his muddy feet on the crumpled sheets. Imagining an expectant audience, I tell them that I want to worship these impressions like the visitors who pray to Mohammed's footprint marked in stone at Murshidabad. Archaeologists say that Mohammed was never there. Soon I will pretend to Maurice and myself that we have never been here in this passionate bed. Sensing that this will only make the worship of Subhrasheel stronger, I withdraw from the anguish of inevitable loss and imagine an audience again. Following a Kama Sutra inventory of aphrodisiacs, I tell them of the smells of jasmine rising from the salt-caked sweat on the sheets and of cardamom on my lover's breath.

The lights from a train passing over Kharagpur junction flash through the room. Startled from these poetic excuses, I remember that we are close to the longest platform in the world. The plane for Hiroshima is rumoured to have refuelled in Kharagpur on its way to Japan. Here a British army base has been overlaid by the Indian Institute of Technology and the site of an old colonial prison repossessed by a colony of Anglo-Indians. We have thrown aside railway-issue regulation red blankets and the still air carries Hindi train announcements. Above us rats gather on the outside of the mosquito net. Unperturbed by our movements, they watch with the boredom of old residents who have seen this seduction many times before. So far my story is nothing but a stilted, exotic postcard. Desperately trying to recompose myself, I was grabbing at old, dog-eared images of India. For generations these have provided excuses for lust and they feel strange in this place.

Subhrasheel interrupts my troubled thoughts and says, 'Why don't you read me something while I touch you?' He turns me over to face the pages of the textbook that traces the history of colonial fantasies, which he had made me discard earlier. As I read the words that map the longitude and latitude of our passion, we laugh at the shattering of their calm by our rhythms reverberating in my voice. Sweat staining the pages, I try hard to maintain the serious tone the book demands and Subhrasheel is fascinated by the dissonances produced by our growing passion. But still I am unmade. I can't piece together my voice, the pleasure filling my body and my thoughts. Sensing my distraction, Subhrasheel shifts position, pulling himself up on his elbow. He whispers gently, 'This isn't working. Let's tell each other stories again.'

With childish expectation, I nestle in the curve of his body.

'My mother had an old schoolfriend, Nupur, in Calcutta. They used to climb over the walls that separated their houses, play together for hours and swap hopes about their futures. At the age of twelve, they decided to seek professional advice about the turns their life stories would take. So they went to visit an astrologer who displayed his *jyotish* stones and cheap copper rings on the pavement near Gariahat Market. He was reassuring about my mother's life, but he told Nupur that she was destined to go mad and die an early death. On the bus home my mother laughed off his prediction, joking about the astrologer's crass Bihari accent and ragged clothes. But Nupur was lost in thought. Just before they reached their stop she said to my mother, "How can I get married now? I've heard my destiny. I can't inflict this certain madness on a husband and children." They continued to play together, yet her friend remained distant and behaved like a tragic heroine. My mother, scrubbed of her childish ways, went off to college and married. Nupur hung around her family house, refusing to marry.

'Years later my mother received an invitation to

Nupur's wedding. Overjoyed, she dressed for the event in her best heavy-silk sari. In the wedding house her friend looked resplendent and a mistress of her own destiny. Explaining her decision to marry, she told my mother, "Finally, I realized my life couldn't be mapped by the tales of a ragged old charlatan."

'Five years passed and my mother woke up sweating in the middle of the night, nothing could calm her fever. She told my father she had dreamed she was back in the cavernous hall of her school. Nupur was there and as my mother stepped out of the hall into the sunlight, her friend said, "Goodbye, I don't belong with you any more." The next morning they read the announcement of Nupur's death in the newspaper. Suddenly my mother feared that the astrologer's prediction had been right all along.

'With trepidation she went to visit her friend's husband. He was desolate, his sadness growing as he told my mother what had happened. Nupur had started to feel confused, heard noises that weren't there and saw things upside down. Crying, she confided all that the astrologer had said and sobbed, "It's really happening as he told me, all of it." She insisted on going to a psychiatrist, who prescribed anti-depressants. Her condition worsened and she began to murmur, awake in the middle of the night, "It's my fate, my fate." She constantly washed her forehead and palms, trying to wipe away the lines of the future written on them. A few weeks later she collapsed and her husband rushed her to a nursing home. Furious at the misdiagnosis the doctor said, "Why didn't you bring her here sooner? We could have saved her. She's got encephalitis." Nupur sank into a coma and died.

'So, my baby, be careful what stories you weave here. Nupur chose her life story unwisely and it led to her death. Treat all our tales with sceptical tenderness, questioning why you believe them to be true.

You're making our future out of the past. We made our passion happen with all our stories of Anglo-India, but to make it last we will have to forge something new with them.'

He enfolds me in his arms and I think of all the stories Hope Dover, Begum, Antoinette Fantome and Marigold Jones have told me. They confide Anglo-Indian tales, which are shut out from the official ledgers of Indian and British history. Like Subhrasheel and me in this moment of illicit passion, they have nothing left but their stories to make themselves real. Imagining other pasts, presents and futures, they unravel myriad threads from the grand traditions of India and Britain. These stories resist the official histories that attempt to prescribe their futures as a continuation of a wayward past. They show that these conventional histories are little more than ragged old charlatans similar to the astrologer who sealed Nupur's fate. There is so much to learn from their courage. But do I have the will to weave stories strong enough to bind Subhrasheel and me together? I am married to Maurice who has done nothing to deserve this infidelity. His only mistake is to love me enough to let me go wandering far away from him.

Pulling away from the heat of Subhrasheel's body, seeking rest, I say, 'I can't speak now. Please don't make me.'

'If you are feeling bad about your betrayal then perhaps you should comfort yourself that even if we had just been friends everyone would have assumed that we were lovers. Pobon, the Assistant Additional Divisional Manager and Mrs Gupta would all have expected this seduction. So come and kiss me again. What's the fault in doing something everybody expects?'

Moving further away from Subhrasheel, I feel claustrophobic. This passion was waiting for me in the rumours on the street as I passed. Whatever I say about it will make no difference. There are already a million explanations on those lips. They'll be some variant of Mrs Gupta's *memsaheb* envy: 'Well, she seemed to be such a Bengali girl, but we all know she was really a Western woman looking for another bed-partner. We know what little marriage means there.'

I beg Subhrasheel, 'Let me sleep for a while, let me rest.'

I sleep quietly, but then I have a dream that interrupts the calm. A beautiful woman stands in the middle of Kharagpur's maidan. She invites me back to her railway bungalow. There, reclining on crimson velvet cushions, she starts to stroke my hair and sing a lullaby. I drift in and out of wakefulness. Then she jerks me upright, pushing me away from her silky jasmine-scented frock, and points to a group of people lined up just inside the oak-panelled door. I can make out Subhrasheel's face among them. She whispers in my ear, sadly tender again, 'You have to choose. Will you sacrifice Subhrasheel or yourself?' Not able to send him to certain death, I reply, 'I'll sacrifice myself.' She reveals herself, long crow-black hair lashing through the air, surrounded by a halo of gold and, as Kali, she devours me into death.

I wake up twisted in Subhrasheel's arms, crying. Pouring out my dream, I say, 'We have to stop.'

He draws away, icy cold, but I feel colder, wanting that death my Kali-dream offered more than this barrenness that is now here between us. He promises, the sentences heavy on his tongue, 'I'll leave tomorrow.' Then, growing cruel with the pain of my rejection, he says, 'You're just a word-thief anyway, collecting everyone's lives into files like the Eastern Railway.'

Veiled again under my separate mosquito net, I try to learn to like this blank emptiness. But the next morning, after Subhrasheel has gathered up his mud-stained clothes and left on one of the early trains for Calcutta, I collect his black, black hairs from the sheets. Treasuring them in my palm, I fold them into a piece of paper and stash them between the pages of my diary. Now I have just my diary, myself and an imaginary audience as silent witnesses.

9

Ghosts and Callipers

Since Subhrasheel's departure the monsoon rain has beaten into Kharagpur's tarry earth for a month. The water runs from the tarmac avenues of the railway colony into the ditches on its outskirts, which then spill over into the potholed narrow paths of Hidgely. Here the waterlogging disrupts the routines of the inhabitants, rain leaking through roofs, dripping into *dekchis* and seeping upwards through mud floors. Each house steams with an old, damp, sooty smell released from the earth that was once the foundation for a colonial prison. In ink-black puddles the refuse of a day – train tickets, the page of a child's exercise book, a lost string of flowers that was being carried home to adorn an ancestor's picture, a broken red bangle – mingles with nameless ancient deposits rising to the surface. They reflect with a shimmering stillness the faces of passers-by: the frown of a shawl-seller turned away from a sale; a hint of a smile on the face of a convent schoolgirl self-conscious about the village boys playing cricket with a tennis ball beside the track; and the pinched lips of a railway wife delivering a tiffin carrier to her husband. But as a bicycle wheel slashes through and a bird swoops in to scavenge, the pools stir into ripples, reshuffling the detritus of the past and present. At night or in the premature darkness of a stormy afternoon the rain falls, its hot, liquid steel drops sending the puddles into relentless turmoil, confusing the strata that have temporarily settled. Like the monsoon mud and water that pervade Hidgely, in this Anglo-Indian colony there is no escape from the traces of the past that swirl about the present. There is no illusion that with Independence they have settled peacefully into distinct strata. Here the past and present are in restless turmoil. Unmarked on any map of the Indian subcontinent and outside the municipal order of Kharagpur, Hidgely fills with the cast-off refuse of the nation.

My home is now in Hidgely where the discarded past collects and churns. I have moved in with the Delijahs to be closer to the Anglo-Indian families who live here. Trying hard to work through the guilt of my betrayal of Maurice, during the day I absorb myself in the pursuit of their family secrets. Yet in the small hours of the night when I am curled up on a makeshift camp bed, Subhrasheel haunts me. The room becomes silted with memories that rise up with the drumming of rain on the roof. They seep from the darkness with the feathery touch of a mosquito net mistaken for a darting fingertip and the smell of fresh starched sheets which only reminds me of their unsoiled whiteness. I conjure up Subhrasheel by shaking his hairs from their paper casket, clasping a blanket until the heat from my body suffuses it with human warmth, or by pressing my fingers into the places on my neck which used to be marked by bruises so that their dark purple shadows will return. Each trick turns into a memento mori of our passion. At night, when the monsoon rain falls, the traces of a scandalous past swirl around me as well.

But in the afternoons around five, like today, I sit on the same bed rigged up in a long corridor trying to forget Subhrasheel. I write down in my journal the stories gathered from Anglo-Indian families, putting the tumult of memories to rest in rigid, ordered lines. The pages fill up. They are like the quivering puddles I can see through the window, reflecting on and mixing Kharagpur's past and present, but still I want these lines to be frozen pools, layers of memory held in place by full stops. Above me on the wall is an icon of Mother Mary blinking with fairy lights to which the Delijahs direct all their private confessions. As usual, muffled thunder is just audible under the shunting of a passing train. Once the carriages have rattled past other sounds from the Delijah household are carried on the mounting gusts of wind that herald the approaching storm. The hiss of a pressure cooker drowns out Esmarelda teaching her grandniece to count by its whistles, '*Ek*, one, *do*, two.' Mr Delijah curses his sulky unmarried daughter, Elsie, 'What, that frock again? You're no spring *murgi* any more, to be wearing polka dots and ribbons.' Mr Delijah's daughter-in-law returns from teaching in St Agnes convent, her rickshaw, named after her as 'Emma's Taxi', screeching to a halt outside. Rats scuttle and scratch somewhere above, while Carlton, a nephew sent here to cure his bad habits after an unnamed scandal at his boarding school in Asansol, recites Hindi verbs. A door slams and the Alsation, Dennis the Menace, howls as Elsie's heavy footsteps angrily splash off into the distance.

In this house there is an unspoken agreement that I can stay as long as I don't get involved in their squabbles. Each evening, after listening to stories from other Anglo-Indian homes, I return to a table laden with delicacies such as salted ham and biryani, accepted as part of the family routine. After dinner Emma knits a moss-green sweater to protect her husband from the chills of the Cape of Good Hope and scolds her daughter who tugs on the wool: 'Don't be naughty. When your father gets back from the ship after a few months he won't give you any presents. I'll send him a letter saying how dirty you are.' Distracting myself from Emma's small acts of fidelity and chastising letters that are so different from my own behaviour, I join Esmarelda, Elsie, Mr Delijah and Carlton in front of the flickering television screen. We lounge on the sofas and sink into the solitary entertainment of watching the *Zee Horror Show* or a Miss India contest, the television faltering as the current drops, overburdened by the demands of the local Tata Steel ball-bearings factory. Occasionally I glance at Carlton, wondering if he has forgotten his scandal or if it lingers in his mind as mine does.

Sometimes, tired of writing my journal, I compose letters to Subhrasheel and Maurice. These, like Emma's promised letters to her husband, reveal all my misdemeanours. But I never have the courage to post them. The only thing I have sent so far is a love poem. I wrote it with Subhrasheel in mind but then, as if to underline my own confusion, I posted it to both my husband and my lover. Perhaps I hoped that if I sent to Maurice the sentiments composed for Subhrasheel he would become interchangeable with him. Picking up the poem from the piles of papers spread out like tarot cards on the camp bed, I murmur it as a daily prayer:

Mohammed's footprint at Murshidabad
the cool, stone impression fragrant with *belful*
    sacrifices
traces a faithful history,
solidly questions the rationality of time and
    distance.
The scholars say Mohammed was never there.

Our love follows this pilgrimage
we will refuse to excavate the marks of hands,
    mouths, tongues on our soul's country
Apostates with trigonometric grids
divining absence with our archaeology

But your tracks that run through Kharagpur
    monsoon mud will continue in Michigan
    freezing rain
binding the world with a sacred geography
sanctifying the earth in streets you have never
    seen
Your *didi* lays flowers at your feet even where you
    have never been

For Maurice's eyes I changed *didi* to wife and swapped round Michigan rain and Kharagpur monsoon mud. Then with shards of guilt pressing as sharply into my skin as my lover's fingernails at this double betrayal, I had written to a close friend in London laying bare all the details of the seduction, begging her to bring me to my senses, asking her to feel shock so that I could feel it too. But this letter remained unsent; instead its pages still stare back at me. I needed her to be my conscience, to prick me into feeling how much pain I would cause Maurice and myself. But even so, my head was still filled with Subhrasheel. Next to the letter on the cheap chintz counterpane is another poem, composed in Bengali, in which I am Kali begging her husband Siva to still her *kandokarkhana*, her chaos machine. This too I had cast aside, smiling painfully at the irony of confessing to my husband in a language he wouldn't understand. And here I am again with all these scribblings scattered on the bed around me, shuffling through them to try to find a solution.

The sky outside is streaked now with green-grey clouds and the thunder is so close that it silences comforting domestic noises. Between its rolls Emma calls to everyone to shut doors and windows against the storm, but I turn towards the window grilles, breathing in the abrupt coolness. Beyond the mango tree shivering by the rattling gate passers-by lift the hems of dhotis and saris to protect them from the mud, put up umbrellas as silky black as crows and rush across the emerald grass that sinks its roots deep into the soil. As the rain breaks into full flow, Hope Dover's shack, Colt Campbell's villa and Santa Barbara compound, barely visible across the maidan through the streaming drops, float, creak and heave on their foundations. They seem cast adrift by the swirling rain and mud. In the growing humidity the tuberoses strung over Mother Mary's icon on the other side of the room release their intoxicating velvety scent. Her face is unmoved by the clamour around, but suddenly a gust shakes her and she falls, glass splintering on the concrete floor. Feeling responsible, because I haven't heeded Emma's instructions to batten down the house, I run to the smashed glass and begin collecting up the fragments. Animated by a furious blast of rain and wind, my papers fly apart, sweeping off through the window, caught on the grille, cascading down the sides of the bed or plastered to the wall. The words run into spreading stains. I clench my hand on the glass, dropping it from the pain, and then chase the letters round the room, small drops of blood smearing the dripping ink. Panic drives me into a whirlwind. Will all of Kharagpur and Hidgely find my confidences pasted to their front doorsteps? In the instant before slamming the window shutters to, I see white sheets from my diary turning to sludge beaten down by the rain.

Retrieving blotchy papers from the four corners of the room, I try to separate the Anglo-Indian stories, my poems and my confessional letters to my husband and lover. But the damp pages are stuck to each other. Here are words from Mr Vanjo's life blurring on to a poem I wrote for Subhrasheel after our first meeting in the graveyard. They are almost translucent and I can't quite peel apart the damp pages or separate his stories from my own:

Ganges water runs down the smashed angel's face
Mr Vanjo baptizes his wife's grave
Beside the Catholic cemetery gates
the scavenged angel's lips prop up a *paan* stall
dissolving with a laugh
like Mrs Vanjo's Irish blood
into the indifferent Indian earth.

You too washed death from my marble body
On the beach at Digha wounds stung to life with
    salt, sweet kisses
Fragments of our smiles lie here
scattered with rocks at the limits of the land
Waves will caress them
until the Indian Ocean grinds us to sand

Mr Vanjo's fidelity has become entwined with my infidelity in an attempt to express my own state of mind and I remember how, before leaving, Subhrasheel had accused me of being a word-thief as ruthless as the files at the Eastern Railway. So much for being an anthropologist: the journals in front of me are as much about discovering my own identity as they are about the Anglo-Indians I have met.

Yet the storm's violent shuffling of my neatly sorted papers and the destruction of the icon of Mother Mary carries another message. The longings that fill me don't come only from within, they are more like sediments from Kharagpur's past that flow into and churn in the hollows of my being. They belong as much to the storm outside as to this room of private confessions. My journals, poems and letters show my life has become bound up with the stories of Kharagpur. Why else would the image of Mr Vanjo have seemed so apt for expressing my sorrow at the loss of Subhrasheel's love? If I think through his story again perhaps I can learn something about my own restless and mournful longings. Maybe I'll find out why Subhrasheel still haunts me. Mr Vanjo is surrounded by ghosts as well.

꩜

Mr Vanjo's flat in Choto Tangra, halfway between Hidgely and the railway colony, is a turret in the air precariously perched three storeys up a staircase. It rises high above the red dragons of Jimmy's Chinese restaurant and the concrete filigree of a Marwari home reminiscent of a Rajasthani *haveli*. The portcullis drawn over the door keeps out most intruders and once inside all you can hear is wind whistling around the veranda and his grandson, Johnny, singing a nursery rhyme alone in a corner. He didn't choose this home. In his grandfather's time this had been the neighbourhood for Chinese workers. Imported from Tangra, the Chinese settlement in Calcutta, they were sent in during strikes to run the workshops. Turned out of railway quarters after his retirement, he had moved here with his wife, mother and three daughters, Mavis, Marcie and Paula, only because the landlord didn't mind renting to Christians. He is less pious than the Marwari neighbours from whom the Vanjos have to hide their beef bones.

Mr Vanjo spends most of his time as a sentinel on this veranda, his long lean body straining over the balustrade as he listens out for voices on the wind. I join him often and wait for him to tell me what he hears. He frowns at the arrogant yells of students from the Indian Institute of Technology gathering outside Jimmy's who, once they have graduated, will contribute to India's national development. They roam from the dormitories searching for liquor and flirtations, just like the British soldiers who used to occupy the site before the Institute was built, having been posted here to preserve the Raj. Mr Vanjo can't see any difference between them and the Second

World War soldiers his mother told him about, code-breakers, technical specialists and liars. His mother had known so many like Sylvia Upshon, who, when she went through the uniform pockets of her glamorous British lover, had found a letter and shaken it open, only to have a picture of his wife and child back home fall on the floor, 'Yours to the bone' written on the back. Then there was Auntie Iris who was in the WAACI and went with her friend for her six-monthly medical check-up. She sat in the corridor pungent with phenol and waited next to the other nervous women while her friend went in. The doctor called them all into the surgery and told her friend to raise her skirts in front of them. She was 'ruined down there, all eaten up by her British lover's gift to her'. No difference at all between them and the quick-witted Hindu student suitor of his daughter Paula, who boasted that the campus held the largest science library in Asia while playing footsie with her under the dining-room table. They had met at a Railway Institute dance, where the student had been in the band, pounding out on the drums Aerosmith's 'Love in an Elevator'. He left Paula pregnant and headed off for a grand career building nuclear bombs at the Bhabha Institute of Atomic Research. Mr Vanjo's experience has made him sceptical about nationalist dreams. His daughter, like Sylvia before her, had been good enough for servicing the needs of the Indians and British but not quite proper enough to be included in the spoils of power.

Mr Vanjo's favourite joke is about an imaginary Anglo-Indian bomb. He laughs at the idea that if they ever built it they wouldn't know who to drop it on. From the middle ground he occupies, it is hard to identify any enemies of the nation or even the boundaries of the nation itself. He points out that if, as India seems to be planning, Pakistan is a target, Anglo-Indians would just end up killing their relatives, like his Goanese grandmother who spent her last years in Rawalpindi across the border. Sometimes she'd come on visits, carrying the family certificates rolled up around a smuggled stash of diamonds, which she'd distribute like sweets round the family. She always took the family certificates back, though, as if they were more valuable than the diamonds. That's why, unlike their Indian neighbours, they didn't know anything about their family apart from what his grandmother chose to tell them about her Anglo-Dutch husband. Mr Vanjo would always tease her that her husband was really Goan, not Anglo-Indian at all, but not even this would provoke her to unroll the certificates. She would just snap back at him, her angry reply thickened by Urdu intonations, 'You won't find any other Vanjos in the whole of India. Only in Britain will you find that spelling as a surname.' The truth about his grandmother's claims are buried with her in a Christian graveyard in Pakistan, lost along with the property deeds that she always hinted would restore the family fortune.

Here in Kharagpur, according to Mr Vanjo, the only treacherous proof he can offer of his identity is his own grey-blue eyes, eyes that his daughter Paula also has. Her face was her only fortune or more like misfortune. Treacherous, because what good have they done him or Paula? He thinks they are the reason landlords turn him away and why that student found Paula so alluring. He'd rather have those property deeds or more of those diamonds. Then there is his taste for British food, but even this inheritance is a curse in disguise. He has seen Anglo-Indians die off young because they eat only Indian food now. In the past they got pure British food from England, which suited them better, wasn't adulterated and meant they lived to a ripe old age.

It wasn't always like this. His Anglo-Dutch grandfather's fair skin and blue eyes had been his passport to a well-paid job on the railways. His grandmother never talked about how he got to India. Her family stories always started at the point her husband appeared in front of the Chief Medical Officer to get his apprenticeship in Madras. When Mr Vanjo was a little boy he would climb on to his grandmother's knee, tug at her *dupatta* and listen hard, imagining the medical officer as a lanky chap all buttoned up in a cravat, fingers blotted with ink from running them down the lists of railwayworkers' racial types in the books in front of him. His grandmother was proud of the fact that the medical officer was so impressed with her husband's breeding and demeanour that he sent him to visit a friend, an officer of the Ethnographic Survey, who got out his callipers, asked him about his tattoos, tobacco habits and marriage practices and took measurements.

But Mr Vanjo's childhood was full of shadows of this scientist. His father used to scold him that such a fellow would come and dig the sharp points of the instrument into his skull unless he stopped hanging around with his Bengali friends down by the cooling water of the village tank. Later, at sixteen, when he was planning to enrol as a *kalahassie*, he was terrified of being sent for a medical exam, so he kept quiet about his Goanese grandmother and put on his Prince of Wales check suit and a blue shirt that brought out the colour of his eyes. The officer was not bothered at all. He just looked up his father in the service lists of the railway and wrote 'caste, Anglo-Indian' on the form. But Mr Vanjo's fear of the callipers' claws has never completely left him and he makes sure all his family behave as they should, scolding them if they take off their shoes like Hindus when they enter the house. As he speaks I think of the eminent anthropologists and statisticians who, in the dusty back rooms of museums, honed the points of these callipers long after his grandfather's experiences. In Calcutta, Mahalabonis, the statistical architect of

Nehru's five-year plans, cut his academic teeth on the curious physiognomy of Anglo-Indians. Poring over tables of their cranial measurements, comparing them with figures collected from mulattos in America and criminal lunatics in Britain, he claimed to have proved that British racial characteristics predominated in this population. Mr Vanjo lives under the weight of these researches, scared of a unique kind of bogeyman with a measuring tape.

While Mr Vanjo watches from the veranda, the voices he listens out for are not so much those of the living, but of the dead. Since he moved here both his wife, Milly, and his mother have died. Under the shrill chorus of rickshaw bells, speeding trucks and vegetable-sellers there is a small, persistent call as relentless as the presence of Subhrasheel in my thoughts. At first Mr Vanjo wasn't sure he was hearing it; the low moan had to be some trick, the distorted echo of a rock song playing in Jimmy's. But when he paced the veranda in the early hours of the morning after the truck-drivers had holed up for the night in a *dhaba* and Jimmy's had closed its doors to nocturnal revellers, he could hear it still. It was Milly crying from the graveyard, 'Come, come to me.' For the first half of the day he resists the call, but in the late afternoon he puts on a leather jacket and his best dog-tooth tweed trousers sent to him by his brother in Australia, combs his hair carefully like a suitor and climbs on to his motorbike. As he crosses the bridge over the railway heading for the graveyard she grows more insistent and he speeds up to sixty kilometres per hour – as he puts it – almost committing suicide with his lover's eagerness. At the bridge it gets worse because it was here that two young lovers died, their romance and pain amplifying his wife's call. They used to meet beneath the rusting arches by the tracks, an Anglo girl and the Bengali son of an engineer. His father refused the match and they were not allowed

213

even to speak to each other. So they met by the tracks for the last time and threw themselves in front of an express train. Two photographs flew up from the track and the one of the boy landed side by side with the one of the girl on the bridge. Each time I meet Mr Vanjo I encourage him to retell his story of this haunting with its themes of lost and impossible love, searching for an explanation for why Subhrasheel appears to me at night.

Sometimes the murmuring call becomes too much for Mr Vanjo. Then he pulls out his clarinet from the trunk stored under the huge teak bed that had been both his parents' and his marriage bed. Milly had first set eyes on him while he played jazz favourites for the Easter Dance. She loved him for it, but later, when the babies' cries got too much and her clattering of vessels in the kitchen became too deliberate, he would shut them all out with the most mournful tunes of Billie Holiday learnt by heart from Ceylon radio and from records sent by his brother in England. Now he does the same thing to silence Milly, taking comfort in the regular repetitions of intricate fingerwork. He has a theory about jazz learnt from the writings of Cedric Dover. In the 1930s Dover had advised Eurasians to throw in their lot with the struggle of African-Americans, to forget their British and Indian heritage, which would always leave them feeling inadequate, and to follow the example of the Harlem Renaissance, to develop their own fusions and demand their rights on the basis of this creativity. Mr Vanjo explains that, like African-Americans, he is part of a slave population which was produced as fodder for machines, a convenient workforce to keep the railways running. That's why he thinks it natural for him to want to play jazz.

But even as he says this, he laughs bitterly, distancing himself from the experience of African-Americans, asking, 'How would you write our *Roots*? Where could we go back to? There is no continent of

Africa waiting for us to return. I don't even know what was in those papers my grandmother had. Nehru offered Sir Henry Gidney an Anglo-Indian homeland in the Andaman Islands, where the British used to torture the Indian freedom fighters. Nehru thought that was where Anglo-Indians belonged, in the ruins of a Raj jail. Even if we'd got it we would have made a mess of it. How can you found a nation from bastards with no roots? When I play that jazz, I can forget this, pretend I have some roots and shut out my wife who wants me to join her in that graveyard.'

However hard Mr Vanjo tries to root himself, he can never be at peace. The definitions of a nation all around him prevent this. Indians reject him as a sign of a colonial past that belongs to the oppressive Raj. He is forever polluted by his mixed heritage. The authenticity that Hindus and Muslims take for granted, the possibility of a community formed of kinship and blood, does not exist for him. His restlessness is the fruit of the colonial commission reports that consigned Anglo-Indians to bastard status and the Indian nationalism that continued this judgement. Subhrasheel may haunt me, like Milly does Mr Vanjo, but I can silence him any time I want by returning to my husband. I can distance myself from all this history by becoming a British married foreigner once again. This choice does not exist for Mr Vanjo, however often he plays his jazz.

It wasn't until Mr Vanjo invited me to the consecration of the sacred heart picture on the anniversary of Milly's death that I found out exactly why she was so restless. His daughter Mavis came to pick me up for the ceremony and as we rattled along on a cycle-rickshaw she chattered, fingers flying for emphasis through her short-cropped hair to the silver cross around her neck and to my arm. Her voice wavered between the clipped English she maintains throughout her Bible readings in church and a rolling Hindi echo.

She thought it was funny that there we were, two married women out after dark alone, our husbands far away in other countries, and speculated happily at the trouble we could get ourselves into. I hadn't realized she was married and asked her where she'd hidden her husband.

She giggled again: 'My sister Marcie and I look like the carefree unmarried type, but we've both got husbands over there in Britain. Mine, Ronald, is almost an African like yours. We've both joined the coloured clan. He's sort of from Kenya, but his family's from Goa. Ron's father left Goa for Kenya because he hated all the caste and dowry among Christians there and didn't want his children to grow up that way. Then at Independence the family moved to Britain. And now Ron's a proper British gentleman, though to an upcountry girl from Kharagpur like me he seems improper like the rest of those liberal-minded Englishmen.'

Mavis and her sister had taken a long trip to London two years ago, sponsored by her father's brother. There in Southall at a Rangers' Club Christmas dance her sister met her husband, but Mavis couldn't stop looking at Ron. The only problem was he had been married once to her mother's sister. He too was interested, wouldn't stop dancing with her, but she wasn't sure because technically he was her uncle. So she told him, before she returned to Kharagpur, that if he wanted to marry her he would have to come all the way and fetch her.

Sure enough, Ron turned up two months later and took Mavis away to a Calcutta register office for the marriage. In front of an Anglo-Indian registrar who was all done up in a sari, Ron sealed the ceremony 'in the African way, putting the wedding ring first on my thumb then my middle finger and then on my marriage finger, saying, "in the name of the father, the son and the holy ghost". But it doesn't matter how we got married because the British High Commission won't believe in our love. They're giving us, my sister and me, all sorts of problems. That's why we're stuck here and our husbands there, for two whole years now. We have to prove with all kinds of papers we love each other, but how can papers show it? I know all sorts of other Anglos who've had marriages of convenience. They schemed and planned and have all the documents. We have nothing but our love for each other. I can't pull out my heart and lay it on the table in the High Commission, can I?'

Mavis gave some directions in Hindi to the cycle-rickshaw driver and then continued, 'Sometimes I think it's because I don't have those eyes like Paula. When my father's elder brother and wife emigrated to Australia he had no problems. He looked the part and had my grandfather's railway certificate saying he was Anglo-Indian, but his wife had to pass all sorts of morality clauses and medicals and all. These were just excuses because she wasn't fair enough and had no papers. It's always harder for railway girls to prove their caste. We've never had all those railway inspections our menfolk went through, only have the evidence of our manners and looks to go on. That's why my father's always been so strict with us being ladylike and now I'm so much a *memsaheb* that I don't even fit in with liberal British ways. He wasn't like that with Paula. She was allowed to be a Tom, scrambling up and down trees, playing *kabbadi* with the boys.'

Mavis sees all too clearly the particular inequalities faced by an Anglo-Indian railway girl. Her complaint joins the crescendo of voices in the nationality files of the Eastern Railway, which protested Anglo-Indians' eligibility with no possibility of proving it.

We arrived to find the whole family gossiping over rum to while away the time until the priest turned up and loadshedding ended. Gathered in a smoky pool of light from a kerosene lamp, Marcie, Paula and Mr

Vanjo's sister and brother-in-law, Loretta and Colt Campbell, ignored the darkness in the corners of the living room from which the shapes of ancient family cabinets and boxes loomed. Mr Campbell sported a stetson and his laugh and frame were as big as Texas. He slammed the spindly table with his fist for emphasis as he cracked jokes and then with deft elegance rolled his fortieth cigarette of the day. His wife Loretta, despite her showy polka-dot flounced dress and dark curls piled high, was quiet in the rowdy presence of her husband. Marcie and Mavis kept leaping up to tend to the roast chicken, boiled cauliflower and potato chops with which they were going to celebrate the consecration. Only Mr Vanjo sat taut and mournful: glancing at the shadows; whispering to his grandson, Johnny, who squirmed on his lap; and looking up occasionally at the sacred heart picture, where Mary lays her bleeding heart bare for all to see.

Colt tried to draw him into the conversation by teasing him: 'You better stop spending all that time in that cemetery, otherwise Laura will think you're nothing but a graveyard Anglo-Indian, one of those Indian Christians who hang out there choosing some British ancestor from the names written on the gravestones to be their high-class forebear.'

Mr Vanjo rose to the insult: 'Maybe I am a graveyard Anglo-Indian, but not in the way you mean. I've made a study of the occult, like those Tantric priests who live in the burning ghats and all those Lovecraft and M. R. James types. This ceremony won't help, Milly won't leave us alone. What does the priest know of all of this? I'd be better than one of them, always going round to people's houses when there's a bottle of liquor to drink from, pocketing all the proceeds of their charities. You should let me do the ceremony. Should make me the priest and I'll be the devil's advocate.'

Paula took the now frightened and tearful Johnny from Mr Vanjo's lap and tried to comfort him and her father simultaneously. 'Hush, Daddy, you're upsetting Johnny. We all know the real reason Milly can't rest but, who knows, perhaps if we do the proper worship Mary will solve our other problems too.'

The priest arrived, looking like a bearded Afghan freedom fighter, all muffled up in a woolly hat and scarf over his *kurta pajama*, with an altar boy from the church orphanage in tow to carry his holy paraphernalia. After downing two glasses of rum 'for the chill', he unwound his scarf and tied on a white and gold cummerbund. Sprinkling the family and Mary with holy water from a silver phial and jasmine petals, just like a Hindu priest sanctifying a goddess in a puja, he invoked blessings on the household. Before leaving he prescribed a prayer to be said to Mary on Thursdays after fasting that would spread her influence on all their affairs.

Mr Vanjo began his scornful speeches still in earshot of the priest's retreating back: 'What good will that do? I'm sure Laura agrees with me and all.' He asked me if I had ever had any experience of spirits. Touched by his sadness and adoption of me as an ally, I told him about the distant cousin of my great-aunt's who had been a pathologist in Nigeria. He retired to Sussex where he lived in a vast bungalow filled with mementoes of his travels and portraits of his forebears. When he died, my great-aunt inherited the place. I would go for tea when I was little, never daring to go outside the sitting room where my parents and great-aunt chatted politely. The rest of the house had such a strange atmosphere, gloomy and oppressive even when the sunlight was streaming in. One day I was climbing the stairs from the garden into the house when the hairs literally stood up on the back of my neck. I could hear the sound of breathing rising and falling right next to my ear. I hurtled up the steps and resumed my place back among the comforts of Victoria sponge and family news, telling no-one. Later,

I did tell my grandmother and she said that when the relative died he fell down those very steps. His body was found at the bottom.

'But the real question', said Mr Vanjo, 'is why your relative couldn't be at peace. That's always at the root of these hauntings. Your relative didn't deserve to rest, did he, after slicing up all those bodies, peering into them for the truth, like all those damn British officials whether they're in Africa or India? His spirit must have had a guilty conscience.'

I remembered once again the small elegant leather case of gleaming steel scalpels and blades inherited from this relative and kept in our house. Now I knew where they had been all those years in Nigeria, slicing through lives like Mr Vanjo's.

Mr Vanjo was in full flow, much to the embarrassment of the family: 'That's the fate I'd wish on those British High Commission officers, to never have their souls at peace. They won't let Milly rest, so why should they? It's all their fault. Milly first appeared to my mummy on the day she died. She heard a knock on the door and said Milly's come. On his birthday Johnny was outside on the veranda and said, "Look, Milly's smiling from the clouds to me." That night he dreamt she was playing with him all night. Mavis had told him that Milly had gone to England when she died and each time Johnny's missing Milly he says to Mavis, "When you go to England take me with you or else you'll forget me like Milly has." He doesn't need to worry. Only way my daughters will get to England it seems is after death. That's what is upsetting Milly so that she comes back to us, the British High Commission refusing them visas, prying into their lives, asking for love letters, demanding confessions of sins they haven't committed. They have no honour, they have no shame, they are all dirty-minded so all they see is dirt. They ask for the impossible, for my daughters to be like Mary up there, showing them their hearts in some miracle. They won't be happy until they are in front of them all sliced up and bleeding. They've turned our house into a jadu house like the old Masonic Lodge in the heart of the colony. In the old days the British railway officials raised spirits there to help them control the past, present and future. And now the Indian officials do the same.'

The power returned and a harsh strip light whirred into action. As the shadows retreated into the night outside Mr Vanjo stopped speaking and everyone sat up stiffly, suddenly self-conscious under the glare, smoothing down clothes, patting hair into place.

The storm shows no signs of ending yet. The rain still pelts on the window shutters and the wind rattles at the bolts. Yet I'm glad that it has disturbed my routine and cast my papers into disorder because I now know why Subhrasheel haunts me. Milly appears to the Vanjos because she cannot rest. She is disturbed by the cold steely scrutiny of officials wielding the modern equivalents of callipers and scalpels. But Subhrasheel returns to remind me not to rest. When I sent him away I had retreated back into my married British identity. Ironically it was precisely this rigid notion of identity that I came here to escape from, knowing that it rested on an endless litany of colonial stories of inequality. In our storytelling duels Subhrasheel had dared me to embrace these tales, not just to listen to them but to take them to heart and let them reshape my life. Yet my courage had failed and I had lost Subhrasheel for ever. He keeps returning at night to remind me to take up his challenge. Like my relative I don't deserve to be at peace.

Downstairs Mr Delijah draws back the bar on the front door to let Elsie in. Gusts of wind whistle under doors, up the stairs and along the corridor, carrying snatches of their affectionate apologies to each other. Their quarrel forgotten, Mr Delijah tenderly tells Elsie to stop crying and to warm herself by the fan heater. I'll never know what caused the spat. The icon of Mother Mary stares at me through the smashed glass. Unlike her I will never hear all of the private confessions of this family. Yet I have been wandering from house to house in Hidgely, trying to make everyone yield their secrets. Now with Mr Vanjo's fears of callipers and the prying eyes of officials echoing in my mind, my doubts are growing. This isn't the first time I have wished I wasn't so resolute in my questioning. Colt and Loretta had made me ashamed of it as well.

&

On the night I had learnt the truth about Milly's ghost Colt had invited me to his ranch just next to the Ram *mandir*. 'You've heard of cowboys and Indians,' he said. 'Well, I'm an Indian cowboy. My brother-in-law dreams of the West, but I'm from the Wild West.'

Since then I have often visited them. Turning up at the stiff red-brick portico of Dolly Villa I would always find Loretta and Colt sitting outside on charpoys with a parrot squawking in a cage above their heads. Colt was permanently surrounded by a haze of cigarette smoke which he waved away with his stetson, saying, 'Look at all this gun smoke. Got to be some fire in me still to make such a lot of smoke.' Loretta would chime in, enjoying the familiar joke: 'Watch out once he gets you in his sights, no escaping his gun!' When the conversation faltered Loretta hummed tunes to while away the time, spiking country favourites with Hindi words, 'Oh *mera mehbooba* Clementine'. I kept on asking Colt about his family origins and work as a railway inspector but he always deflected my questions. He would joke, 'You know better than that,

Laura, to ask a member of the cowboy caste where he's from. A cowboy's from nowhere, just rides on his horse, or in my case train, to the next job or two-bit town, until he's thrown out after making trouble. A cowboy just keeps moving. That's the meaning of that film, *The Man with No Name*. I prefer to have no name also. All those Wild West frontier towns were full of men like me and some of them, even though you wouldn't know it from those Hollywood John Wayne heroes, had skin as dark as mine. I'd love to make a movie, wouldn't be a spaghetti western, more like a *chawal*, that's rice, western.' But though he was making light of it, I sensed that for Colt and Loretta this perception of themselves was not just a game.

One long, hot afternoon Loretta, Colt and I retreated inside and sprawled on their huge bed piled with bolsters. We companionably munched *papri chat*, relishing the sweet-sourness of the tamarind and the coolness of the curds. Set into the dark teak foliage at the head of the bed was a black and silver photograph on a glass plate of a severe Bengali woman swathed in a sari, hair drawn tight into a bun. The sun that glinted through the gaps in the closed shutters cast her shadowy likeness on the crisp white sheets. Next to her was an empty space where her husband had once been. It seemed an oddly sombre and rather too typically Bengali piece of furniture to be gracing this Indian cowboy's home, so I enquired about its origins. Colt explained that he had bought the bed second-hand at an auction sale, just before their marriage. I asked him if he ever wondered who it had belonged to in the past. He said that was exactly why he had bought it, so he could give this woman a home again. She had stared so mournfully at him next to the *almirahs* and rickety old chairs at the sale that he couldn't resist her entreaties. Colt and Loretta often lay awake at night telling stories about who she might have been and what her husband had looked like. Not letting the subject drop, I urged Colt to explain their fascination.

'Since you've asked I have to tell you,' he said. 'I was an orphan. I never knew who my father was. I was packed off to a railway boarding school and orphanage in the hills before I can even remember. My mother was an Indian Christian, that's all I know. I have no photographs or papers from her so I think of this woman as my ma. I never want to forget that I have Indian tastes in my blood. Other Anglos are ashamed of it, but I'm proud. I hated that school, all the strictness, Scottish pine trees and dark cold churches, barrack-room dormitories where they wanted us to forget that we had anything to do with India.'

The teachers had dressed Colt up in uniforms, drilled him in loyalty to crown and country and criticized him when he didn't have the right manners and accent. One boy was hauled up and soundly beaten for not squeezing his toothpaste properly. Another had his tongue burnt for lying about his father. All the teachers used to call Colt a bloody bastard and he in return had no respect for them.

Silent for a moment, Colt looked at Loretta nervously, then he admitted, 'That's why I became a cowboy also, to escape all of this. I used to read books about the Wild West. Then when I went to the apprentice home in Chokradapur one of my girlfriends gave me the name Colt as a joke and it stuck. After that I didn't have to ever think of what type of British or Indian I was. I just belonged to the rough-and-tumble life.'

Colt's experience was the very image of AB's, the Anglo-Indian orphan who had left St James to work on the railways and in the circus and whose life Subhrasheel had conjured up in our seance a month ago. For both of them learning the art of disguise had become a way of banishing the brutal experience they had suffered at school. Subhrasheel had wanted me to try to learn the same art, but I had refused his offer.

Colt's confession wasn't over. Suddenly losing his swagger, the bed creaking as he sank further back into it, he quietly added, 'Like every cowboy the West has ever seen, I'm a murderer.'

Picking his stetson up from the bed, he stared at it, examining its stiff ridges and valleys as if they somehow represented a map of his life. He had been a notorious wild card in his youth, nothing better than a butcher's son eloping with his landlady's daughter in Chokradapur. They had escaped on the night mail, smuggled into the luggage carriage by a drinking buddy of his. It had been romantic at first, the jute bags cushioning their embraces. But the railway police were tipped off by the girl's father and when they were discovered he felt the butts of their shotguns striking his back. He woke up in jail, where he did a stint for corrupting a minor. Still, even after that he didn't change. He broke each regulation he came across: stopping his train in the middle of runs to hunt for deer in the jungle; swapping his railway rations for bottles of drink in the railway running room; throwing coal to the women along the track just so they would lift up their saris to catch it and he could see their legs. Every Railway Institute dance he went to he would start a fight. The first time he met Loretta was at the Kharagpur May Queen dance. The place was full of Europeans, mainly soldiers, and they had put up Union Jack bunting all around the room. He danced with Loretta, but one of the British soldiers had cut in and said, 'She's too pretty for a bastard like you. Bet you don't even know who your father was.' Despite his attempts to contradict their prejudices, there was only one way the British could identify him. This was too much for Colt, he punched the soldier out in one and pulled down all the Union Jack flags in his rage. Loretta was impressed by this show of pride and

225

shortly afterwards they began courting. But one night he was out drinking with his best friend. The liquor took hold and he woke up the next morning by the railway tracks with his friend dead beside him, all bruised and bloody. He couldn't remember anything, apart from some stupid quarrel about his mother being an Indian Christian slut from Madras. Despite his cowboy marauding, he could not stop himself rising to the insult that reminded him of everyone's disdain for his mixed origins. He wept over his friend's blank eyes until the railway police came and found him there. He had cried in remorse ever since, even though it wouldn't do any good, and from then on he had made a vow to be a non-violent cowboy.

As Colt sat on the bed forcing back the tears he made his promise out loud once again: 'I follow Gandhi-ji's path now. Sometimes I think I wear my stetson just to remind me of what I've done.'

'It's good that he's married a holy woman like me,' said Loretta. 'I manage to keep him in check.'

Colt's reinvention of himself carried heavy costs. The stetson that had once been a symbol of freedom had turned into a sign of its limits. I felt deeply ashamed that I had reminded him of this by my persistent questioning.

But now that the façade of their game had crumbled Loretta had something to tell me. Pulling on the cross around her neck she confided that she hadn't always been a holy woman. It all began when her grandmother, the one who lived in Pakistan, had died, when she was about seventeen. There was so much sadness and uproar in the house but the strange thing was that her parents were most concerned about the loss of the documents her grandmother had kept safely. They quarrelled all the time about how to get them back. Her mother was always trying to persuade her father to find some way to go to Rawalpindi so that they could save the family honour and fortune, and their angry

226

voices warred long into the night after she was tucked up in bed with her sisters. One night she cried herself to sleep thinking about her grandmother and had a dream. Her grandmother was back with her, combing through the tangles in her hair, and she whispered, 'Go and find the place where the book is always open and you will find some rest.' A week or so later she was cycling on some marketing errands through the colony and there she saw it, a big Bible in a glass case outside the Baptist church. She went straight in and spoke to the pastor. After that she converted and took her comforts in Bible study. In the absence of documents that could prove her family history she sought a substitute, an open book to which she would have free access. Shut out from the official ledgers of Indian and British history and with no written proof of her origins, Loretta entered a community of the book which would not reject her.

Loretta started to stray from her religion at the age of eighteen when she met Colt. Then after Independence her brother left for England, her mother died and she came back to the faith again. She started to get depressions. She couldn't stay at home. While she was doing the housework she would feel a presence come behind her, her mind would go blank and she just sat chopping the vegetables for the *subji* with the tears flowing down her face. She began to read the Bible and used the power of prayer to banish the shadowy presences of her lost relatives. This helped, but recently they'd been having problems again, since they moved into Dolly Villa. Once she tried to get up in the night and she was thrown on to the bed three times. Then she felt someone pressing down on her chest. One day she and her niece, Paula, were sitting chatting on the bed and they saw someone walking past the window, an Anglo girl with long flowing hair and a short-sleeved flowery frock. They both felt cold and scared because they knew who she was and that she had been long dead. It was a young girl called Barbara whose parents had left her in the care of another family at the time of Independence because she was handicapped and they didn't want her in their new life. She was beaten and shut up in the room next to this bedroom without any food. She starved to death, forgotten by her relatives abroad and mistreated by the people at home in India. Now she was haunting the villa and had brought Loretta and Colt bad luck ever since they moved here. Staring at the window, Loretta took my hand and said, 'You must pray too, Laura, or otherwise you'll start to see Barbara's ghost as well.'

Looking at the blocked-over door in the opposite wall where Barbara had died, I felt cold and scared. Behind that door lay all the painful histories of Anglo-India that Colt and Loretta tried to shut out with the holy book and cowboy myths. And now I was helping to raise them from their unquiet sleep with my questions.

Colt took Loretta's other hand with tenderness and murmured soothingly: 'Hush, my darling, there's nothing to fear. The holy book will help us both through this, it's much stronger than these evil presences. It's got greater power than that terrible Jadu House, that Ku Klux Klan place that keeps these spirits rising all about us. We'll make our own magic.'

Then he began to sing her a country and western tune. As he sang I felt the soothing magic of the holy book and Colt's cowboy myths once again. And I wished that I was with Subhrasheel creating a new future with our own magic.

❧

Looking up from the pile of re-sorted pages, blurred words and mingled memories, I push open the window shutters. The storm has passed over, leaving behind a glistening vista of broken branches, fallen mangoes and newly eroded streams of water. And I think of Subhrasheel and all the well-worn paths we washed away with those stories whispered to each other in the darkness. He appears at night to remind me that it is not enough just to excavate the past; instead, like Colt and Loretta, I must weave a new present and future from its threads. It is too late to return to Subhrasheel, my only homage to him will be to continue wandering around the houses of Hidgely. My search will not be for painful family secrets like an old bazaar spy, railway official or Raj anthropologist wielding callipers. Instead, in the jadu houses all around I will listen out for the conjuring of new paths.

10

Jadu Houses

At the heart of Kharagpur looms the forbidding façade
of the Masonic Lodge. On first arriving I had thought
that the Divisional Headquarters, where the whirring
lines of telephone wires meet and from which bicycles
stream to and fro, was the centre of command. But
by some trick of planning each journey taken through
the colony to the Railway Institute, maidan, Catholic
church or railway offices inevitably passes the Lodge.
An unnatural silence surrounds it; no-one dares
encroach on the broad lawn of grass on which it
stands. Even the cows that loiter by the steps of the
Institute, trample the maidan and chew on flowers in
the churchyard only graze tentatively around the
perimeter. Hidgely's residents riding by on cycle-
rickshaws observe this silence; the stream of
conversation halts and they make the sign of the
crucifix. In the far distance the towering walls stained
black with age catch the sunlight and in places turn
a strange dried-blood deep red. Almost invisible
windows run around the top floor, too high for any
human eye to look into. The glass panes are divided by
crosses shaped like the black marks on schoolbooks
and the railway's history sheets. Along the front, three
arches draw in shadows, making it difficult to see
if there is a door through which the initiates enter.

Everybody knows that all the railway officers are members and that they have regular assemblies here, but there is never any evidence of anyone arriving. Colt and Mr Vanjo are not the only people who have mentioned the evil influence of this place. Everyone accuses the Jadu House rather than the Divisional Headquarters of being the source of their troubles. Tonight, while the revels of the pagal gymkhana fancy-dress party at the Railway Institute distract all of Hidgely's residents, Hamish Thomas has promised to sneak me inside it.

Hamish is the impresario of the infamous Santa Barbara compound. For a while no-one wanted to take me to visit him there; it seemed as off limits as the Jadu House. Walking through the winding narrow paths of the *adivasi* village, it is very difficult to make out its boundaries. Its burnt-umber mud-brick walls streaked with yellow clay seem an organic outgrowth from the soil around. There is no nameplate or number labelling the gateless entrance, just a break in the curving façade that gives on to a wide undefined space marked by a chaos of footprints zigzagging in all directions. Sometimes early in the morning I would glimpse Hamish, his long black hair flowing behind him, as he cycled off to his duty in a half-buttoned-up driver's uniform. He looked devilishly handsome, like a prince from a Moghul miniature in disguise so that he could travel unnoticed around his kingdom.

Yet everyone knows where Santa Barbara is. They speculate about its inhabitants almost as much as they do about what goes on inside the Jadu House. But in the case of Santa Barbara the rumours are of scandalous confusions. Colt would laugh whenever it came up in conversation, adding, after his guffaws had subsided, 'They've evolved a new species there, the missing link, and the king of the jungliness is that Hamish Thomas.' Mr Vanjo would frown and say, 'That place is full of all sorts mixed up together: *Upma*

Anglo-Indians – South Indian Christians who pretend to be Anglo-Indians but give away their true selves by loving to cook all those typical South Indian dishes like *Upma*; Firinghees who are hardly Anglo-Indian at all; over the wall Anglo-Indians. They wear frocks and ties but don't behave properly like I make my daughters do.'

Hope Dover was the most terrified of it. Here her husband had caught his death from a blue stone slipped into his drink. She whispered Hamish Thomas's name as if she was afraid that mentioning it would act as a curse: 'The wives there take country liquor before their food. They offer it to me, but I am afraid to take. When you start to drink it you can never stop and I always think of my babies and the ruin it would bring to them. That's why the wives there look so fat and plump and alluring to men from that liquid diet and me here all skinny and wasted.' According to Hope, Hamish rules over the compound with his two wives. 'He had his first wife who gave him three children, but he began visiting an orphan in the homes in Calcutta. He took her sweets and everything. One day he took a letter for the nuns saying that the orphan's uncle had died and he had to take her away. The nuns believed it and now they all live together in unholy harmony.'

The Delijahs maintained their usual pregnant silence on the affairs of others. I was very curious about this place that looked like a typical Indian village compound and yet housed an entourage of unconventional Anglo-Indians.

Knowing its reputation I was surprised that my first occasion for crossing over the threshold into Santa Barbara was, of all things, a wedding. Begum and his wife Donna turned up at the Delijahs'. His quiff was freshly pomaded and she was all done up in her green and gold wedding sari from years ago, her muscular arms straining at the seams of the blouse and her blond hair scraped back. Begum explained that Hamish had asked him to bring me to the wedding of Tyrone, a young man who lived in the compound with his widowed mother, so that I could experience some Anglo-Indian traditions.

Santa Barbara was transformed. A purple and yellow awning, with speakers at the top of bamboo poles blaring a Hindi tune, '*Maya Memsaheb*', turned the modest entrance into a palatial *pandal*. Here Tyrone, smeared in turmeric from being mobbed by relatives the night before, was dancing with adolescent energy. Spinning with him was a little girl who looked just like Alice-in-Wonderland in a blue-striped frock and ribbons. He stopped to greet us and said the guests were gathering at his mother's house to wait for the church service, but that Hamish wanted to see us first. The little girl pulled on his shirtsleeve, saying, 'Tyrone-*da*, why won't you tell me if it's an arranged marriage or not?' Begum winked at me and whispered, 'Only arranging that's been done here is between the hearts of Tyrone and Patricia. She's an Anglo and his family's some variety of Indian Christian. Her family's wild about it, especially as she's going to have to wear a white sari instead of a wedding dress to hide her growing stomach.'

Inside the courtyard sunlight filtered through the purple *pandal*, tinting the faces of the caterers who rushed about with giant steel buckets and baby baths full of food. A group of young girls huddled around a huge leaf parcel of jasmine flowers, threading them on to strings for all the guests to wear. Workmen heaved tables into position and chased away chickens and goats. Begum picked up a frightened, braying kid, which had a yellow ribbon tied around its neck, and carried it towards one of the mud houses. Inside on a charpoy sat Hamish in a loose white kurta with a St Christopher medallion glinting at his neck, hair tied back with a ribbon that matched the goat's. He leapt up when he saw Begum and said, 'I've been looking for Shefali. That's her sister Dipali over there. They're my foundlings, rescued them from being drowned. And this here is Diamond the Dog. Ever heard of a black diamond, well, she's one. Turned up at my door one day and she's stayed ever since.'

A Labrador as sleekly dark as Hamish's hair looked up benignly from under the charpoy. Two women in T-shirts and leggings, whom he introduced as Teena and Maureen, sat cross-legged on cushions singing, 'All Things Bright and Beautiful' and 'Jerusalem', copying down the words as they remembered them on to sheets for the guests to follow at the wedding. Donna and Begum sat down next to them and began to help, his rich baritone balancing the women's sweet soprano voices. Above their heads a silver-foil house, occupied by miniature images of Jesus and Mary, jutted out from the wall; below it a picture of a peacock-blue farmhouse in the middle of rolling mustard-yellow fields suggested a bucolic paradise of plenty. This hybrid image of a Christian but Indian homeland hung over us as a hopeful symbol of unity.

Hamish delicately stroked the nose of one of the goats and beamed. 'Welcome to my Anglo-Indian *para*, full of waifs and strays like Shefali here. You must have heard a lot about me,' he continued. 'I'm known as the Godfather, the Don, the Good Samaritan, pick anybody up from the road and rescue them, I will. I'm like St Christopher, the saint of travellers, I protect all the wandering types and give them a home. Gandhi told us to get back to the villages and we're just following his schemes. Everybody tells all sorts of bad stories about me because they don't understand the rhyme or reason of my big family here.' Continuing to caress the goat with one hand, he swept his free hand round as though to indicate his domain. 'No regulations here. It's not like that Anglo-Indian Association, having to prove your lineage, or the rail-

234

way colony where they inspect the rights of people to abide together. Take Maureen over there, I rescued her from one of those orphanages. The nuns were just keeping her locked up until they could marry her off to any old fellow who would have her. She ended up there because her Anglo mother was divorced from her Bengali husband and they both wanted to get rid of her. Aunts and uncles on her Anglo side disowned her, didn't even send her rice or sweets or visit her because they were ashamed their sister had married a Bengali. And as for the Bengali family, they just married off their son as fast as possible to someone more suited who could cook *chingri mach* and tie a sari, claiming he was an "innocent divorcee". People say Maureen's my wife, but she's like my daughter.'

As he continued to speak it became apparent that his scepticism was a long tradition in his family. Unlike Mr Vanjo and the Campbells, he was not haunted by absent documents or nationalist definitions.

Hamish explained that his grandmother had founded the *para* in the 1930s. She had been a mysterious lady, a dance-hall crooner who travelled between the railway colonies with a band of musicians. Somehow wherever she went some union trouble started. The authorities had tailed her for a while, but could prove nothing. She always hated the colonies and their paperwork. She used to say to Hamish, 'Nothing but evil follows the railway's forms, calling someone European or Anglo-Indian so they turn their back on their own mothers.' She regularly told the cautionary tale of when their family had bought a job lot of plots in Kharagpur cemetery from the colony committee and she warned, 'Just you watch, the people who hold them will all die off young,' and they did. The documents made things come true. That's why she spent all her money on the deeds to this land, because she wanted a living paradise, not a right to death. Hamish, as her favourite grandson, had continued her tradition of rejecting the authority of documents.

About the time his grandmother had bought the land there was a lot of talk in the Anglo-Indian Association magazine about founding a homeland called McCluskiegunj. The leader of the community, Sir Henry Gidney, supported the plans to build it in Bihar. This promised land would be a separate *mooluk* or nation, complete with its own Five Year Plan and Anglo-Indian anthem. Hamish's grandmother had been sceptical about the place: 'Just like one of those damn aristocratic railway colonies or hill stations pretending to be Britain, complete with Gidney Castle and the Anglo-Indian Association checking your credentials before you can even buy a plot there.' She wanted her *para* to welcome all comers, building it among the *adivasi* villagers from mud bricks so that Anglos could become like them, children of the Indian soil. She even set up an open-air chapel at one corner of it, so everyone could worship the spirit of the place as well as God. Hamish still holds services there and asks no questions of those who turn up wanting to join the family.

Those who arrive in Santa Barbara have many reasons for coming. The Evanses used to live in Calcutta near Park Circus, but their landlord started to give them trouble. He wanted them out, so he printed up posters that defamed him with the fake signature of Mr Evans at the bottom and pasted them all round the house. Then he instituted a case against the family for slander. The case ruined them and no other landlord would rent to them, so they moved out here. Mr Marchand had become a Marxist during the railway strike in 1974 and had helped to found a union in Addra. He was a telegraph operator and used to send code words through the network, innocent things like 'business is good' that spread the union's plans to other colonies. Once the strike started the railway police tried to arrest him, but he escaped and hid out in the jungle and villages. Then he found his way to sanctuary in Santa Barbara. Buddho Johnson had emigrated to Australia with the rest of his family, but he hated it, all the food tasted rotten and he missed Indian ways. So he left his family behind and moved into the *para*. Mrs Xavier, Tyrone's mother, had settled here because every other house she lived in she saw ghosts. One day, at her wits' end, she came to worship at their open-air church to ask for release from the spirits and she liked the place so much she moved in lock, stock and barrel. Now she wasn't bothered at all by people returning from the past. Within the walls of Santa Barbara a community of people has collected which has overcome obsessions with origins and identity. This, I suspected, was why the local villagers and other Anglo-Indians found it so scandalous.

Hamish broke off his stories to announce it was time to go to the wedding in the Catholic church, and that he wouldn't be attending: 'I don't like to get lined up all stiff and rigid in those pews. Those priests just want to claim the community for their own – clean it up, make us confess to sins, write us down in their books, buy our souls from us for the price of scholarships to church schools and a few new clothes. We have our own ways here or at least we make them up as we go along.'

Inside the church it was hard to distinguish the stiff formality that Hamish was so keen to avoid. The congregation was a glorious sea of magenta saris, lilac frocks and lime-green shirts. The priest, in gold-lurex robes, led the bride up the aisle. Patricia looked nervous and uncomfortable in her daisy-white sari and long white net gloves. Her blouse crowned with puffed sleeves was worthy of an Elizabethan costume and her face was almost invisible behind a flowing veil. Below the chords of the wedding march played on an electric organ by Terry, a travelling ticket collector, the guests gossiped about her pregnancy. Her white stilettos clicked on the concrete floor, which had been painted in pink, green and blue diamonds. Waiting to bless her union at the altar were three images of Christ. He smiled with crusader's flag unfurled, grimaced under the weight of a cross, and looked upward with compassion, illuminated by a halo of red light bulbs, his hands nailed to the cross. In front of the altar were two cast-iron white filigree chairs with huge red-velvet cushions straight from a Bollywood Moghul Emperor's durbar. Tyrone looked a little drunk, turmeric paste blotches just visible on his neck above his father's old cream suit. Begum and Donna sat next to me, whispering about who from the bride's side hadn't turned up, criticizing them for their misguided sense of their pure Anglo heritage and speculating what they would do with the family jewellery if they weren't going to give it to the bride.

But when the priest started his sermon, I began to understand Hamish's absence. With a deadening solemnity the priest intoned, 'The Anglo-Indian community has no history without the Church. All your lives will pass unrecorded unless you take the blessings of the Church at birth, marriage and death. Your existence will come to nought. We have gathered today to celebrate a moment of recorded history willed by God, who is the only one who can give you true immortality. Recorded in the Church register it will be found by generations to come who will recognize the significance of this day and its holy bond. This couple, even if they might not have intended to come together in marriage a few months ago, have been brought together by God and are part of his larger plan. When all their friends have left them and they face hard times and temptations, God will be the only one to guide them. The only true community is the community of this Church, but only the pure and obedient of spirit can enter it.'

Hamish's plan for his community certainly didn't fit this rigid mould and he wanted to follow his own path and history. I looked forward to seeing what the Santa Barbara traditions would be at the reception later.

I wasn't disappointed. The *pandal* glittered with fairy lights and pounded to a bewildering soundtrack of Europop and Hindi film music. At the entrance Hamish smeared each guest with sandalwood paste and sprinkled them with rose water. Tyrone and Patricia sat in state on the filigree thrones raising glasses of raisin wine as Begum found increasingly bawdy excuses for toasts. Hanging above them was a white crêpe-paper and lace wedding bell. Seven young men threw handfuls of rice over them. They were followed by seven young girls, dressed in everything from slick miniskirts to embroidered Lucknawi *salwar kameezes*, who garlanded the couple and all the guests with flowers. As Tyrone and Patricia cut the sponge wedding cake, Hamish swiped at the bell and they glistened under the cascades of silver confetti that tumbled out. This was a dizzying mix of South Indian and European Christian traditions, not ashamed of its own eclecticism.

It was now Hamish's turn to give a sermon: 'Here is my wee bit of advice for the bride and groom. Our lives follow our own geography. They flow like a river finding their own paths to the sea, wearing the earth into new shapes as they pass over it. In the Bible the river they tell us about is the river Jordan. They say the river Jordan flows into the Sea of Galilee and ends in the Dead Sea. In the Sea of Galilee it gives out all its sweetness and in the Dead Sea all its salt bitterness, ending in death. In Hindu mythology they believe in the holy waters of the Ganges that will make you twice born if you reach it on death. But here today what we are celebrating is the source of a new river with no fixed path yet, no known destination. I say to this couple, make your own way and leave this Indian soil different once you have passed over it. You will give something new to the generations to come.'

I enthusiastically joined in with the toast and applause. At last I had found someone who loved to improvise, to bend the traditions that were usually held in such reverence.

The toasts over steaming mountains of *pulao*, *subji*, mutton and *papads* enticed the motley parade of guests to the tables. The Alice-in-Wonderland little girl ran about with a white silk cushion covered in pink and blue ribbons, pinning them on to guests' lapels, saris and Tshirts.

Begum whispered to me, pointing out a matronly woman in a lemon-yellow chiffon frock and a man in a dark charcoal suit more suitable for a funeral, 'The bride's mother and father, Dora and Leonard, have finally arrived. Let's see if we can fill them up with liquor. It always acts as the spirit of forgiveness.'

Dora scowled and patted her fringe back into place, trying to cover up the sandalwood paste on her forehead. Begum pulled me over towards them brandishing glasses of wine and Dora's whole aspect brightened. She grasped my hand and said, 'I never expected to see a Britisher at such a wedding. Welcome, you can be our lucky charm.'

Leonard grumbled, 'Don't start now, Dora, on all your charms and potions and magic,' and knocked back both the glasses of wine proffered by Begum.

But Dora paid no attention and rattled on anxiously: 'My daughter there, she's had a love spell put on her by Tyrone. From when she met him she's been breaking every caste and creed. I've got a lovely statue of infant Jesus, baby Jesus. From that day all the trouble started. My daughter took the statue and threw it at me. She was mad in the head.' Dora was convinced that Patricia had been 'given witchcraft' by Tyrone and when Patricia announced that she was going to marry him, Dora knew something was up: 'So I went to a

Tantric fellow in Ripon Street in Calcutta to get his advice. Before I even said anything he told me, "You've come regarding your daughter." I didn't even tell him I had a daughter and he said somebody had witch-crafted her. He said, "Do you want to know who witchcrafted her?" I had an idea, but I didn't say. Anyway he said, "I'll show you." He took a piece of paper and said, "Don't say anything, don't do any-thing." He picked up a candle and put the paper over the candle and Tyrone's face came. On the flamed piece of paper from the smoke the image came and on the side was a chocolate. The chocolate was penetrated and I asked him why is it like that. "It's because witchcraft was put in," he said. That's how Tyrone got Patricia to marry him, a no-good South Indian Christian from Santa Barbara *para.'*

She sniffed in disgust, but Begum hadn't yet given up on his mission of reconciliation. He pointed out the obvious flaws in Dora's account: 'Dora, what's a good Catholic woman like you doing consulting these Tantrics and believing in all this witchcraft? Not very godly yourself, are you? You remember how everyone made a fuss when Donna and I got married in the Muslim rights, well, nothing bad has happened from our mixing. What harm will come from Tyrone and Patricia's union if they love each other?'

Leonard became animated again: 'What have I been telling you, Dora? My ma was an Indian Christian too. You know how it hurt me when I was little and she couldn't go with me to the Christmas party at the Institute. I used to take food wrapped up in a napkin back to her, I felt so bad. And now we're all Indian, even you believe in that Tantric stuff.'

Dora's lips set in a hard, obstinate line, but when the little girl rushed up to her with the wedding ribbons and cake she accepted them.

Much later, once all the leaf plates had been taken away and the tables pushed to the side of the room, Begum pointed Dora out to me. She was dancing a speeded-up foxtrot with her husband to an old Amitabh Bacchan movie tune mixed with disco beats.

'Why is it a full bottle of liquor doesn't dance, but when a man or woman is full of liquor they do?' Begum said. 'Dora's dancing to a different tune now. She'll accept the match for the love of her daughter. Same thing happened with Donna and me, after we got married.'

A few hours later Dora was jiving with Tyrone. Hamish slipped up behind me and whispered, 'Look at the magic of Santa Barbara. Seems like witchcraft to everyone outside but once you're inside, even if it only lasts for a few moments, all those castes and creeds seem like evil spells. And the worst place for conjuring them is the Jadu House, the Masonic Lodge. When you walk past it you lose your senses. All your will about where you want to go deserts you. The spirits of the past possess you and you wake up hours later, far from your own home, thinking you've been in Britain or some such nonsense.'

Banging on the Delijahs' door at midnight when the celebrations were finally over, I clutched in my hands a collection of talismans from Santa Barbara: a demure red ribbon and a lace handkerchief embroidered in fine turmeric-yellow needlepoint with the date of the wedding, which unfolded to reveal coconut slices, *paan* leaves and a small enamel peacock-blue box with a mirror inside. Suddenly worried about what the Delijahs would think of my dissolute appearance, I checked my face in the mirror. Streaks of sandalwood paste anointed my forehead as if I was a devout worshipper returning from a dawn visit to a temple, but my cheeks were shamelessly flushed red with raisin wine. Having passed through the magic of Santa Barbara, I am neither a respectable British *memsaheb* nor a Bengali lady, but some strange mixture of the two. If only there was a way to make this spell last.

I'm expecting more of this magic tonight at the pagal gymkhana. Hamish is the impresario of this event too; he has rented the Railway Institute for the night. Excitement is palpable in almost every house in Hidgely. For the past week piles of yellow chiffon, green nylon, old saris and gold fringes have been piled in corners, waiting to be stitched into costumes. On top of them are pages torn from magazines: photographs of James Dean, cartoons of gods, goddesses and nationalist leaders, and publicity shots of 'sixties Hindi movie stars that will provide the patterns for the cloth. Even the Delijahs have broken their usual reserve to speculate about what Elsie and Carlton should wear to the dance. Eventually Elsie decided to go dressed up as the singer Alisha from her *Made in India* video, while Carlton would go as Elvis.

Only Hope was reluctant to let her young daughter take part, warning that 'All the fruit-sellers dress up and disguise their caste. I won't let her go because they will take her out and make trouble with her. They're worse than *chamars* and she won't know they are fruit sellers from their looks. And all those people from Santa Barbara will go dressed up nicely, when they are only from the bottler caste, the one that trades in old liquor bottles. No-one will be able to make out what they really are.'

Nonetheless I'm looking forward to this riot of colour and fantasy. Like Gary's description of the pagal gymkhanas of his youth and Subhrasheel's story of the Attorney General this evening will be a celebration of the fluidity of disguises. I couldn't think of what to wear, but once Hope told me that I was becoming too Indian-looking, 'all thin and dark', I decided it had to be a sari, so I borrowed one from Donna. When I fold and pin it into place, the cascades of embroidered Lucknawi cloth feel very different from Mrs Gupta's borrowed clothes because later I will jive and drink in them and not sit sedately admiring a classical musician's skill.

Begum will be taking me to the pagal gymkhana and I'm very proud to have him as my companion. My choice to borrow a sari from Donna was not accidental. Their multifaceted love creates daily the spell that I had felt that night returning from Tyrone and Patricia's wedding. Begum and Donna have made their home neither in the red-brick villas and shacks of Hidgely nor in the mud huts of Santa Barbara. They live in one of the yellowing concrete houses built in the railway colony since Independence. Their rigidly functional lines have sprouted on the site of the Raj pleasure gardens, where at dusk the railway officers and their ladies once took the air and contemplated flower-clocks daily clipped by malis sweating under the midday sun. They are a homage to the modernist schemes that gripped the imagination of new nations, which erected Corbusier-inspired concrete and glass blocks from Abidjan to Chandigarh. Railway bureaucrats calculated the exact dimensions required by each individual worker so that all their needs could be met and they could take an equal share in India's glorious new industrial future. The most complete realization of this vision was at Chittaranjan, a town named in honour of a nationalist leader, in which refugees from East Pakistan were resettled and at the heart of which is a locomotive works that ended India's reliance on imported rolling stock. Nehru took Tito on a state visit there in the 1950s. Young, enthusiastic railway officers often tried to persuade me that I should conduct my research in Chittaranjan, calling it one of the 'Temples of Modern India'. Here, they suggested, the concrete blocks at one fell swoop annihilated economic inequalities, the communal violence that had accompanied Independence and the inheritances of the Raj. I had the suspicion that this hopeful refounding was less representative of the fate of nationalist utopias than places like Kharagpur, where concrete blocks jostle with makeshift shrines to Vishwarkarma, the god of craftsmen, built from materials stolen from the loco workshop, and with the old palatial bungalows of divisional superintendents. Yet each time I visited Begum and Donna's home, I felt that perhaps nationalist, secular dreams had found some kind of unplanned realization here, as they had in Santa Barbara compound.

The railway bureaucrats would not recognize their utilitarian designs in the changes that Begum and Donna have made to their allotted space. The house bulges with a series of ramshackle conversions that overspill the boundaries of the property. Lean-to shacks for animals, palm-leaf screens, bamboo verandas and a clay tandoor oven have grown like secretions around its walls. Since her sons left for college, Donna has tutored neighbours' children in Bengali, Hindi and English under the cover of the improvised veranda. She cajoles them in a dizzying mix of languages, so intermingled on her tongue that they seem like one: 'Shabana, Cecily and Nila *kuch aur nahi*, don't be doing, *cholo* concentrate *korcho*.' Visitors call in a regular stream, looking for Begum to help write petitions or to catch up on family news. Donna refuses to let them touch her feet in greeting, although some of her sons' friends insist. Then, embarrassed by the respectful gesture, she bends her almost six foot Amazon frame, reaching out her hands and raising them up from the ground. When Begum isn't hanging out at the stadium or sports club offices, training up children, playing cards with his retired sporting friends and fixing up jobs for the needy, he joins her here.

One day Donna, Begum and I were sitting on the veranda steps. The harsh sunlight, filtered through the woven bamboo screen above, turned into a honeyed

245

glow and chickens pecked for crumbs at our feet. Donna combed out and oiled her long flaxen plait like a Bengali housewife, while Begum leafed through an old scrapbook filled with wedding photographs and newspaper cuttings about their sporting victories. The scent of the sandalwood oil mingled with the lingering aroma of *keema*, which waited on a sideboard inside in case anyone showed up and felt hungry. As Begum turned over the pages, Donna chuckled at the pictures that showed them stiff but happy in their wedding finery.

She explained the fluid passage of her life: 'I wasn't brought up to be a Muslim bride. It was the last thing my parents expected. When I was growing up in Addra colony my parents stuck to British habits, all sitting down to dinner together in the evenings and singing round the piano afterwards.' Her mother allowed her and her five sisters to go to dances at the Institute, but watched who they danced with carefully. 'My God, my mother used to sit to the end, so strict, *arre baba*! If she found somebody under the influence of liquor she'd say, "Don't get up" and if she thought that a particular partner is not very graceful in his behavement also the next time, "Don't get up." For the Coronation Dance my mummy told me I should dress very simple with no proudiness, so she bought dress material in red, white and blue like the Union Jack. I asked her, "Who's going to wear?" She said, "Shut up," but I said, "Like this I won't get the prize, India's independent now." My mummy said, "So you want to get up with mascara and make yourself known." She always insisted on respectful, simple frocks, none of those short skirts and all. And now look at what I wear.'

She picked up a sari blouse lying next to her, waiting for stitching.

Donna explained that when she was young she wasn't much into all this make-up and frills. Instead, she loved to lace up her keds, put on shorts and sprint round the colony or to skip school and sneak into the swimming pool. Looking at Begum with a wicked smile, she added that the first time she was kissed was there: 'I shouldn't be telling my husband about old boyfriends. It'll only make him jealous – but maybe that's a good thing, it'll keep the home fires burning. The boyfriend I liked at that time was there at the pool. I wanted to know how deep it was and I didn't know he was hiding under the diving board. These girls said you must see how deep it is. I walked out on the board carrying my books, fully dressed in a lacy frock, and the boy pulled the board down. I landed in the water and he kissed me. My mother told me if I kissed a boy I would get a child, so now I thought I would get pregnant. I went home all soaked and my mother already knew I'd skedaddled from school. She came towards me with a malacca cane smeared with oil and chillies. She beat me and for two months I was never allowed to go outside to run or to the pictures and all. I still thought I would get pregnant so I ran a bath and took down some potash disinfectant and mixed it in the bath. Luckily my father came in and said, "What are you doing, girl?" I started crying and said that I was going to get a baby. My father said to my mother, "Why did you tell her she'd get a baby that way? You are worse than a red-faced monkey filling her mind with nonsense." After that I never listened to my mother's rules and concentrated everything on running and sport. I felt so strong and free that way.'

Donna thought that her mother was strict because she had been left alone so young: 'Her mother had died and we were never sure what happened to her father. My mother was put in an orphanage with nuns. Her relatives swindled her out of the property that was rightly hers and all alone in the world she devoted herself to following the nuns' ways and that marked the rest of her life and the way she treated her own babies.' Donna, however, had rejected all of the lessons that tried to teach her how to be a demure *memsaheb*. Instead she built her identity around the strength and speed of her own body.

She took after her father's mother, the sister of Dr Ghosh who founded a famous hospital in Calcutta. She was a swimmer: 'Very massive yah, ouf. She swam where the Hooghly enters the Bay of Bengal. In one breath she swam the breadth of that. It's called the gondola, strong current and all, no halting. My father thought I would be a swimmer too, but my shoulders weren't strong enough to match my grandmother's record.'

Donna was the first Anglo-Indian I had met who spoke openly and proudly of a formidable Indian, Hindu ancestor. All the others had struggled with the shame and contradictions of having mixed ancestry. Begum put down the scrapbook and urged Donna to tell me how it had been predicted that she would be a sportswoman.

'I was born at my uncle's house in Jamuria, in the middle of the coalfields,' she said. 'My mummy at that time came in for a bit of a nervous breakdown and she didn't want to stay in the house when she was expecting, so my father took her to Jamuria. After she had me, she didn't want to see much of me either, nerve things happened.' As soon as her father saw Donna's blond hair and strong limbs he started to call her his own dear *koila* cat, meaning his coal-black cat. 'The joke was I was born in a coalfield, I had that strength and fire that coal has, the speed and wickedness of a cat also and it was funny because I was looking so fair.' Then when she was three days old her father laid her on the bed and went to bathe her mother. The house was on two floors and in the trees outside the window there were often monkeys, big black-faced baboons. A monkey came in through the window and grabbed Donna and was sitting with her in its arms when her father returned to the bedroom. 'After some time she left me on the window sill. But say what you like, they say now, the Hindus, Hanuman is the monkey god and Hanuman is also the god of strength, massive strength like that, and so massive strength I had from when I was very young, god-gifted. I didn't have to build up strength, I was Hanuman's child.'

This story showed me how far Donna had travelled from the British identity her mother had tried to impose on her. Here was a Muslim, Anglo-Indian wife drawing on Hindu traditions. The magic of this moment had the same power as the conjuring of Santa Barbara.

Donna was proud that she had used her prowess to represent Orissa in the national school games. Then she represented Bengal, followed by the South-Eastern Railway team, Rangers' Club and finally Mohameddan Sporting.

Donna took the scrapbook from Begum and turned to a particular cutting: 'When I went out to a national competition in Jamuria, my father was very proud because I was racing for India on the soil where I was born. But the crowd who came to watch and the journalists reporting didn't know I was representing the Indian team. Here, look, it's a photo of me and it says, "Russian girl wins," they thought I was pure Russian. When I was doing the march past, the crowd kept saying, "There goes the Russian girl," and very close photo they took while I was doing the shot-put and there they put on the photo, "The Russian girl wins the day," big block letters. It makes me so angry and all. They couldn't recognize I was Indian.'

Begum held her hand: 'Don't worry, my little straw doll. We know we were doing it for our country. It's just that we are too cosmopolitan for them to understand.'

I asked Begum how he had got so interested in

sports. When he was a little boy he used to sneak into the south side of Kharagpur to watch the Anglo-Indians and British running round the stadium. He envied the sheer expanse of the pitch after the cramped quarters his parents lived in by the mosque on the north side of the colony. He wondered what it would feel like to have all that ground to sprint across. When he started working in the loco plant under the regimentation of the time clock, he dreamt even more of beating the clock in races and stretching his muscles against their own limits rather than exhausting them against the hard sheets of steel. One year he was taking part in the annual Vishwakarma festival in the workshop, when they had tiger dances and walking on coals, and the potential of his physique was spotted by the railway coach, an Anglo-Indian chap. That was his chance to earn respect and to become, as he put it, 'half Anglo-Indian', fulfilling his dreams of entering the stadium at last.

'It was lucky this happened, otherwise Donna and I would never have met. One South-Eastern Railway tournament was going on and I spotted Donna across the field. Ouf, such a looker she was and she won the race and my heart that day. First prize my heart! Then after that we used to court each other at the weekly tournaments in Calcutta and Kharagpur.'

Begum thought that he won Donna over because his physique made him look more Anglo-Indian than the Anglo-Indians. He shared Donna's sense of identity as something malleable, determined by one's own life choices rather than by permanent markers of religion, class and race.

It took much longer to win over Donna's parents, however; seven years in all. His mother loved Donna because of her beautiful long plait and respectful ways, so there were no problems with his family. Her parents didn't even come to their marriage and Donna paid their part of the expenses on her own. They went through the full Muslim ceremony. A year afterwards her sister, a travelling ticket inspector, managed to bring about a reconciliation with her parents because they saw how happy Donna was and how loving Begum was.

Donna didn't feel properly married until her parents had accepted him as her husband: 'Laura, all these religious ceremonies are only for families to come together and share in joys and sadness. If they don't, then the heart of the thing is not there, however many blessings and rituals and incense is burnt.'

'So few people understand this,' Begum sighed wearily. 'Donna and I try to make them see that what is important is the heart, but religion here in India is a show with everyone acting like high-caste Brahmins, looking down their noses at people of other faiths, wearing their religion tied like a thread round their bodies.'

For a moment Donna looked down at the folds of her sari, lost in thought. I imagined that she was musing on the painful divisions between Hindus, Muslims and Christians that fill the pages of Indian history books and newspapers. But I was wrong.

'I remember the funeral of one of my uncles,' she said sadly. 'He was a high-up Mason who died in Calcutta. The body was motored in from Calcutta and the Freemasons had put it in a full bronze coffin, airtight. It was kept in the Masonic Lodge, not brought home once for us to sit up and mourn with him and look at his face for one last time and remember all the sweet and good things he had done for us. They didn't open the coffin for us to say goodbye once. That doubled, tripled our grief. I don't believe in that kind of thing, people belong to their families and friends, not to evil places like the Masonic Lodge. It's there that all the trouble starts.'

Once again the building that lay at the heart of Kharagpur was described as the source of sorrows, but

I couldn't understand the connection that Donna had made between it and religious strife. Then Begum spoke and made everything clear.

'You know, the Masons are a strange thing,' he said. 'All their secrets, even the way you are sitting, your hand position is a code. Their way of talking, their way of standing, their way of holding the spoon and fork is a code. They have their own unholy wicked codes. Just the same as this thing that happens between communities, always watching and saying, this behaviour means you are British, that means you are Muslim or Hindu or Christian. Just like trained monkeys – but I say we should not follow such codes, we should run the race of life whatever way suits us.'

Taking me inside the house and through to their bedroom, Begum proudly pointed to a framed document on the wall. It was presented to him on his retirement by fellow workers in the railway. 'This is our philosophy,' he said:

A Tribute to Abdul Ahmed alias Begum

Shri Abdul Ahmed is widely known as Begum. It is not a strange exception that one such as Begum has sprung from nowhere, on the contrary, he has been born and brought up among all the people of India and knowing them all, shares sympathies and works for their greater benefit.

An exemplary citizen, Begum has got free access to Church, Mosque, Gurdwara and Temple only due to his superb human friendships and his true temperament. Although he is from an orthodox Muslim family he is married to a Christian lady. His life is an example of cosmopolitanism. Half India's problems would have been solved if the politicians, administrators, religious supremos could follow Begum's radical humanism.

Last and not least the outstanding trait of his character is generosity of spirit. And through this spirit Begum will move on through this rumbling universe with his incorruptible innocence. We wish him and his lifelong companion, Donna, a long and happy life.

Members of Bengalee Club, Kharagpur
14 April 1992

Begum and Donna's love was not merely a private victory. They had persuaded the respectable Bengali officers of Kharagpur that their unconventional relationship held the seeds of India's future. Tonight, wearing Donna's sari, I will sneak into the Jadu House. Her stories and borrowed clothes will protect me from its evil influence and its attempts to keep old divisions alive.

Begum's motorbike splutters to a halt outside and Dennis the Menace greets him with a yelp. Hitching up my sari I run outside, eager to know how he is dressed tonight for the pagal gymkhana. His costume is hidden under a long leather jacket and he urges me to climb on to the bike. I hang on side-saddle as we speed over bumps through the darkness, until we shudder to a halt outside the Railway Institute. The classical columns have changed for the occasion as well; they are festooned with red, green and orange bunting, the colours of the Indian flag, and flickering lights. A group of pirates is loitering by the lines of motorbikes, swigging from paper bags. One of them teases Roger, who had come as Indiana Jones: 'Where's your Temple of Doom then? Must be the church over there, they've been trying to get your soul to no effect for years now.' Clarice, dressed as Elizabeth Taylor playing Cleopatra, gazes proprietorially at her young men and waits to cause wars with her fading beauty. Tarzan, painted blue and in a lungi, is Baby Krishna. He pulls on

Henry's arm, begging to be shown Govinda's latest dance steps one more time.

Alice is looking me up and down with curiosity. Then, laughing, she says, 'I've heard of *Indian wallah vileti saheb bangeya*, an Indian or Anglo becoming a Britisher, but now we've got Blighty *memsaheb* trying ever so hard to be an Indian lady. Give it up, child, not even the Indian women are ladies any more!'

Before I can reply Begum chortles, 'Wait till you see my costume, Alice.' He peels off his leather jacket to reveal his waistcoat, which is pinned with Indian and British flags. Taking a courtly bow he places a Nehru cap on his head and says, 'I'm a patriotic Anglo Muslim Indian. No bluffing tonight, laying all my cards on the table.'

Everyone claps at the show and starts drunkenly but fervently to sing the National Anthem and *'Sare jahan se accha.'*

As we climb the solemn white stairs, the bass pounding from the dance hall at the top of the building grows louder with each step. Huddled figures look up towards us. Mr Marchand is in *khadi* with a *jhola* bag and round glasses glinting in the half-light. He interrupts an intense discussion with Maureen, who wobbles in stilettos and a leopard-skin skirt, to say, 'Look, I've found my Helen, she's stepped right from a Hindi movie.' Maureen's heavy eyeliner and long red fingernails do make her look just like the 'sixties actress renowned for her nightclub scenes and impersonations of Anglo girls. She smiles and replies, 'And me my revolutionary.' At the top of the stairs lines of chairs are laid out in the ante-room for wallflowers to sit on. Mavis and Marcie, in short white frocks that look like wedding dresses, laugh as they encourage the assembled hopeful women to sing, 'Some day my Prince will come.' Paula frowns at Johnny squirming on her lap. He is kitted out as the Undertaker from the World Wrestling Federation and tugs at her flapper dress and pearls. The only man sitting on the chairs is Buddho Johnson and he doesn't really count because he is wearing a red-spotted head-scarf and a lilac short-sleeved frock from which his biceps bulge, tattooed with an anchor and the eyes of the Buddha.

Inside the dance hall, fragments of silver light from a glitter-ball sparkle on the faces of couples, who have found their own rhythms to the speeded-up Bryan Adams number. Dora and Leonard stick to a foxtrot. Tyrone tries to persuade Patricia to follow his posse rap moves. Colt and Loretta, who have just come more in character than usual, twirl and step-dance. Mr Vanjo sways peacefully in a corner with his eyes closed, arms stretched out for his invisible partner. The band, a group of Indian Institute of Technology students in their best Benetton, Megadeath and Lacoste T-shirts, begin reluctantly to bash out, 'RRRasputin, Lover of the Russian Queen', turning up their noses at the special request. Hamish whirls up beside me and asks me to dance, his monk's robe and long beard making it clear that he has asked for the song. As we dance he bends towards me and says, 'What else could I come as? Known as I am for poisonings and witch-craft. But later tonight, we'll go to that place you've heard so much about, the Jadu House, where all of that really happens. The caretaker will be so drunk after the dance he won't mind.'

As the night wears on, Elsie takes over the micro-phone and in her gold *lengha choli* belts out 'To Sir With Love'. Buddho Johnson heckles her from the back of the room in a high-pitched voice, calling, 'Let a real Miss Oldie Goldie take over the tune.' One of the pirates distracts him by offering him more liquor outside. Ignoring the disturbance courting couples, pretending to be Romeos and Radhas, Juliets and Krishnas, stare into each other's eyes. Sweating from all the dancing and wondering where Subhrasheel might be at this moment, I walk out on to the long, wide expanse of the balcony and into the cooling air. Hamish leans against the balustrade, supporting an elderly man in a fraying railway guard's uniform and *pagri* with coils of red ribbon around his neck. Calling me over, Hamish introduces Mr Francis, the caretaker of the Masonic Lodge, who drunkenly salutes and then folds his hands into a *namaskar*.

'I'm a railway public servant with all my red tape, like the joke?' laughs Mr Francis.

'Mr Francis is going to let us into the Jadu House, *cholo* Laura.'

Mr Francis rattles a huge bunch of rusted keys: 'Where has my faithful service got me anyway, keeping the secrets for all these years with no reward? See, here are the keys to the castle.'

As we stumble across the grass I hitch up my sari to protect it from mud stains, suddenly thinking of Subhrasheel's grandmother and her night-time discovery. The Jadu House is almost invisible in the blackness. The only hint of its closeness comes from the abrupt dropping away of the humid wind on our faces. Then it is there, a looming inky-black shadow of towering walls with no windows to reflect moonlight. Using fingers to feel our way along the craggy bricks to the entrance, we come to the trinity of whitewashed arches that seem like the grand portals of railway tunnels. Following their curves leads to a blank teak door, which could once have been railway sleepers. Mr Francis fumbles at the lock and Hamish lights a *biri* in his impatience. Once inside I follow the glinting light of the *biri* up stairs that creak as we climb. Hamish's long robe sweeps away the dusty footprints of Masonic initiates who have been there earlier in the day. At the top of the stairs Hamish strikes a succession of matches, which light up an antechamber with a grand ancient Egyptian arch guarding the entrance to the spirit room. Its details are so similar to the hoarded relics of the British Museum, but it is as fake as the Moghul arches of the Eastern Railway. Next to it are pegs that Mr Francis says the Masons use to hang their clothes on before they enter the room. Photographs of railway officers in full Masonic regalia of gloves, whips and ropes, line the walls. Their suits are swapped here for the naked tools of power. We cross the threshold on to a chessboard floor flanked at each end by wooden thrones and plinths with masons' hammers lying on them. Here the railway officers arrange souls like chess pieces. All the religious books of the world – the Koran, the Bible, the Bhagavad-Gita – lie piled up as if they were civilizations collected for the pleasure of the officials. In a corner on a purple-velvet-covered table are a skull and a pair of phrenologist's measuring callipers. Bumping into something propped against the wall, I look down to see a picture showing a railway track that progresses onwards and upwards to the heavens, the signals looking like crucifixes.

Everyone in Kharagpur had mentioned the power of this place. For Mr Vanjo it is the source of his own lack of control over his family's destiny, which lies in the hands of Indian and British officials. For Colt it represents the origin of the Ku Klux Klan-like racial categories that constantly disqualify him from belonging. For Hamish and Begum it is the font from which all distinctions of community and national traditions emanate. And now inside it, I realize that their speculations about the rational bureaucracy of the railways are absolutely true. Here railway officials admit to themselves the secret occult obsessions of the Raj, dropping all the pretences of its benign influence. The only magic against the divisions the Jadu House preserves is the delicate tracery of Anglo-Indian stories. In their own jadu houses they reveal the occult absurdities that pass for reality, bringing other truths of identity into being.

Hamish kicks one of the mahogany thrones and says,

'So here's where they conjure up and keep souls. Not so impressive when you get inside, is it? I'll have to tell everyone now about its hollowness.'

Back at the Delijahs', lying in the bed rigged up in the long corridor, I know my quest is almost over. The still weak early-morning sunlight strikes the crumpled, mud-stained sari draped over a chair. Subhrasheel's grandmother many years ago had woken up next to her husband and worried about the guilty stains on her sari. Her discovery of his obsession with British elegance had filled her with terror, but I don't feel fear. Kharagpur has given a gift to me, a myriad of family stories that reveal a present and future that don't rest on the false divisions between communities. This is a joyful pagal gymkhana. But even though there is no reason to stay here any longer, I'm afraid to leave. Perhaps all of this Anglo-Indian magic will seem unreal beyond the boundaries of Santa Barbara, Hidgely and Choto Tangra. How can I make it last? Yet tossing in this bed where Subhrasheel still comes to me at night, I know there is another cause for my reluctance to admit that my quest is over. There will no longer be any excuse not to return to Maurice. And I'm not sure I can go back to him now. Nor can I face the pain of shattering the home that we have built together. Getting up from the bed, I'm happy for the distraction of a morning visit to Hope. A little resentful of my friendship with Hamish, Begum and the Vanjos, she feels neglected so I'm going to see her today.

Hope is sweeping away a pool of mud that had invaded her house. She greets me with an oddly relieved smile: 'Thank God it's you. I thought you were my stepdaughter coming across the maidan to worry me about the house. Roger's stolen all the land papers from his father's railway box and given them to her. She's trying to evict me. They're starting a legal case for what they're calling a rightful share of my property. We're under Indian law now, which means all the children are supposed to have a part. I still can't believe my husband's dead. I keep expecting him home; while sweeping I could just see him coming across the maidan.'

Inside, the living room is littered with *dekchis* to catch the water leaking through the roof. As drops splash steadily into them, Hope wraps a shawl around Henry, who is lying ill on one of the couches. He has lost all his gangster bravado and is deathly pale. Hope confides that he drank acid out of a battery last night, but won't say why. She is convinced that some girl must have refused him at the pagal gymkhana. The rickshaw driver took one look at him when he became sick and refused to take him to the Railway Hospital. 'It'll be a police case,' he'd said, so Hope had to carry Henry all the way there.

Henry turns over on the couch and whispers, 'It wasn't any girl, Ma. I got to thinking too much about everything without work.'

Hope tries to comfort him, but she is obviously distressed herself: 'When my husband was alive everything was alight and everybody visited me. When the light is burning bright everybody will come, but when it's darkness no-one will even come and strike a match. All our relatives abroad used to send us foreign clothes, and now look at the state of us. We even send *rakhi* friendship bands to all our Indian neighbours' children at that festival with *barfi* sweets and all, but in times of trouble they don't want to know.'

Trying to distract her, I change the subject by telling her about some of my new friends.

'I don't know why you're spending your time with all those evil types,' she snaps. 'Colt's a bad man, he just makes it all up about that ghost to keep people away from their house. He took one knuckleduster and killed a man and was in prison for it. And one of their sons is really his servant's child by him. The Telugu community took him to court and made him adopt the son, so they took him on. And that Mr Vanjo, what's the use of all his mourning? When Milly was ill he neglected her, no doctor was sent for. Now he has one beautiful carved gravestone with Bible words all over it. What's the point of spending money on that and washing the grave every day? I'm not like that. I try and do everything for my babies while they're alive, not after death.'

I don't want to hear these things. Hope is ripping apart the magic of Mr Vanjo and Colt's stories and showing me the failures of love that she thinks are hidden behind them.

'I found something of yours. I've been keeping it safely for a whole month, but you haven't visited me. Wait here.'

Getting up, Hope disappears into the kitchen and returns with two crumpled pages from my diary that had blown out of the window during the monsoon storm. They are a little browned at the edges from drying beside her kerosene stove.

'I knew these must be yours when I saw them, such a fine neat hand and all these poetic words about our community. My daughter's written something for you, the elder one who's married an Indian Christian.'

She hands me four pages from an exercise book identical to my diary and overflowing with flowery italics:

We Anglo-Indians don't think of the future because we don't have one. The housewives have to go to church and seek help for her children. For example for books, uniforms, etc. Some of them take the money, enjoy themselves in hotels or in liquor. The men are terrible. They smoke, gamble, take tablets, pop articles in the shops. The sons are no less. They beat their parents. If they don't get any money they throw knives or axes. They beat up all the little kids badly, without having pity.

260

The young generation just want money to drink or even have a lot of fun with women. They have no respect for Grandma. Sometimes the girls in our community go the wrong way in their young age due to poverty and family disturbances. From childhood they see their elders are self-interested and they like to enjoy their lives by any means. The same child grows into a young girl. She learns to do the same. For a little dressing, movie, make-ups, hotels or some gifts, they go in the wrong way. Most of our young girls know we have to get married in our own caste and have to face the same problems. So they think, 'Why not enjoy our lives after marriage?' and get married so they can have freedom and pleasure. Some wives enjoy themselves when their husband is away or at work. This is the life of our community. But the widow suffers. As you can see my mother. After this there will be no pension. Three younger kids will suffer.

I don't want to believe this relentless summary for so many reasons. It is too close to Bengali and Raj judgements on Anglo-Indians and it doesn't fit with what I have learnt from the pagal gymkhana and the traditions in Santa Barbara. But suddenly I realize that Hope's daughter couldn't have written anything other than this. Once she took up a pen she was constrained by every document that has ever been written about Anglo-Indians. She thought of her audience and wrote a plea that would suit the expectations of a Blighty memsaheb. This is what I am still, a representative of all those generations of railway officials.

Hope interrupts my thoughts and suggests, 'But you must take more back to Britain than this. Roger's been teasing me that we should ask you to take Tarzan with his foreign ways. He doesn't belong here. Take him as your brother.'

In this moment I know that stories and words will never be enough, but that they will be all I will leave Kharagpur with. Taking Tarzan with me would only confirm the idea that somehow he is a foreigner to the land in which he was born, a Lord Greystoke returning to claim his inheritance in an unreal Britain of aristocratic stately homes. Whatever disguises I wear, I will always be a Blighty *memsaheb* to Hope. The weight of this is painful. It is time to leave Kharagpur. Taking these stories with me, I will try to make them affect the world outside Hidgely. Then perhaps Tarzan's future can be different.

11

A Crystal Globe

Taking with me a sari, a present from Donna, and the
talismans from Tyrone and Patricia's marriage, I left for
Calcutta. After a month back in Mrs Gupta's castle,
answers evade me. Tonight, as on every other night,
pacing around the flat, I try to distract myself with
anthropological texts. *Bustee* dwellers shout *quawali*
songs, jackfruit fall from the tree, a Hindi video plays,
pipes shudder, the Guptas' bed creaks and the fan
clicks as it completes another circuit. The pungent
mosquito pesticide belching from a municipal lorry
overwhelms the usual undertones of incense, mould
and mothballs and then fades away. These are sounds
and smells so familiar they offer no distraction. I don't
know who or where to think of to calm my mind.
Thinking about Maurice just makes me fearful. I can't
remember what loving him felt like. My love must
surely exist somewhere inside me, waiting to be re-
awakened. What can I do with all this desire for
Subhrasheel? Britain and America are abstractions; all
my daily routines – washing in buckets, folding a
dupatta and pinning it in exactly the right position,
carrying a flowered handkerchief to mop my brow,
putting up an umbrella to shelter myself from the
midday heat, scattering Bengali words into English
conversation and sitting with the right degree of

composure on crowded buses – have made me forget the rhythms of other countries.

In Calcutta I've been having a recurrent dream. Strangely, when sleep finally comes, I don't dream of Maurice or Subhrasheel. Instead in the distance there is an old Anglo-Indian woman. She walks from the door of a rose-entwined stone cottage along an avenue of Scots pines and hedgerows that are part of a railway hill school. She is carrying something in her hands. She gets nearer; white streaks of talcum powder on her arms smell of lavender and cupped in one of her palms is a small crystal globe. She gives it to me, saying, 'Here is our inheritance. Take it, but be careful what you think of because this globe will alter everything around,' and my fingers tremble from the cold of the glass. Inside the globe is an exact replica of the homely scene surrounding us and I think of flames. Suddenly the quaint hedgerows and grass are a bonfire. Waking up sweating, arms and neck stiff, I know this is just a dream. Hope Dover can't evade the poverty and pain of her situation with her thoughts and wishes. And yet Hamish, Colt, Begum and Donna's lives do come close to a wilful annihilation of the weight of their surroundings. But what fascinates me is that in the dream I don't want a home. Instead I will its destruction. In my waking hours everything is less clear.

When I first arrived from Kharagpur on the morning train, Mrs Gupta fussed over me as if I was a prodigal daughter returned at last from dissolute wanderings. Trying to tell her about Kharagpur I lost my way and she was soon bored, closing down every story with 'That's what I expected, now you understand, you don't have to go there ever again.' She gave me a small notebook in which she had itemized the exact hour and number of times Maurice had called for news, but only after much questioning and with great reluctance did she admit that Subhrasheel had been phoning as well. She sat at the huge oval dining table respectfully chatting with her mother-in-law, who was swathed in her white widow's sari, and watched with great curiosity from across the room as I lifted the crochet cover off the phone. She wanted to see whether I dialled an international or Calcutta number first. My fingers felt like lead as I called America. My meandering tales of Kharagpur sounded increasingly fantastic and Maurice waited for an opportunity to speak his mind. Finally he said slowly, 'Laura, everything is different between us. That poem you sent was all very romantic about love bridging distance, but it's not enough. You should come back home.' I made wild promises about buying plane tickets that I wasn't sure I'd keep. Next I called Subhrasheel. Before the dull click of the receiver being put down, he said only one thing to me: 'You just want another ride on that Kharagpur express, don't you, my *tesu*?'

Afterwards, going downstairs to my flat, I met Ashok, Mrs Gupta's son, climbing towards me, on his return from work. He greeted me by saying, 'I answered the phone to all your men while you were away. They wouldn't leave their names. Perhaps we two should go out to dinner alone some time to discuss all of this?' Making hurried excuses about the pressure of work, I retreated to look for privacy again.

Later that night, a slow knocking on the door startled me from unquiet sleep. It was one in the morning and I couldn't imagine who it could be. Sliding back one of the four barricaded panels, I saw Subhrasheel in a kurta and fine white embroidered shawl smiling wickedly. I was shocked by his traditional clothes, the unbearable closeness of him and his decision to return. As I lifted up the heavy wooden bar it let out a low moan and the door creaked open. Thinking of Mrs Gupta's watchful presence in the bedroom above I flinched at the noise, motioning to Subhrasheel to stay silent with my fingertip on his lips. He grasped it, refusing to let go or be silent, whispering, 'I'm supposed to be at an all-night classical concert with my ma. I told her I'd spotted some friends in the audience and I wanted to sit with them. I never much liked such pious musical performances of passion. So here I am – what are you going to do about it? You better make good use of all the time until the morning *raag*.'

Then inside, the weight of our bodies pushing the doors to, he made fun of my poem: 'Sorry I forgot my strings of flowers, I'm not planning for any sacrifices, faithful histories or sacred geography tonight.'

'But you look dressed for a religious ceremony. Let's do something about that.'

It was my turn to unwind him from the shawl and remove the last defence of his kurta. Pulling away laughing, he defiled the Bengali elegance of his clothes with the cheapest of Chippendale stripteases.

But this was only the beginning of more unveilings, so many that the bed became a pagal gymkhana of words and gestures. He sang snatches of *rabindra sangeet* and Pulp songs, his breath searing my breasts. Taking on academic tones to lecture him in Kama Sutra techniques, ancient Japanese erotica and Masters and Johnson, I stroked his hair chastely like a sister and watched for small pulses of arousal in his body. We improvised experiments in pleasure, giggling at our skin's all-too-eager and predictable responses, pretending to note them with cool objectivity then tumbling into the sheer taste of each other again. But all the images intermingled like our limbs and mouths until we laughed at the impossibility of stillness. There was no pain here, I could burn in the fluidity of this for ever, but of course dawn broke and he put on his creased kurta and sneaked out of the flat, leaving me alone with the sounds and scents of the Guptas' morning routines: water being pumped, *loochis* frying and the patriotic songs of All-India radio.

Now I'm waiting for Subhrasheel to arrive for

another night of restless passion. It's late and he isn't here yet. The crowd from the last Hindi film show in the nearby cinema is dispersing, quarrelling over fares home with autorickshaw drivers and looking for trouble with the *hijras* who hang out in the park.

Subhrasheel and I have set up a collection of smokescreens and mirrors around our affair. For his parents, girlfriend and Mrs Gupta, we have concocted the excuse that he is helping me with my research. When his parents became too suspicious, he told them that I was just a close friend who would become his *didi* in the Bhai Phota ceremony at the beginning of November. Meanwhile at random hours he sneaks into the flat, avoiding the glances of neighbours, hiding from Mrs Gupta and her household of servants. We venture into his college canteen, concealing any signs of affection between us. Among the students playing cards, and under the eyes of his girlfriend, I perform the part of a researcher and a loyal wife. I tell her at great length how much I miss my husband. She just stares at me coldly, saying things like, 'Is your work going well? I'm sure Subhrasheel is being a hindrance rather than a help in your researches.' But the alibi of Bhai Phota troubles us, hanging like a threat or a promise of a simple solution for a reality that does not fit with all those around.

I often visit the American Institute of Indian Studies guest house, a haven which other researchers use to maintain a balance between venturing into the city for interviews and remembering their other selves. Telling these new friends about Kharagpur, I hate the way it changes into a series of exotic or theoretical points. The research students are all caught up in their own quests. Sufia, who grew up in America with a Bangladeshi father and a Puerto Rican mother, is achieving a subtle, brilliant revenge on her Muslim relatives in Sylet who always looked down on her mixed origins by becoming an expert on Bengali translations of the Koran. Debashish, raised in America, is pursuing stories of partition that were an unspoken shadow over his parents' lives. He avoids his relatives in Calcutta because he cannot bear the pain and poverty they want to draw him into. Tony, from a jute-mill company town in Scotland, whose father worked in the factory, is researching the universal struggles of the working class in India and Britain, building alliances with Calcutta's Marxist academics. Then there are the more itinerant artists and scholars who arrive to take photographs of festivals, to retrieve a single manuscript or to give a lecture, swooping in and out of the city with single-minded earnestness. I find some solace at Anjan and Sheta's book-lined flat in their extended family house. They are old friends with their roots deep in the debating ferment of Calcutta's politics and academia. But they know Maurice well from time spent at the University of Michigan. I fear their judgement on my disloyalty, and that they will read my passion for Subhrasheel as a misguided attempt to become part of a place they have a prior claim to.

Subhrasheel and I shouldn't really be bothering with subterfuges. Mrs Gupta is clearly suspicious and has been for a long time, even before it was justified. She was reluctant to resume our Bengali lessons, saying, 'What's the point of learning more, you're not going to marry a Bengali so why do you need it?' Now that she has been persuaded, she uses the lessons as an opportunity to ask me why I have changed so much and to say that she wants the old Laura back again. She makes up elaborate reasons for needing Subhrasheel's parents' telephone number, all of which I manage to deflect. She even made one last-ditch effort to pull me back on to the right path, planning a four-day trip for us to Murshidabad and Malda with Sufia in an attempt to distract me from Subhrasheel long enough for me to forget him. I half-hoped it would work.

As we drove over mud roads, swerving to avoid speeding lorries, I picked grass seeds off the folds of Mrs Gupta's sari. They had attached themselves during our contemplation of some ruin. Removing them was an arduous task worthy of a fairy-tale trial of devoted endurance. To while away the hours of travelling, Sufia told stories of djinns, spirits that possessed humans and gave them ravenous appetites and glowing eyes. Her father used to tease her that they could be attracted by women who wore nail polish and flaunted themselves. So she always makes a point of delicately painting her long nails with deep golden browns, blues and reds. I wondered idly whether I had been possessed by a djinn and if that could explain my desire. At Gaur crumbling minarets and domes were all that was left of the medieval Islamic capital of Bengal. Now the walls were decorated not with lapis-lazuli plaques but with drying fishing nets and gaping holes. Sal trees sprouted from the arches that had been built large enough to admit parades of elephants. Farmers walked through the gates bearing loads of grass they had cut from around the foundations to feed their animals, not to reveal a layer of their history. This neglect of the Muslim heritage of Bengal reminded me of the denials of the past that produced purist versions of Hindu India, the versions that the equally neglected stories of Kharagpur contradicted. The only part of the city wall kept in good repair was the section that serves as a boundary between Bangladesh and India. Here soldiers with threatening arrogance checked the lorries and foot passengers who were making their way across the border. In a mosque near Murshidabad we appreciated the picturesque vista of paddy fields shimmering beyond the single wall left standing and heard the tale of a nawab's daughter who was walled up alive by her father when he discovered that she had fallen in love with a servant. Her only reward was to be worshipped now at a shrine in the grounds. Mrs Gupta talked with reverence about the glory of this chaste end to an illicit passion.

Mrs Gupta's attempts to induce amnesia in me finally failed at Suraj's palace on the banks of the Ganges. As we approached the palace the villages were overshadowed by eighteenth-century stately homes. These were cornucopias of unicorns, lions, coats of arms, elegantly proportioned steps, Corinthian columns and colonnades in fine yellow stone. They could have been the setting for a novel by Thackeray. Yet these were the homes of *zemindars*, landlords made rich by the Raj permanent settlement, in which they lived out the dramas of caste status and quarrels over marriage alliances. Mrs Gupta sighed in appreciation of this aristocratic heritage and could not see the ironies of it, the ironies that Subhrasheel had told me about months ago in his grandmother's tale. Suraj's palace, built after his defeat at the battle of Plassey, was a more grandiose version of this aristocratic style. A goat chewed grass in a rusting bandstand by the river. White cows gathered by the wrought-iron fence, searching for shade under the regularly placed palm trees. They were framed against a vast turmeric-yellow Buckingham Palace façade. Inside elegant corridors housed suits of armour, cannons and Constable paintings. At the heart was a domed durbar room. A giant crystal chandelier imported from Paris hung above the silver and red velvet throne. Long before Mrs Gupta's purist version of the present, the trappings of power had intertwined British and Indian traditions. However much affection I showed to her, I would not submit to her amnesia. Everything we saw reminded me of Subhrasheel and Kharagpur's versions of history.

After we returned, I started to spend time again

at Gary and Carol's flat. One day I arrived to find Carol sweating over three stoves in her tiny kitchen, surrounded by bulging shopping bags full of *keema*, fresh *dhania* and chillies. As I sat on the concrete floor beside her and chopped onions, she explained to me that a British film crew had turned up in Calcutta to collect recipes from all of its communities. They had asked her to prepare a typical Anglo-Indian feast. She'd had lots of problems agreeing on the menu with them because every dish she listed as Anglo-Indian they had told her wasn't really theirs: 'They kept saying this was Muslim or that was Bengali. I started to get angry with them, but they wouldn't listen to me. So finally we agreed on mango fool, spicy sausages and meatballs. Doesn't seem very typical to me, but then who am I to tell them?' Carol was delighted at the venue for the filming, the Calcutta Golf Club, although she wasn't sure that it represented the family's background: 'See, Laura, we've never been allowed in such a grand place. Only with the help of them would we get inside. They said it was perfect because of the golf clubs, caddies and Raj architecture. They wanted a cricket match at first. I'm pleased and all, but I'm getting the feeling they think we are some old *saheb* British types, when we're not.'

The cooking over, we snatched a lunch of mango *achaar*, crab and coconut curry, rice and *daal*, then hastily packed the food for the programme into huge tiffin carriers. We all piled into one taxi and as we made our way slowly through the traffic, Carol told the children to cross themselves each time we passed a church, echoing the respectful gesture of Hindus passing a temple. The well-heeled golfers at the club looked down their noses at our ragbag crowd: Lorissa in an Elvis T-shirt, Carol in a light blue nylon frock, Isolde in a Hawaiian shirt and shorts, Gary in an American football shirt and me in a *salwar*. As the crew set up the shot on the manicured lawn in the shadow of the clubhouse, which had the predictable air of decaying colonial luxury, I played on the swings with Lorissa and Isolde. They gossiped about their boyfriends, joking that they had been 'hit in the heart, but you'll just get hit tight and hot if ma and pa find out', and complaining about the comments passed on them in the street when they came home from school. Then in the long tedium of takes and retakes, the crew urged me to be filmed in the picnic scene as well, so I was presented to the viewing public as just another Anglo-Indian. From my vantage point at one corner of the red-chequered tablecloth I watched sadly as Gary and Carol were turned into mildly comic and safe snapshots of Raj nostalgia, wondering whether when it came to my turn to tell their tales the same thing would happen. This was a version of that small crystal globe that didn't have the power to change anything.

꙳

I'm still waiting for Subhrasheel. Has he had a failure of nerve? Or has something happened to him? The street outside is almost silent now; all the lights in the house apart from mine were switched off long ago. Phoning his home is out of the question because it will arouse suspicions. All I can do is spend a few more hours listening out for him; if I fall asleep I may miss his arrival. When I strain my ears to distinguish the low thud of a *paan*-shop shutting up for the night from the sound I want to hear, the place becomes alive with rustlings: cockroaches scuttling, mosquitoes whining, the refrigerator whirring. Then finally there are footsteps shuffling their way down the narrow passage outside the door. They are heavy and unfamiliar. Confused, I look through one of the panels to see Debashish. His speech is as slurred as his gait and his round, kind face is smiling apologetically.

'Sorry, I need to talk to you tonight,' he says. 'It's all so stupid and melodramatic like a Bengali movie, but it's my birthday today and I just heard someone I thought I loved is getting married and it's not to me. I've drunk almost a whole bottle of whisky.'

I welcome him inside, just managing to get him into a chair before he falls over.

Mrs Gupta is calling through the window grille from her bedroom upstairs, 'Who is it, Laura?'

'Only Debashish. It's all right, don't worry,' I reply, thinking she just wants reassurance that it isn't one of the footpath drug addicts she fears will invade her house. With curt anger she says, 'It's not all right, come up and talk to me immediately.'

Cursing each padlock I have to undo in the darkness on my way upstairs, I reach the final metal portcullis. Mrs Gupta is on the other side, hair loose and falling wildly on to the huge lace collar of her housedress. She doesn't unlock it. Grasping the metal trellis, her knuckles turn deep red as she speaks: 'Debashish has to leave. I always knew something like this would happen with all these men visiting at odd hours. I've woken up my son, he'll take him home in a taxi. You must move out of this house within a month. Everybody in the neighbourhood has been watching your every move because you are a European woman and now they have got to thinking that my children have been associating too much with you. You will spoil their prospects of a good marriage. Everyone will say they've been spending too much time with a high-living European.'

Her outrage vented, she sounds a little sadder: 'And I don't recognize you, Laura, you've become too Anglo-Indian from all your researches.'

Ashok appears, smirking at me from behind his mother's back. There is nothing I can do to alter any of this. I am furious that I can't help my friend Debashish when he obviously needs me, but even more I am bitterly disappointed that Mrs Gupta thinks that all her predictions have come true. Why does our relationship have to end in a way that confirms all her prejudices? Debashish is bundled into a taxi.

Now that Mrs Gupta has given me notice to leave the flat, I suddenly want the security of my old home again. Perhaps the best thing to do is to try to return to Maurice to remind myself of what that home is. With sad resolve I pick up the receiver and dial his number in America. I tell him that I will break off my research for a month and book a ticket to come home to him via Britain.

❧

The next morning, as I wander to the local vegetable stall the threat and promise of Bhai Phota is becoming visible on Calcutta's streets. Workmen are starting to put up bamboo poles and canopies that in a week will house images of Durga slaying a lion, beginning a season of celebrations which will progress through the full-moon Lakshmi puja, the moonless night of Kali puja and then Bhai Phota. When I return, Subhrasheel is waiting for me, watching as another pole is heaved into position. Inside, I tell him of the previous night's events and of my decision to leave for a while. His eyes glitter with an unreadable emotion and he says, 'But you knew all along that what we had together was a lie.' Twisting my hair in his hands and pulling me towards his mouth with tender anger, he insists, 'Just come and taste the lie.'

After hours in the bedroom hiding embraces from Mrs Gupta's ancient gardener who is sweeping under her jackfruit tree, Subhrasheel abruptly stops, pulls on his clothes and says, 'I want you to come back from your trip a changed person. I want everything to be different.'

I can't take the truth in the wake of our lovemaking,

but he continues, 'I would push you back into the arms of your husband, if I could.'

I feel a bitter liberation, replying, 'There is a solution to all of this. Is the offer of Bhai Phota still open?'

'Yes, if that's what you want I'll give you the very *rakhi* band my sisters gave me. But this is not a matter of indifference, it's a serious bond and if you break it I will hate you.'

'We have no choice: now that what we have can only be destructive, we have to change it into something fertile. My *bhai*, I renounce you, I renounce you.'

He is quiet and stunned. Then he sits at my feet staring up at me, trying hard not to look at my lips, and we hold each other, shielding ourselves from the pain we both feel. With this vow suddenly all fear of loss disappears in the hope of a sanctified friendship outside of time, decay and the momentary satisfaction of desire. Now I'll return to reforge the sweetness of my old life – but how will I feel in Maurice's arms? And that dream is still haunting me. How do I take the old woman's inheritance, that small crystal globe, to London and Michigan without thinking of the flames that will consume all domestic comforts?

In London there are three letters waiting for me. Maurice has written pages of hope and love, full of plans for when we are reunited but laced with sentences that chastise. Asking me why I have sent only two letters to him during all the months away, he revives the theme of how different our lives have become and that it will take work to draw them together. He lists new friends whom I don't know. I read all of this as fast as possible, casting it aside. The handwriting on the other envelope is unfamiliar. Inside is a letter from a cousin of my mother's, who has spent years investigating the family history. She wants my help. Enclosed is an extract from the diary of my great-great-grandfather, a publican and horse trader in Leicester. His diary has a reputation in my family for its detailed confessions of amorous exploits, which were excised by a later, more prudish relative. Poring over its pages, my mother's cousin had found a single cryptic reference to India.

My young life was peaceful and spent under the kind care of my mother and father. My elder brother James and I spent many hours playing among the hedgerows. This all changed when I was sent to a dame school where all the teachers were too strict for my liking. The fortunes of the family were not so prosperous in 1818, so out of necessity James was forced to seek work. One day I was called out of school and my mother was there with James. She said to me, 'Kiss your brother goodbye. He's going off to India as a soldier in service to the King.' I never saw him again nor heard another word of him.

This is a puzzle that I will try to help the family solve. It is a small chink in the walls between Indian and British histories. And I wonder if this is why my grandfather sent me on this quest and underlined those words in *The Satanic Verses*: 'The trouble with the English is that their history happened overseas, so they don't know what it means.' Maybe he had heard stories of James's disappearance. Perhaps this was the secret that, for all his irreverence, he could never quite tell me. Instead he had left me to find it on my own. I will not disappoint him. It should be possible to trace James Batten in the records of the India Office Library, which I am planning to visit anyway in a couple of days to follow up on railway records. The third letter is an invitation to an Oriental night and lecture at the British Museum, sent to me by a friend who organizes events there. This is a challenge that I can't resist either.

The next evening I take my place in the audience at the British Museum lecture hall. Imogen Francis's spiky black hair, silver jewellery from Rajasthan, short skirt and wiry body, thin from long, hot third-class train journeys, look odd in the sedate setting. She has spent the past year researching the lives of female Victorian travellers and retracing their journeys in India. She introduces us to some of these women and their motives. Fleeing the restraints of Victorian domesticity, the home and the hearth, they set out on obscure quests for botanical specimens. Often they remained in their fashionable crinolines even as they crossed rope bridges, but sometimes they wore Indian dress. Now projected in front of us is a sepia photograph of a lady crossing a picturesque mountain stream, lacy hat on head, waist corseted. At first glance she looks like the stern, elderly queen in burning white marble who still sits outside the Victoria Memorial in Calcutta. But this *memsaheb*'s skirts can't hide the paradox of her liberty. Two Indians are bearing her weight on their backs, carrying her to another adventure. The audience laughs at the quaintness of it all and I burn with sadness and shame. I remember the Kalighat print that presided over my flat in Calcutta, which showed a woman just like this one treating her husband as a coolie, and I know that Imogen is related to Mrs Gupta. Calling on the audience to make sure that these women are not forgotten – many of them died in India but their monuments are decaying from neglect – she urges us to support the work of the British Association for the Preservation of Cemeteries in South Asia. As she speaks I think of the graveyard in Kharagpur and imagine a member of BACSA meeting Mr Vanjo there. At first they would appear to share an emotional investment in the same monuments, but if they lingered in conversation what would happen?

Would homages to the sacrifices of the Raj feel so comfortable and uplifting? How can I make them speak to each other? Can Milly's ghost appear to the crowd assembled here?

The next day these questions follow me to the India Office Library. Crossing Blackfriars Bridge the dull grey Thames flows under arches and ironwork similar to those that grace the Eastern Railway headquarters in Dalhousie Square and Suraj's palace. A cold wind sweeps around the tower block that is now the home of the records of colonial rule, part of the same modernist dreams that produced Chittaranjan and Begum's home. Inside, the quiet of the reading room is broken only by the rustling of leather-bound volumes, which are startlingly white and well maintained, as if these orders and indents have only ever existed within the neutral confines of a library. I grow a little nostalgic for the worm-eaten, dusty records in the Eastern Railway headquarters. At least those documents were marked by the inky fingerprints of the hands that they had passed through. And in the corridors of the Eastern Railway you could never imagine that the pages were time capsules of long-dead struggles. The reading room is filled with an international congregation of academics on quests that all still have to be routed through London. They learn the intricate departmental structures of the India Office so that they will find the notes in the margins that hint at the stories the bureaucratic records try to hide. I am hunting for such clues in the personal papers of British railway drivers. These letters were sent for safe keeping to the India Office after the death of the drivers in India, and never claimed by their relatives. I can't stop reading one set of letters between a husband and wife. Their love, longing and accusations make me shiver with recognition:

Alabaster Villas
Stratford New Town
Essex

George Cole
Albion Hotel
Calcutta

December 19 1861

Dear George

You would never lissen to your wife's words,
dear George. If I never see you again I have
nothing to blame myself for. I tried to persuade
you not to go, but it was no wise. If you loved me
you never could have left me and mine. I hope
by the blessing of God I shall still continue to
love you as I always have done. I shall always
blame you for not trying for something here.

Mr Drake, my lodger, is very fond of the
children. He bought them some sweets two or
three times a week. I think it seems so kind of
him. If they are gone to bed when he comes
home he is quite in a way. He says he wishes
little Lucy was his. I try to make myself as happy
as I can. Dear George, I must tell you that
everybody says a single life agrees with me.
Several people say if you were to see me then
you would be surprised to see what a nice figure
I have got. I hope, dear George, that you are not
lodging in that Hotel now.

Love
Lucy

February 26 1862

My dearest husband

My dear George, we were all very pleased to hear
you had left that Hotel we all began to think you
did not mean to do yourself any good. You say
that you love me very dearly. I am delighted to

think you do. I knew that you did but actions speak louder than words.

My lodgers treat me with the greatest respect and everybody else that I know. So my dear George now you are away you say you are not expected home so I can have any one in I please. I should not have anyone coming into my house at any moment. I never do anything I am ashamed or afraid of. It is cruel, very cruel to be accused as so wicked a thing. I hope my dear husband I shall never be any disgrace to my dear dear children and likewise for my husband.

Your last letter has indeed made me feel truly unhappy. God knows I am not deserving of what you accuse me of. I should have sold my home off before now and followed you long before this, only I am afraid my children are not strong enough to bear the voyage. What must that woman feel when she goes to bed at night with a married man and she a married woman? Thou shalt not commit adultery I do not forget that my dear George.

March 1862

Dear George,
I feel as if my poor heart would break. I thought of my husband and wondered whether he would forsake his poor children for the sake of another man's wife. I fear some dreadful end will be the end of this.

You say if I want someone else I am to have them. Perhaps, my dear George, you are measuring my bushel by your bushel, if so I hope you will be happy. I hope if you form attachment to anyone out there she will prove as faithful to you as I have done. You are threatening to stop my money from the railway company, but

remember I am your lawful wife, I have my
marriage license to show. I have heard from
Dick Watkins you do not go to bed very often
and when you do you are so easily persuaded
by others that you get up again and go out
pleasuring.

I wish I had never loved not never been a wife
or mother, but that is no more now. My dear
husband I shall come out to you. Mrs Furman
says every woman that has a husband in India
can get to be with them. She says it is a dreadful
place for gambling and all other games for them
that go. You are never out of my mind sleeping or
waking. I very often come to India and back of a
night in my sleep.
Love
Lucy

The last letter in the file is from George to Lucy. It
was found in his possessions after he died of fever in
Calcutta. Lucy never read it.

Howrah, Calcutta

2 Alabaster Villas
Stratford New Town
Essex, England

September 8 1862

To my wife and ever dearest children,
Our Lucy, dearest Lucy, I feel as if I loved you
more and more every day. You cannot imagine
my feelings when I am awriting to you. I just
fancy I am in Bed with you once again I often
dream about you all my dear Lucy. My oft
repeated prayer to our Heavenly Father is that
we all shall meet once again and not to part again
till death. I do not think I shall want to roam and
leave you any more. Has Mr Bench come home

yet? I think I told you that he got the sack for being drunk on duty and assaulting his foreman Mr Higby. I hope you won't listen to any more tales that is carried home it is only done to part us. But my own dear wife such a thing as that must not happen while we are alive it would break my heart if I knew another man was enjoying your charms, my own darling wife.

Have you got my likeness and one or two silk Indian handkerchiefs that I gave Bench to bring home to you? I do believe you my dear wife when you say that if you had the money you would send for me. The lavender you sent smelt very nice, it made me think that I was beside the old tree picking a sprig or two. If you ever hear of anyone acoming out here do tell them that it is not all gold that glitters.

Love

George Cole

I am deeply moved by this lovers' quarrel and the sparse details of the letters that are so different from the embroidered memoirs of civil servants and their wives. But reading them, I also realize that I can never send such a letter of love home to my husband. I have no tokens of nostalgia left that are equivalent to George's lavender sprigs.

My list of research tasks over, I can now check for records of James Batten. Taking out the diary entry that tells of his disappearance, I begin in the most obvious place, the drawers of index cards that list births, marriages and deaths of Europeans in the colonies. Next to me is an elderly man frowning over a thin Indian notebook that looks out of place among the glossy files. Confused, he asks, 'Will Eurasians be listed in this section? I've been trying to track down my family without much luck. My relatives in India need the papers to come.' I tell him they may be, attempting to explain which department they may accidentally show up in. He looks disappointed but still hopeful as he starts to rifle through a guide to the India Office Collections.

Turning back to the card catalogue, I immediately come across an entry for a Batten. It reads, 'Matilda Batten, baptism 4 February 1819, birth 20 December 1818, illegitimate, St Helena, to James Batten and Sarah Benson, slave of Mary Alesworth.' St Helena was a stopping-off point on voyages to India and here my relative enters history again as a father who left behind a child, moving on to his destination with barely a backward glance. This is the same desertion that has filled the pages of Anglo-Indian history. I will not abandon Matilda, she will be my chosen link to the past. Remembering Edith Batten from the Eastern Railway, I know that these scattered links will make the magic of Hidgely and Santa Barbara continue. It is through them that Anglo-India can be made to speak to India and Britain, reconfiguring the relationship between them. I am holding that crystal globe in my hand and this time I'm awake. Now the flames burn up even my own family's treasured visions of where they belong. Their home is not only composed of rose-covered cottages in a rural idyll, but also of stories of conquest. A few months ago in Subhrasheel's arms I had wondered what was inside and what outside of my identity. In this moment I know that this is a false division: India and Britain are part of the same crystal globe and my self is suffused with the contradictions of their historical relationship. Memories of my grandfather had sent me on a quest to India, but ironically the journey ends here, back in London among the familiar suddenly rendered strange.

All at once I understand my mistake that night a few months ago in the railway inspectors' guest house when I sent Subhrasheel away. I misinterpreted the dream of Kali. I thought she was offering me a choice,

283

death for me or for Subhrasheel. What she promised was that if my old self died then I could gain Subhrasheel as well. I don't need to renounce him, just my previous self. All of Subhrasheel's names for me, 'True-blue *memsaheb*, Mrs Chatterjee, Kharagpur girl, *tesu*' now hang in the air together at once. Their seemingly contradictory allusions that confused me before now make sense; my identity is composed of fragments of all these interlinked histories. The distinctions between them have been carefully preserved for generations, but the source of all of them is the history of Anglo-India, its illicit desires, mixed origins and brutal reality. Subhrasheel does not offer me either India or a peaceful end to contradictions, instead he offers restless stories that divert me from comfortable, homely lies. If, as he told me in Kharagpur, we are all making myths out of ourselves and one another then I want to choose the myths he makes of me over the ones that India and Britain have long been living under. I will not return to America. Instead I'm going back to Subhrasheel, Calcutta and Kharagpur with no desire to find a home. I will be changed as Subhrasheel wanted me to be.

Subhrasheel picks me up from the airport. As we pass Sealdah station villagers are pouring into the city for the moonless night of Kali puja. Children let off chocolate bombs, home-made fireworks, in the path of the taxi. Cascades of sparks fly up around the wheels and the driver curses them good-humouredly. Strung along the route are blinking shocking-pink, yellow and green fairy lights formed into peacocks, a family sitting in armchairs watching Kali on the television in front of them, and filigree strings which echo the *chandan* patterns that are painted on the faces of brides and goddesses.

Anjan and Sheta have agreed to let me stay in an empty flat that once belonged to Sheta's parents. Once we have reached it and the taxi has left, Subhrasheel takes out of a plastic bag two fireworks he has made. He lights them on the pavement, renewing our spirit of anarchy. Fountains of golden stars rise upwards. Inside, on a huge family bed, we while away the hours until midnight when the drumbeats of the daks will deafen and the priests will chant. Like Colt Campbell's marriage bed this too has teak leaves that curl around a photograph of a severe Bengali lady. We stare back with fondness and insolence, not bothering to hide our embraces from her.

At midnight Subhrasheel tells me the story of how Kali visited his grandmother. After partition she lived in a village in rural Bengal. It was an hour after Kali puja when everyone was sleeping. In the quiet of the night his grandmother heard the jingling of anklets from the roof terrace. Looking out of her window, she saw the huge shadow of a woman with long dark hair to her ankles outlined against a tree. She danced and danced. His grandmother knew who she was because who but Kali could cast a shadow on a moonless night? The next morning she went up to the terrace and saw scatterings of *sindoor* like blood on the terrace. We look out for shadows on the trees outside, knowing that if Kali is dancing tonight it is from joy.

Epilogue
Ceremonies of Dust

Four years later our marriage is a foregone conclusion and a reality that we are living without the necessary papers in our flat in New Delhi. Janakpuri is now our temporary home, a colony of sun-bleached middle-class houses that sprawls on the outskirts of Lutyens's city. Far from the elegant façades of civil servants' bungalows and the palaces of the state, it is famous for less benign symbols of government: Tihar jail and the Raj military cantonment. In this status-conscious city the local joke is that if you spend long enough here you will be the neighbour of top-level politicians who will all at some point be held on corruption charges within the walls of the largest jail in Asia. We have joined older Punjabi residents, refugees of partition, and newer immigrants, families from Bihar and Uttar Pradesh, whose aspirations of affluence could only be realized here.

The colony is bordered by the competing towers of the Arya Samaj, a Hindu organization founded to convert Christians and Muslims, and a small, neon-lit church. Slick Marutis swish past filled with the brash young men of Delhi on hedonistic quests to Nirula's and Thank God It's Friday, windows rolled up to seal them off in air-conditioned comfort. When they stop outside one of the concrete villas, Aqua or Hindi pop blares out from the open car doors and the local vegetable-seller plying his wares from a cycle-cart looks on with curious envy. Their consumption of pleasures is insulated by wealth from the city's recent conservatism. The ban on kissing in public places, which has just been officially declared a Western threat to Indian values, will not affect these rich kids. The colony's respectability is guarded by *durwans*, ironically paid for by a local *goonda* who lives in a villa at the centre of the enclave. Outside the walled enclosure maids and day-labourers are encamped in huts, gambling on the roadside and rifling through stalls for bargains among the plump mass-produced agricultural yield of Haryana. In signboards above the entrance each slum proclaims its allegiance to a political overlord. These are the same politicians who, in the name of sanitation, have recently knocked down lean-tos inside the colony, sending in municipal workers to destroy the huts that housed the local *istri-wallahs*. Lorries from the surrounding regions, autorickshaws and Maruti vans speed past the compound, only slowing down at roadblocks. Here the police search for the home-made bombs that with deadly regularity disrupt religious processions in old Delhi under the walls of the Red Fort. At all major crossroads soldiers stand with rifles slung over their shoulders outside white canvas army tents. Despite the stately buildings at the heart of the city, New Delhi is a place suffused with the violent disputes, nomadic nonchalance of temporary residents and get-rich-quick schemes that usually characterize border towns. When the municipal government tries to reassert its authority over these seething entrepreneurial hopes it does so in the name of Hindu cultural purity, public order and fears of Muslim terrorist attack, playing on the mutual distrust of neighbours who share little apart from monetary exchanges.

We chose New Delhi for its indifference and opportunities, seeking the neutrality of a city too occupied in making deals to pay close attention to our lack of a legal certificate. It is a safe haven where we can live together far from the scrutiny of Calcutta, and Subhrasheel has found a job as a strategic planner for an ad agency. We lie to our landlady and neighbours that we are married, otherwise renting a flat would be impossible. In spite of our precautions a network of distant relatives who are settled here are whispering about our living arrangements and Subhrasheel's parents have told him that he really ought to marry me. Other relatives are rallying to our cause and our relationship is bringing to the surface a rich seam of unconventional family tales.

Mr and Mrs Roy are now convinced of our passion. Recalling three generations of love marriages in their own family, they are determined to welcome me with a lavish wedding that will silence all gossiping tongues. Subhrasheel's ex-Naxalite uncle is delighted by his nephew's choice, which provides him with a glimmer of rebellious hope in the context of the smooth professionalism and political traditionalism of 'nineties India. His own wife, a comrade he met while underground in the villages of Bihar, has never been accepted by the family because of her lower-middle-class origins and he relishes Mr and Mrs Roy's refusal to continue this pattern. Subhrasheel's twin sisters, Sohag and Sohini, report with glee the general amazement at Presidency College that the daring marriage is going ahead and defend the suitability of the match. Chattering over the telephone and snatching it from each other in their excitement, they tell of other precedents: the aunt whose beauty was spotted by her husband, a Sikh, at a dance performance; another aunt who had an arranged marriage, but then ran away with her childhood sweetheart; and an uncle who married an Indian Christian. Even more sober relatives are coming round. An uncle has pronounced that if

Subhrasheel had sought an arranged marriage his qualifications could never have been traded for someone as well equipped as myself with a doctorate and a Cambridge education. So our plans to elope to a temple in Rajasthan or to have a registration with only two witnesses have been swept aside in a flurry of preparations for a grand wedding in Calcutta. Mr Roy is planning every detail down to the arrangement of trellises of jasmine flowers and the type of leaves on the *pandal*. Mrs Roy is carefully choosing pieces of family jewellery to give to me so that the guests will be able to precisely calculate her approval.

While Subhrasheel is out at work, and loadshedding interrupts my writing, I often take out Tyrone and Patricia's marriage tokens. At the wedding I want our union to be sanctified in the same way that Hamish blessed theirs, wishing that it would be the source of a new river with no fixed path and no known destination, a river that would leave Indian soil different once it has passed over it. The spirit of Santa Barbara that questioned all rigid versions of tradition should be the foundation of our marriage. But in a sense Mr and Mrs Roy's plans to dress up a foreign, divorced, older woman like all Hindu brides as the goddess Lakshmi will revive the atmosphere of Santa Barbara. They are refusing to bow to public judgements on my morality and suitability. We are acutely aware of their generosity, especially after hearing from new friends about Delhi's climate of cultural prohibition and avarice, which means that differences of community, class, caste or regional origin create real barriers. One friend sees his girlfriend once a month when she can sneak away from her family home because her Sindhi industrialist father disapproves of his Bengali origins and earning potential. Another couple, a Hindu and a Muslim, are now married – but only after the wife was kidnapped by, and then rescued from, her relatives. We attended a desultory wedding of a Bengali friend and his Punjabi bride that was overshadowed by his mother's refusal to be present. Even among the cosmopolitan chic of Subhrasheel's agency his colleagues are bemused by our engagement. The head of the branch has enquired about his parents' response and was surprised to learn that they were not worried about the effect our union would have on his sisters' marriage prospects.

I'm looking forward to walking around the fire, shimmering for a moment in the red and gold of a Hindu bride, bending traditions to new meanings, for other reasons as well. All around, in the public spaces of New Delhi, tradition is being appropriated to a rigid conservatism. Apart from the ban on kissing in public places, it is reduced to debates about the pernicious influence of satellite television and the banning of cow-slaughter within the city limits. Plans are afoot to take possession of history as well. Administrators are being appointed to academic institutions who are sympathetic to the amnesiac versions of the past, which write an exclusionary story of Hindu India. Christians as well as Muslims are becoming targets of attack. Reading an article about the increasing rate of vandalism of Christian cemeteries in Uttar Pradesh and violence against church members in Madhya Pradesh, I remember Mr Vanjo. These are attempts to intimidate tribal Christian voters into the right-wing fold. All these schemes use the symbols of *swadeshi* and *bideshi*, Indian and foreign, that have long sliced through and been refused in the multifaceted lives of Anglo-Indians. These debates distract from even more dangerous and apparently neutral schemes to issue identity cards to all of Delhi's inhabitants. These will stamp the socially mobile population with the boundaries of community affiliations and disenfranchise its itinerant members. Given the history of voters' lists being used to target

Sikh families in New Delhi and Muslim families in Bombay during the riots of 1984 and 1993, this is disturbing. If I could I would paste the tribute presented to Begum and Donna all over the walls of this city. Delhi's inhabitants make brusque shorthand assumptions inspired by the political rhetoric about the opposition between traditional Hindu morals and westernization. Strange men at telephone booths ask me if I'm Russian. The question is full of innuendoes because of the brisk trade in Russian prostitutes outside the seamier hotels of the city. A fridge repairman returns on the flimsiest of pretexts and demands to be let into our flat when I am at home alone, assuming that I will comply with his desires.

These are minor annoyances for me, but the same attitudes produce recurrent contradictions in the lives of the professional women in Subhrasheel's agency. By day, dressed in jeans or miniskirts, they clinch deals. On leaving the office, they climb into the cocoon of a car so as to escape the lewd stares on the streets and speed off home where their parents list the latest bio-data details of a suitor. Later, beyond parental scrutiny once more on the dance floor of a nightclub, they drink, smoke and flirt, while their male colleagues discuss their lapsed morals, pointing out those who are easy game. It's as if all the historical judgements made on Anglo-Indian women's loose westernized behaviour have been transferred to them. A recent Hindi film, *Beranarsi Babu*, shows Govinda converting his westernized wife to demure Indian ways, a resolution that owes more to contemporary right-wing attitudes than to the requirements of an ancient tradition. This is a happy ending that has its origins not in Sanskrit texts, but in the colonial history that produced Mrs Gupta's respectability as well. The battle lines between Indian tradition and modernity produced by the Raj *Kali yug*, which are questioned in

Anglo-Indian histories, are growing sharper and taking on new forms.

Our wedding will not follow this plot. When I am dressed as a Hindu bride, we will for a fleeting instant seize back tradition from this path, following the route of Subhrasheel's unconventional relatives and that of Santa Barbara compound. The gift Mr and Mrs Roy are giving us is a moment when our private myth-making will be sanctified in a Hindu ceremony. Wrapped in a sari and painted with *chandan*, at the same time I will be Mrs Chatterjee, a *memsaheb*, *Tash* and Lakshmi, confounding all simple categories and celluloid happy endings. Subhrasheel is less content with the idea of putting on a dhoti and sitting for hours beside a fire in the heat of May in front of distant relatives whom he hasn't seen for years, but he promises, 'At last all our so-called lies will become true.' We giggle, remembering how many we have been forced to invent during our time in Delhi.

🍂

On arrival in Calcutta for the wedding, during the taxi ride from Howrah station, we treasure each sign of the city's anarchy. We are happy to have left behind the municipal order of New Delhi and its dark undertones. The derelict warehouses, waterlogged streets, crawling traffic and argumentative political graffiti look like some apocalyptic vision of the future. But this tumult is strangely comforting because it makes it less easy to believe in a triumphant, prosperous Hindu Raj. The taxi driver launches into a heated debate about the government, with a candour a stranger wouldn't risk in New Delhi. Traffic police wave ineffectually at the brawling congestion with none of the omnipotence they exercise in the capital. Bustees lean against grand concrete tower blocks, not banished yet to separate zones. On the buildings towering over the tumult all the layers of the city's history are written. An abandoned Armenian church crumbles next to a mosque. The colonial police headquarters are encroached on by stalls. Massed protesters shout slogans on the Maidan opposite Fort William, on land owned by the army and designed long ago for taking the air. New Delhi, by contrast, is divided between the domes of a Moghul past decaying beside modern highways and a different, efficient administrative present. It is easier there to think that the battle lines have always been only between Hindu and foreign Muslim and Christian invaders. If there is to be a future apocalypse it will probably come from this kind of amnesia.

Calcutta welcomes us with an unseasonal shower, huge drops splattering down as we run into the guest house, where my parents and Mr and Mrs Roy are waiting for our arrival. Mr Roy says the rain is an auspicious sign for our wedding, before he rushes off to make sure that the damage it has caused to the *pandal* is repaired. Like most couples, Subhrasheel and I have few clues as to what all the elaborate ceremonies will involve. As Mrs Roy describes the timetable, we grow nervous about whether we will get everything right and the huge potential to offend by a misplaced gesture. Our unconventional match makes it even more important to get all the details right because those legions of relatives and friends who may still be sceptical are waiting for opportunities to criticize or to find evidence that Subhrasheel's parents are half-hearted about the wedding. Mr and Mrs Roy, Sohag and Sohini have exhausted themselves hand-delivering every single one of the four hundred and fifty invitations, on a sort of campaign trail. Some friends have enquired about whether my parents have contributed towards the expenses and have subtly checked out their monetary and personal credentials. Others have not replied to the invitations because they have cherished hopes for years that Subhrasheel will marry their daughters. At risk in the next few days are all of Mr and Mrs Roy's social relationships. Non-attendance of guests or mistakes on our part will mark their lives for years to come. We realize that despite my dreams in New Delhi of bending tradition this process has a dynamic of its own, which has little to do with our wishes. Like the unseasonal shower, there are many unforeseen events that can occur before the marriage, and all will have to be turned into auspicious signs on the day.

Conscious of the watchful eyes of close relatives staying near their house, Mr and Mrs Roy insist that Subhrasheel should not be allowed to be alone with me until the night of flowers, four days away. So he disappears, leaving me at the guest house with my parents and two close friends from London, Fiona and Patrick. It is a huge grey concrete building put up in the 1930s to house the hopes of an extended family. The proprietress, her children now living far away, rents out a floor to suitable guests and the grounds for weddings. Our use of the premises as the bride's home and for the wedding has been permitted because of my Cambridge connection and fluency in Bengali. Yet the landlady still sends her brother, a barrister visiting from London who complains constantly in clipped English about the dirt of Calcutta, to check us out. He was underwhelmed by my parents' efforts to blend into the city by wearing modest ready-made *salwar kameezes* and kurtas, but cheers up immensely when he sees us dressed up in suits and tailored clothes for a meal at the expensive Oberoi Hotel.

After the meal we sit up late into the night and my parents and Fiona are full of enthusiastic questions about the rituals, few of which I can answer. Their freshly arrived eyes see the intricacies of Hindu tradition and the chaos of Calcutta's streets, but I want to tell them about something else. The guest house is in the heart of Beck Bagan, the Anglo-Indian and Muslim district. Through the window just beyond the branches of the giant flowering tree and bamboo scaffolding under which we will be married is the roof of Gary and Carol's flat, one of the places where this story started. Now sponsored by a relative, they have left for a home in America, seeking a place where they will be less visibly different. I am unsure that they will find their dream realized there. As I am about to be enfolded in all the markers of a Hindu bride, they have vanished from Indian soil. And there will be no Anglo-Indians at the wedding: the social mores of Bengali middle-class society would not permit this and it would cast doubts on the associations of the bride. The Bengali proverb, 'Tasher biye thakbe ki kore, oto tin miniter biye?' 'How can a Tash's wedding last? How can you promise a lifetime in a three-minute wedding?' would hang in the air reminding the guests of my divorce despite the long ceremony. Once I have explained that this is an Anglo-Indian district, Fiona is intrigued by the idea of finally seeing an Anglo-Indian and asks me, 'How will we know when we run into one on Calcutta's streets? How can you tell the differences between an Anglo-Indian, an Indian and a British person?' I reply, 'You can and you can't. It all depends on who you are and with what perspective you are looking. Your vision of the world is revealed by whether and how you see them.' Everyone is puzzled by the cryptic answer and we turn back to questions about the Hindu ceremonies, which seem so much more tangible.

The next morning, Lotte arrives to spiral *mehendi* on my hands and feet. She runs a beauty parlour plastered with images of Hindi movie stars in Lake Gardens. Her name on a signboard above the co-operative housing provides a shimmer of glamour in the respectable neighbourhood. Mrs Roy has promised that her origins will give her the skills to decorate my fair skin and tutor me in exactly how to wear a sari. She has the added qualification of having gone through a similar transformation for her own wedding to a Punjabi. Lotte is delighted to chatter to me about the negotiations with relatives that she has had to manage. And I feel strangely comforted that I will be turned into the perfect image of a Bengali wife by an Anglo-Indian; accepting tradition from her will seem less purist. As the cool green henna paste winds its way across my palm, Lotte comforts me that I am marrying with the blessing of my parents into a liberal, loving family, which will make no dowry demands. Her experience has been different. Her parents won't visit her husband's house and his relatives come just to pass comments and criticize. Even after their wedding they have had to keep all of them happy with lavish gifts, which silence their complaints. Her sister never wants to get married, having seen her choices: either an Indian family always carping or a good-for-nothing Anglo husband who just wants her money. Lotte couldn't resist her husband from the first time that she saw him, he was so good-looking. They are happy, like newly wed lovebirds, but only when they are alone. Taking her responsibilities very seriously she promises that she will make me so beautiful and demure that not a single guest at the wedding will have anything to complain about.

Unable to move, eat or wash for the next few hours, I wait for the green paste to dry and fall off leaving behind deep orange curlicues. To repossess my unfamiliar hands and feet, I tell myself they look like the spirals on the shells found on the beach at Digha. Then wondering how to conceal these signs of a bride from our landlady back in Delhi, I start to spin excuses. Interrupting Patrick from his search on the balcony for his adopted crow, Eric, whom he has been imagining as his Calcutta familiar, weaving together the city's strangeness with stories of his feathered friend's exploits, I tell him of my worries. He says, 'I almost blew your cover. I met a journalist in London who writes the society column for an Indian newspaper and told him of all your subterfuges, divorce and so on. He decided to write an article about the wedding. Later, I realized that if your landlady or neighbours read it in Delhi, you would be out on the streets, so I rang him up and made him promise not to do it.' We laugh at the narrow escape and continue to gossip until it is time for us to leave for the legal registration of the marriage.

In the taxi, wedged between Mr Roy and my parents, I think of the history that lies behind the legal ceremony. Our union is going to be rubber-stamped under the special marriage act at Bhowanipore register office. In the ledgers of the state, Hindu, Muslim and Christian weddings are all classified and recorded differently, with separate legal rights inherited from Raj-era codifications accruing to each of them. Anomalous cases such as ours were not recognized under the law until the secular enactment of 1950. This reflected the refusal of British administrators to sanctify such marriages between communities or to bless homes that wove together different traditions. There was one loophole: the bride or groom could convert to their spouse's religion. This, however, was not as easy as it sounds. For example, if an Anglo-Indian Christian had sought a state marriage with a Hindu, it would have been hard to convert to Hinduism because only a few sects accepted people who were not born into the religion. The Hindu spouse would have been ostracized by their own community if they had converted to Christianity. The lack of legal recognition for mixed-faith marriages meant that religious boundaries between communities were reinforced. The criticism of Anglo-Indians for living in concubinage relationships with Indians and Chinese that filled the pages of government reports reflected

298

the absence of legal rights rather than a choice on their part. The lack of legal rights also meant that there was no standardized law to cover such cases. If a British or Anglo-Indian woman did manage to convert in spite of the obstacles, they forfeited the legal rights of a British citizen. We are not presented with such difficult choices but, unlike other marriages, our papers have to be scrutinized at the highest level of the state government and there is a long waiting period in which people can raise objections.

This ceremony is a secret. As far as the wedding guests are concerned, it had already taken place on a trip to Calcutta several months ago. In reality, what had happened was that, just before arriving in the city, we found out that the advocate who was charged with submitting the papers to the state government had failed to do so because he had broken his leg. For a moment we were faced with a choice that partly echoed those of older generations. There was one way we could still get married at short notice: if I converted to Hinduism by signing a certificate at the Arya Samaj, then we could be immediately united under the Hindu marriage act. I refused, not because of a religious conscience – my agnostic parents hadn't even baptized me – but from a hesitation to become part of this organization even just for the sake of convenience. The Arya Samaj was founded in North India in the late nineteenth century on the principle that Christians and Muslims were in fact all Hindus who had been forcibly converted. It sought to erase these corrupt foreign influences from Indian soil and to establish a Hindu Raj by permitting a process of 'reconversion'. This is not a vision of India that I would have wanted to condone. Mr and Mrs Roy had, nonetheless, urged us to come to Calcutta for a small party with close relatives. If we hadn't gone through with this party and maintained the fiction that we had been legally married that day, my living in New

Delhi with Subhrasheel would have continued to be a scandal.

As we climb from the taxi outside the domed building almost concealed by *paan*-shops, curious onlookers watch our odd marriage party. The gloomy, creaking wooden stairs wind past offices filled with sheaves of files falling from the dusty shelves. Stopping by one of them, Mr Roy checks nervously with a large Bengali woman wedged behind a desk that everything is in order. As stern as the ancestral lady from Colt's marriage bed, she wields her pen and hands the necessary document to a peon, who passes it on to Mr Roy. The close, musty atmosphere does not betray any hint of celebration and is most reminiscent of the Eastern Railway. But I am ridiculously happy because there is Subhrasheel in the circular room where a bespectacled clerk waits officiously by a ledger to marry us. I haven't seen Subhrasheel for twenty-four hours. He is as scruffy as the student he was when I first met him, in jeans and a crumpled shirt, but this time, seated on the benches round the room, encircling us with their blessings, are our families. We pay our last respects to my old marriage by presenting the clerk with the divorce certificate, which he examines intently. Subhrasheel whispers to me, 'Look, Kali's here.' Above the noticeboard pasted with the legal announcements of forthcoming marriages is a small clay figurine and behind the clerk is a calendar from which her eyes stare down at us through cascades of jasmine. After signing, we say husband and wife for the first time and exchange gold rings with our names written in Bengali on them. Everyone claps and the next marriage party waiting in the doorway witnesses our shocking public kiss, a foreign practice we have insisted on.

We are immediately parted and instructed not to let slip anything about the registration. Back at the guest house I wait for the evening's *sangeet*. Sohag and

Sohini have insisted on the North Indian custom of a singing competition the night before the wedding, inspired by recent celluloid extravaganzas such as *Hum Apke Hai Kaun?*, in which such events provide the seeds of romance for the groom's younger relatives, and by the practices of their Marwari friends. They are a little disappointed that Subhrasheel has not brought a flock of good-looking, eligible men from his advertising agency to take part, so they are making do with gossip about the prospects of matches with his older Calcutta friends who will be attending. Carefully dressing in the one outfit I have chosen for myself, a pale cream silk *ghagra choli* embroidered with purple flowers and bound at the back with laces, I realize it looks like some combination of a Victorian crinoline and a Rajasthani princess's robe. I feel unsure about the demure visual effect. My mother has on a showy pink glittery *salwar kameez* and Fiona has concocted an Asian fusion fashion statement with *bindi* and *dupatta* draped over a dress. I am happier about their blithe irreverence towards Bengali good taste than about my own capitulation.

The *sangeet* is in full swing when we arrive, male guests gathered around the bar, extravagantly drunk and swaying, female guests clustering around a harmonium at the other side of the room rehearsing under their breath. Subhrasheel, flushed with rum, keeps his young cousins and friends laughing with risqué jokes, as Mrs Roy starts to lead the chorus in Tagore's song, '*Bideshi Mai*'. The words tell of a foreign woman who has come across the sea and captured hearts. Two portly matrons draped in cotton Dhaka saris dance towards me as if I am their lover and the crowd laughs at my blushes. The men continue to drink seriously while the songs unwind the erotic tale of Radha and Krishna in the demure style of *rabindra sangeet*, which is most reminiscent of a Methodist prayer meeting. Yet I am moved and can't shake off the shock of our love becoming so public. A younger aunt, Papiya, sits down next to me on the floor and whispers, 'You must promise to tell me everything that happens in the bed of flowers on the third night, us married women must stick together.' She giggles at my embarrassment and I worry if I am appearing innocent enough. It's the turn of my parents to perform. My father pulls out an old poetry book and reads, voice thick with emotion, 'Come live with me, and be my love.' Across the room, Probir has placed a comforting arm around Mr Roy's shoulders because his eyes are filling with tears. After the recitation he explains, 'That was the first poem I gave to my wife when we were courting so long ago. It's time for me to dance with the lovely mother of the bride.' A 'fifties Hindi film tune plays in the background as my mother does a jive to Mr Roy's comic Raj Kapoor moves. Probir, not to be outdone by my father, recites by heart the speech of Cassius from *Julius Caesar*, the one he used long ago to woo an Anglo-Indian. Then everyone joins him in 'Mona Lisa'. Subhrasheel's friends and cousins take over, strumming on guitars and humming drunkenly a range of tunes from Eric Clapton to the latest Daler Mehendi song. Sohag and Sohini weigh up their assets in a corner. Winking at me, Subhrasheel gets them to play Anjan Dutta's Bengali homage to an Anglo-Indian woman, 'Mary-Anne'. The pop song tells of his childhood love for the daughter of a railway driver, whom he abandoned for a more appropriate match. The singer glimpses her on a rickshaw many years later, her youth faded, her once long, glamorous finger-nails worn down from years of work as a secretary, but still Jesus looks down on her from an icon under the stairs with hope in his eyes. This could almost be a night of revels in Santa Barbara; the Indian and British cultural references are equally interwoven, yet the gathered guests would never admit this. I want to continue the mood as Subhrasheel will, by going out for late-night drinking at one of the dives on Park Street with his friends, but this is forbidden and we have an appointment for five in the morning at the Kali temple to bless the wedding bangles. Disentangling Patrick from his new blood brothers by the bar and Fiona from the unending questions from aunts about her marriage status and whether Patrick is her husband, we leave.

Autorickshaws, lorries and taxis cluster in the street beside Khalighat and their drivers wind garlands blessed at the temple over their engine grilles to protect them for another day from accidents. The trade in religious tokens is brisk this morning; as the sun rises it takes over from the night-time commerce in prostitutes on the same streets. Beggars and pandits loiter, waiting to reap the financial rewards of religious conscience. Subhrasheel and I expect little from this place apart from the symbolism of Mrs Roy taking us here and binding me to the family's ancestral goddess. This means more to us than the extravagant stories about how Kali's little toe touched the earth here thousands of years ago and the gothic, bloody rumours of ancient human sacrifices on this spot. Subhrasheel is enjoying telling these to Patrick and Fiona and then destroying the effect by describing the current professional struggles between different pandit unions. I almost expect him to ask our pandit to present his credentials as a card-carrying member. Sohag keeps warning us about the crush inside even at such an early hour, but the path leading into the temple grounds is a scrubbed municipal pavement, with orderly stalls arranged all along it. Barefooted, with the pandit carrying our allotted basket of flower garlands, *prasad* and red bangles, we feel the stark mosaic of the pavement pressing into our feet. The pandit sprints through the entrance to the temple grounds, which look like a Victorian public baths. Inside, a street-dog licks the post where the daily sacrifice of live goats is made and worshippers streaked with vermilion *tilaks* saunter around, rearranging rumpled kurtas and saris and munching on *sandesh prasad*. Following the bobbing head of the pandit, Sohag warns us again, but we can't really see anything that presages the chaos she promises.

We reach the temple building where worshippers are lined up single file on the steps below the domed roof, which stretches like terracotta thatch down the walls. On the exterior are art-nouveau tiles and a plaque recording the patronage of a Raj administrator. The windows are too small and high up to see inside; it must be very dark indeed within the temple. As we join the crowd on the steps, our backs and limbs are forced against them. The pandit calls instructions over the heads of my parents and Subhrasheel. Now is the moment to enter. The pandit disappears over the threshold beyond which nothing is visible, only the scent of sandalwood and incense rise along with shouts from inside. Following Subhrasheel, my feet slip on crushed flowers, I'm held upright only by the pressure of hundreds of pandits straining to hold their baskets of offerings aloft, their bodies pressed against a metal cage below us. Curses and prayers compete in a deafening roar. There must be steps down to the goddess, but where are they and how will we reach her? The priest instructs his friends to hold back the force of the crowd with their bodies, arms outstretched, palms interlinked to clear a path between the black wall slick with sweat and oil and the mass of humanity. He commands us, 'One, two, three,' and then we sink, as if plunging into the midnight waters of the Indian Ocean, pushed down by the next wave coming from behind. We don't know if we will drown or rise to the surface again.

We are not here for a simple blessing of bangles. Ten feet above us the arms of less favoured worshippers strain through a metal screen showering the goddess they can barely glimpse with flowers and shouting their praises. The flowers cascade on to us too: we are face to face with her, in an intimacy that is unbearable. She can see us better than we can see her because we can't move our heads to take her in, there is no room. There is no trace of delicacy about her, unlike the images of Durga and Lakshmi, no arms upraised in *kathakali* poses, no demurely straight nose or pouting lips, no voluptuous curves concealed behind a sari. If she has hair, then it is made of the hundreds of jasmine and orange-blossom garlands falling about her. If she has a tongue, then it is that gigantic strip of gold pouring from where her mouth should be. All she has are three huge blood-red eyes staring from a formless blackness. They are as big as my hands, which are now being bound with garlands from her neck to Subhrasheel's. Her guardian priest, six foot tall, sweating, semi-naked in strips of white cloth, rhythmically intoning mantras, staring somewhere else far beyond our eyes, is marrying us. His hard thumb roughly imprints vermilion on us from her forehead. What are we doing being married here? We haven't chosen this but it is happening, the flames from a brass *anjali* waving around her eyes and then so close to our faces we draw back in fear of burning. Rising up into the blinding morning sun, Subhrasheel says, 'That's it for ever, Auntie Kali has bound us. She's always been the goddess in front of whom runaway lovers and star-crossed couples have been married. The pandit must have decided to help us out by blessing our match before it could be undone by considerations of caste or suitability.'

Even though I will wear Kali's bangles at the ceremony this evening, the day is taken up with transformations into a more demure icon of womanhood. While I am still rubbing the vermilion *tilak* from my forehead, Subhrasheel's aunts arrive bearing the groom's family gifts, the *tatwah*. They are composed of elaborately wrapped jewellery that has been worn by brides for three generations, and new saris chosen by his parents. Enveloping me in a white and red plain cotton sari, with house-keys tied to the fall so that I look like a nostalgic vision of a Bengali housewife, they smear me with a mixture of mustard oil and turmeric that burns my skin, cleansing it for the wedding. Subhrasheel is somewhere else, going through the Gaye Halud. I can't wait to see him again this evening; our conversations have been monitored and brief for two days now.

Then Lotte and Mrs Roy arrive for four hours of dressing. Mrs Roy instructs me that I must not raise any objections to anything Lotte does to my appearance, because only she knows how to make me into a proper bride. Recalling her own wedding, Mrs Roy remembers the gossip that floated around their ceremony with a thousand guests. Elegantly smoothing out the creases in her sari with her long silver-shimmering fingernails, she says, 'You won't have the problems I did. My mother-in-law was scornful of the love match at first. She took one look at me and said, "She's so dark and black-faced, we don't need another image of Kali in our family." I was terribly hurt by that and so nervous about how I looked during the ceremonies. But everything has changed now, our generation is trying to be different, we understand the problems caused by such attitudes. You know what happened at my wedding? My husband's brother had just married the Indian Christian nurse of his father and the family members were so ashamed that they locked her up in the house and wouldn't let her come to my ceremony. They didn't want anyone to know about the scandal. But they were all wrong, she is a wonderful woman and they have made a good life for themselves in America.'

In a coded way she is explaining why they have

accepted me as a bride for their son. They have already seen and experienced the pain caused by disapproving relatives. And I realize that Mrs Roy has taken her mother-in-law's insult and turned it into a source of strength. The powerful Kali, not demure Lakshmi, is her model of womanhood.

Reflected in the mirror, Lotte smiles and looks at me pointedly as if to say, 'See, what did I tell you about your mother-in-law?'

Mrs Roy leaves me to Lotte's expertise. She delicately outlines my feet with red *alta*, turns my eyes into giant black-rimmed orbs, slicks my lips with bright red lipstick, paints a nosering on and weaves *chandan* in an arch above my eyebrows. Scraping back my hair she adds a huge fake bun, from which jasmine flowers cascade. The gold-threaded red sari weighs down heavily on my petticoat and I can't believe the force of gravity will not pull it off at some point in the night. The gold *tikli* on my forehead and chains stretching from rings on my fingers to a bracelet dig deep into my skin and the hairgrips holding the transparent net veil dotted with gold stars scratch painfully. Looking in the mirror my lurid smile looks unfamiliar: here I am, Suhashini, the name Subhrasheel's family have now christened me with. Great-grandmother's ornaments, gigantic discs that press into my neck like Boadicea's wheels, seem to want to repel the alien invader who wears them. For generations women, whether they were too low caste or dark, have been transformed into brides by this gold. Passing into the husband's caste, taking on his name and status, they have glimmered in this jewellery that erases their old self with its light. I don't recognize myself.

Lotte assures me that I look like a typical Indian bride as she pins on the finishing touch, a filigree pith crown, which the puja images of Lakshmi usually wear. But I can't help feeling like someone taking part in a pagal gymkhana. Staring back from the mirror is somebody who looks more like Helen than a Bengali bride. In the 'sixties Helen was the archetypal Hindi movie Anglo-Indian vamp, who purred in leopardskin with junior artistes dressed as Africans through a thousand tropical nightclub scenes. Once in a movie plot Helen played a British girl who lived in an England of stately homes, filmed in Simla, and tempted a young Indian engineering student with her seductive charms. When he is about to leave Britain, she gets drunk and threatens suicide if he doesn't take her back to India with him. He agrees and they visit his Indian extended family. By the end of the film, impressed by the celluloid religious values of India, she discards miniskirts, lipstick and cigarettes for cotton saris. But this won't be my story, even if I am Lakshmi for one night and touch all the relatives' feet, *pranaming* them in a gesture of respect; everything I have gone through here has shown me that this is a false version of India and Britain.

Patrick puts his head round the bedroom door and says, 'Hello, Princess Alpha from the planet Zephron. Are you on an intergalactic peace delegation?'

My mother, anxious for Lotte to help her into her sari, pushes past him and stands shocked for a moment by my appearance: 'My God, where are you, Laura? You look like a Victorian fantasy of an Indian queen.'

It's almost dusk, the sky is beginning to turn dark and the crows are roosting in the trees glimmering with fairy lights outside the window. We are going to have a *goduli biye*, a wedding at the time when the sun is dimmed by the dust raised from the hooves of cows returning from the fields. At the point of transition between night and day, the ceremony will look to the future surrounded by the stirred-up dust of the past.

The voices of guests rise from below and my mother is taking lessons from the aunt who married a Sikh, in how to welcome Subhrasheel to the bride's house with a rice-winnowing basket. It is filled with offerings painted with bright yellow, green and red flowers. Descending the stairs with difficulty, I go to greet some of the guests, but we are interrupted by the shrill blowing of conch shells and ululations that mean Subhrasheel has arrived.

Hiding on the stairs from his eyes, I wait for the *subho dristi*, the auspicious first public sighting of the bride and groom. The daughter of his Naxalite uncle and aunt calls me out. There he is, a handsome stranger in an embroidered dhoti and shawl, but this time, unlike that night years ago when I had returned from Kharagpur, I can't unwind him from them, for there are relatives watching now. Subhrasheel is serious and composed, so unlike his usual self. Patrick, as my brother, leads me around him seven times and I can't take my eyes off Subhrasheel or stop smiling. His aunts keep laughing and calling to me not to look at him; I'm supposed to be shy and fearful, full of *lojja*. Our arms become entangled in huge garlands as we place them round each other's neck three times. Ironically, in spite of her own past, the aunt who ran away with her childhood sweetheart shouts instructions about the etiquette of the ritual. Subhrasheel is led off to sit on the *pandal* surrounded by the trellis of hanging flowers. With him are my father, Probir and the priest, for it is the moment of the *kanya dan*, the gift of a virgin. They invoke the Roys' ancestors, offering them *til*, but mine are not remembered because I cannot be given by my father as we are foreigners with no caste. Instead Probir stands in for my father and gives me away. I had carefully consulted with my family so that my father could quote eight generations of ancestors at this point in the ceremony, but now I find that they have been written out as witnesses. Instead I make a private invocation of Matilda Batten.

Then I too am led to the *pandal*, seated opposite Subhrasheel on hard ancestral wooden boards painted with fish, symbols of fertility used for generations, and the priest joins our hands under a cloth. The heady scent of tuberoses and jasmine rises all around. While the priest murmurs Sanskrit mantras Subhrasheel tickles my palm, and I try hard not to giggle with relief at this return of his naughty self. Children and curious guests wander on and off the *pandal* as the priest continues. One little girl, blissfully unconcerned, sits reading the story of Dracula, unimpressed by the wedding fantasy in front of her. Hands hold back my veil and protect my sari from splatterings of *sindoor* with a handkerchief, as Subhrasheel paints the mark of a married woman into my parting. My sari and Subhrasheel's dhoti are tied together and we stand up, reeling back from the spitting flames and acrid smoke of the fire dangerously close to our feet. He clasps me to him from behind and I feel the whole length of his body pressing against me, our hands joined round a clay bowl of *moori*, which we pour on the leaping flames. His sweat drips on to the back of my neck and with something approaching prideful *lojja*, I realize this is the first time we have ever touched openly under the eyes of relatives. But this intimacy witnessed by the crowd is swiftly over and I follow him seven times round the fire with his aunts laughing and urging me not to go too fast because I am so eager for the *phul shojjo*, the bed of flowers.

The witnesses of fire, earth and water have blessed us, but now I must spend the rest of the evening seeking the blessings of all his relatives, by *pranaming* them each in turn. Mrs Roy leads me to all of them and Subhrasheel is nowhere near my side. I want to parade my union with him, but this is an irrelevance to this event which is all about the joining of families.

The photographer keeps praising my fair skin and the guests my *pranaming*, congratulating Mrs Roy that I am doing this more fervently than a modern Bengali bride would. I would really like to be sitting in a corner with the little girl reading Dracula to get her view on all of this. Papiya keeps teasing me about the inelegant shawl tied to my sari that represents my husband, saying, 'Now you're a married woman, you understand the inconvenience a husband is.' Under a glistening chandelier too large for the maroon canopy the guests feast on Bijoli grill fishfry served by waiters wearing turmeric-yellow uniforms and white gloves. On the street outside Probir has set up a makeshift bar in his car boot and men return from it reeling from his strong doses of rum. Tired children fall asleep on the *pandal.* Priti, the daughter of the once scandalous match between the Indian Christian and Mr Roy's brother who lives in America, watches the proceedings from a corner, resolutely out of place among the delicately draped silk saris in a tight mini-dress. Seizing a moment when I am alone, she says in her New Jersey drawl, 'It's all too strange for me, I don't know how you're coping so well. I wouldn't wear a sari, whatever my relatives say about it.'

Close to midnight the guests have left, but all the younger cousins are waiting for Subhrasheel and me to arrive at a nearby aunt's house for a night of teasing. This should be the duty of my brothers and sisters, but since I have none, Sohag and Sohini, and Subhrasheel's cousins Biku and Kunal who now count as my brothers-in-law, have stepped in. My sisters are supposed to steal the groom's shoes and ask for ransom for them, bargaining late into the night before allowing the groom to be alone with the bride, a sort of affectionate prostitution of their own sibling. Instead a night of guitar-strumming and liquor has been arranged. With relief I undo Lotte's labours, removing safety pins and smearing the make-up from my face. At the aunt's house, we all lie around on hastily spread-out mattresses and tell jokes, and my new brothers-in-law indulge in *boudi baji*, flirting safely with their sister-in-law. The charged atmosphere spreads throughout the gathering, Sohag and Sohini dancing with their cousins. Priti sits apart and when I try to draw her into the dancing she snorts in disgust, 'I don't have much time for the Indian national sport of flirting with cousins.' Finally, at three in the morning, Subhrasheel and I are allowed to be alone but the bed Biku and Kunal have prepared is laced with tennis rackets and hidden alarm clocks that go off unexpectedly all night.

I ask Subhrasheel how I looked all done up as a bride. Twisting my body around him, he replies, 'That's not the point. It wasn't for me, all that show, it was for the relatives. Now our myths can start again, my *tesu*, I want you like this and this and this.'

The next evening, I am prepared as Lakshmi again for the final passage into Subhrasheel's family. The bride has to be welcomed into the groom's home, taking her first step across the threshold barefoot and staining it with an auspicious footprint of *alta* and milk. Over the last few years I had sneaked into this place while Subhrasheel's parents were out, watching for the neighbourhood spies, or was invited as a strange foreign guest to parties. Now the local *para* boys loiter on the narrow street, looking on at my entry heralded by conch shells. This time the rooms are filled to overflowing with excited children running about, tripping over the long saris and dhotis of their elders. Nostalgic for the promise of chaos and defiance of respectability that hung in the air the first time I visited here, I wish that Pobon was present to witness the fulfilment of his suspicions about the relationship between Subhrasheel and me. That night I had heard the story of Subhrasheel's cousin who was taken away from India to forget his past-life memories that did not fit his surroundings. Since then Calcutta has given me the gift of the revival of a dissonant identity, the whole past life of colonial Anglo-India that hovers around the Indian and British present, but that is not being acknowledged tonight. Instead, as Mrs Roy touches our lips, ears and mouths with honey so that we will experience only sweet things with our senses and each aunt feeds us sweets and blesses us with *til*-grass, I am being wrapped in Bengali traditions. I greet Subhrasheel's parents as *Baba-ma*, father-mother. All the guests call me Suhashini. Mr Roy affectionately uses his own private nickname for me, *notunma*, new mother. Mrs Roy calls Subhrasheel and me her two babies. My father winces visibly at each of these appropriations, but I want to tell him not to worry: as one identity is overlaid on another I will not allow the new one to wipe out past incarnations. The vow Subhrasheel and I have made is to let them all hang suspended in teasing debate with one another. This is what our stories whispered in polyglot sentences of Bengali and English have always done and in this way we will continue the magic of Kharagpur.

The last night of celebrations is at the Tollygunj Club, the palatial residence of a civil servant turned in the late nineteenth century into a secluded pleasure ground for Calcutta's British elite. The sign by the swimming pool, 'No Ayahs Please', remains along with the malis who snip the golf course daily with scissors and the stiff social requirements for membership. Sohag and Sohini are particularly excited that we are having a reception here as it marks our union with a social cachet that augurs well for the matches they will make. The more snobbish members of Subhrasheel's advertising agency, who were underwhelmed by our residence in the unimpressive area of Janakpuri, have been amazed that

313

we have secured such a place for a reception and our social stock has risen as a result. In the garden outside the Far Pavilions guest house among the clipped hedges decorated with fairy lights and dressed in a blue and gold sari worthy of a Bombay socialite, I *pranam* each guest.

Seeking an occasional break from my duties I make a point of chatting with Prashanto Roy, Subhrasheel's sociology professor from Presidency College. Prashanto more than deserves this attention because he was Subhrasheel's mentor after St James and had given Subhrasheel the tools to criticize its traditions. He has long been at the heart of the Marxist politics of Calcutta and has turned up in his simple white dhoti in a sartorial defiance of the Tollygunj Club's traditions. He delights in lashing out at the institution around us and its colonial mentality.

Apart from Fiona, Patrick and my parents there is only one other guest I have invited, Indrani. She is an old friend, an academic and political activist who has made it her life's work to confront oppressive versions of Indian tradition. Over the heads of the guests, I glimpse her smiling face framed by boyish cropped hair that contrasts with her conventional purple and white Dhaka sari. Sneaking an opportunity to sit with her on one of the lawn chairs, I am rewarded with a gift from her more precious than the pearl necklaces the other guests are proffering.

'I've been saving a story for when you had gone through all these Bengali traditions,' she says. 'You are the last person to be taken in by all of this, but just in case listen to one of my mother's memories. She had a childhood friend named Protima. When the friend married, she disappeared into an elegant, crumbling home in north Calcutta. They wrote letters once or twice a year to relive their childish exploits. But one puja my mother came to Calcutta to visit her parents with her eldest son. Once Bijoya had passed and the duties to Durga and the endless stream of relatives were over, she left her son in the care of her mother and went to her friend's house.

'They sat on the long veranda outside the kitchen. Her friend rattled the keys to the storeroom she had held in her possession since her mother-in-law had died and they laughed about how, when small, they had longed to untie them from the saris of their eldest aunts and run away with *gur* which turned their fingers into sticky brown delights. The two friends could spend precious uninterrupted hours together because Protima's husband was on outstation business and his younger brother and his wife were still caught up with duty visits.

'As the afternoon turned cool towards evening Protima abruptly left her alone to take a long bath, appearing afterwards in a translucent Dhaka sari that made my grandmother feel shabby and maternal in her plain cotton. She fussed with the cook about the exact amount of masalas in the *singhara* and ushered my grandmother into one of the outer rooms for receiving guests, dusting down the low seats. Protima explained, "My husband's best friend from his Presidency days is coming. Hiresh is such a brother to me. Please excuse this interruption, but stay longer."

'Hiresh arrived and greeted Protima as *didi*, stabbing the air with his strong expressive fingers, filling it with compliments. Then in mid-flight one of his fingers settled to remove a *singhara* crumb from Protima's cheek. Watching her friend's eyes looking downwards with embarrassment, my grandmother then knew everything. Later, after Hiresh had left, she asked Protima, "How long has it been going on? Don't you have any shame?" Her friend now had no trace of fear and looked as courageous as the images of Durga slaying the lion. With her *sindoor* catching the light and her sari carefully folded around her, she said, "Don't worry, my husband's away so often, the servants like their bribes from the storeroom and anyway I'm behaving just like Draupadi who had five husbands."

'So, Laura, even the most demure of Bengali women can find precedents in the myths of the Mahabharat for her romantic dalliances, twisting and turning tradition to new forms. The name Protima means "the image of a goddess", but that image can be reinvented many times. Good luck reinventing it as you can.'

Remembering Indrani's advice, after the party is over Subhrasheel and I reject the prescribed bed of flowers. We slough off kurta and sari for jeans and head for a nightclub. Dancing with friends through to the next morning, my Kali *shakha pola* rattle to the trance beat. I think of Helen in her nightclub scenes, the vision of Kali's womanhood that Mrs Roy has adopted as her own, and of Donna's cosmopolitan Muslim bride. There are many choices that India's current public culture is trying so hard to deny.

Returning to New Delhi we unlock the stifling rooms of our flat. The last few days have seen a heatwave more intense than usual and a layer of sand has been carried on ferocious blasts of wind from the Rajasthani desert. The roof terrace and all the furniture are covered in the yellow dust. However hard we sweep the floor, our feet scrape against the grit. This is not the romantic dust of an auspicious *goduli biye*, a dusk wedding. The local rumour is that the unseasonal weather and sand are fallout from the Hindu bomb just let off in Pokhran. Remembering Mr Vanjo's joke about the impossibility of an Anglo-Indian bomb, I wish that a Hindu bomb was equally unimaginable. Also in my mind are the Eastern Railway petitions and Milly's restless ghost as we sort out our love letters, preparing them as proof of our emotions for inspection by the British High Commission. Our passions may, if they are rubber-stamped as real, at some point qualify Subhrasheel for a visa to cross the border into Britain. Sadly we wonder whether private myths and reinventions of India and Britain will ever be enough. Can Anglo-Indian histories ever be heard?

Glossary

Achaar – Spicy pickle.

Adivasi – Indigenous non-Hindu groups outside the caste system, literally 'original inhabitants'.

Almirah – Large cabinet.

Alpana – Filigree patterns of white paint used to decorate houses and shrine-rooms during festivals.

Babu – Male clerk, usually in government employment.

Bandh – Political strike.

Barfi – A sweet.

Beta – Son.

Bhai Phota – Ceremony that celebrates the relationship between brothers and sisters.

Bhisti – Person employed to deliver water.

Boti – Blade mounted on wooden handle used for chopping vegetables, meat, etc.

Buddhu – Stupid one! Affectionate, teasing name.

Bustee – Slum.

Chamar – Cobbler, leather-worker caste.

Chandan – White lacy patterns made of sandalwood painted on the faces of brides and images of goddesses.

Charpoy – Bed made of a wooden frame with bands of coir rope stretched across it.

Chingri mach – Prawns, shrimps.

Chokra – Lad.

Darshan – Viewing of the idols of gods and goddesses in temples.

Dekchi – Metal vessel.

Desh – A country, or the original village home of an individual or family.

Dhaba – Roadside eatery.

Dhoti – Folded cloth worn by Bengali men, more elaborate than the lungi (see below).

Didi – Elder sister (term of respect).

Diwali – Festival of lights held in North India in November to ensure prosperity. Associated with the deities Lakshmi and Ganesh.

Dotara – Stringed instrument played by Bauls.

Dufteri – Watchman in offices.

Dupatta – Scarf worn with *salwar kameez*.

Durbar – Originally the gathering of courtiers in the presence of the monarch, but now used to indicate the gathering of people in the presence of any form of authority. A ceremony of power associated with the Moghul emperors and lesser rulers and land-owners. Also incorporated by the British into the Raj bureaucracy (for example, the Imperial Assemblage of 1877).

Durga – Consort of Siva. One of the incarnations of Shakti (female power).

Durwan – Watchman.

Gaye Halud – Purification ceremony for bride and groom before Bengali Hindu wedding.

Ghagra choli – Blouse, scarf and long skirt.

Ghazals – Urdu couplets about lost love set to music.

Godown – Warehouse.

Goonda – Troublemaker.

Hanuman – Monkey-god, signifying strength and courage. Devoted aide of Ram.

Haveli – Houses for the gentry, built around a central courtyard.

Hijras – Eunuchs.

Holi – Spring festival of colours. Associated with Krishna and Radha.

Istri-wallah – Person employed to iron clothes.

Jai Hind! – Victory to India!

Jater dosh – A pollution of a family line, literally a mistake in the family line.

Jhola – Bag popularly associated with radicals and students.

Jyotish – Astrological.

Kabbadi – A team sport.

Kandokarkhana – Literally a chaos machine. A person or thing that creates disorder.

Kanya dan – Part of Bengali Hindu wedding ceremony in which the bride is handed over to the groom's family.

Kathakali – Indian dance form.

Kathi rolls – Meat wrapped in paratha.

Keema – Lamb mincemeat cooked with spices.

Khadi – Hand-woven cotton.

Kintal – Antiquated term used by the British in India in the nineteenth century to refer to slums, particularly in Calcutta.

Kobi gaan – Bengali duelling songs, performed in the late eighteenth and early nineteenth centuries by poets sparring with each other. Known for their acerbic wit, satire and daring.

Koila – Coal.

Lakshmi – Goddess of prosperity.

Lengha choli – Similar to *gagra choli* (see above).

Lojja – Shame.

Loochi – Fried, small roti.

Lungi – Cotton cloth worn by men.

Masala – Spices or spicy, as in 'Masala movies'.

Mehendi – Henna-paste patterns.

Memsaheb – Term used to refer to the wives of English civil servants. In the late nineteenth century Bengali playwrights and social reformers criticized the behaviour of such women and the word still carries a double meaning of apparent respect mixed with disdain.

Mistree – Workman, painter, carpenter, etc.

Muharram – Muslim festival of mourning.

Murgi – Chicken.

Nawab – Regional overlord.

Nimbu pani – Lemon mixed with water.

Paan – *Paan* leaf wrapped around betel-nut shavings, rose syrup, spices and sometimes tobacco.

Pagri – Turban.

Pallu – The part of a sari that falls from the shoulder down the back.

Pandal – Marquee.

Para – Neighbourhood.

Phul shojjo – Literally 'bed of flowers'. The third night after a Bengali Hindu wedding.

Pranam – Touch someone's feet in a gesture of respect.

Prasad – Food offerings to gods and goddesses.

Quawali – Urdu songs similar to *kobi gan* (see above).

Raag – Musical composition.

Rakhi – Thread-tying ceremony between brother and sister, similar to Bhai Phota (see above). Primarily North Indian.

Roshogollas – Fried round sweets made from curds and rose water.

Saheb – Term of respect for male figures of authority.

Sandesh – Flat, round sweets made from curds.

Shakha pola – Bracelets worn by Bengali married women.

Shilnora – Grinding stone.

Shorshe mach – A dish of fish and mustard seeds.

Sindoor – Red powder worn in the hair-parting by married Bengali women.

Singhara – Samosa.

Subho dristi – First sighting between bride and groom in Bengali Hindu wedding ceremony.
Subjhi – Raw vegetables.
Subji – Dish of cooked vegetables.
Thana – Local police station.
Tiktikki – Lizard.

Appendix

'Anglo-Indian': Historical Definitions

From the seventeenth to the early eighteenth century people of Indian and European parentage were called *Firinghees* (derived from Persian), *castees* and *mustees* (derived from Portuguese). In the mid-eighteenth century they were named *half-castes* or *mixed bloods*. Until 1786 the East India Company encouraged the unions of local officers and Indian women. It granted five rupees per month for the upkeep of children born to British soldiers from these relationships. There were no legal limits on the employment of half-castes in the Company or on their movement outside India.

In the late eighteenth century the East India Company started to define half-castes as a distinct legal and social group. In 1786 a school was set up in Calcutta for the half-caste orphans of British soldiers and civil servants. An edict prohibited such children from proceeding to Britain to complete their education. Between 1792 and 1795 Cornwallis reformed the East India Company bureaucracy. The new regulations prohibited high-level civil servants and military personnel from marrying Indian women and women of mixed parentage. People of mixed Indian and European parentage could not be employed in the upper or official cadres of the Company or military except as musicians in the British army. In 1808 they were prohibited from holding any rank in the British army. As a result they sought work in the service of the Indian princely states and used their older business links with the Company to trade with it as intermediaries.

In 1823 a political organization, the East India Club, was founded in Calcutta to campaign for greater rights and for half-castes to be called *East Indians*. It funded a grammar school, an apprentice school and a commercial academy. At this time the term *Indo-Britain* was also used. In 1830 J. W. Ricketts, a founding member of the East India Club, took a petition to the British parliament. This petition protested against the limited employment opportunities for and the confusion around the legal status of East Indians. They could not be employed in the 'superior' and 'covenanted' offices of the army or civil service because they were not British. They were excluded from most of the 'subordinate' posts in the judicial, revenue and police departments and from the army because these were intended for Hindus and Muslims. They were under English common law if they lived in Calcutta, but elsewhere the legal status of their marriages, the legitimacy of their children and their rights of succession to property were unclear. Regional courts ruled according to Hindu or Muslim law. East Indians were largely Christian and therefore had no courts in which to seek redress. Ricketts's petition for a decision on these issues was rejected.

The East India Company's charter act of 1833 resolved the problem of employment. In the act East Indians were classified as natives of India with the same rights of employment in the army and civil service as Indians. But their legal status continued to be uncertain up to Independence. Even after the introduction of laws in the 1830s and 1860s to administer the rights of Christian converts in India, decisions on which marriage laws and inheritance laws applied to people of Indian and European parentage were made on a case-by-case basis. It was difficult for them to produce documents to prove their status one way or the other because records were kept for only a few years by the different departments of the government. Baptismal records just listed an individual's religious affiliation. Often the decisions were based merely on the opinions of judges as to how Indian or European an individual appeared to be from their demeanour, accent and skin colour.

By the mid-nineteenth century the employment opportunities for East Indians had expanded. Railway companies actively recruited East Indians to work as drivers, guards and stationmasters. British railway officers thought that their mixed parentage gave them a greater aptitude for technology than other 'castes'. After the rebellion of 1857, they were employed in the Indian army and the lower levels of the civil service in preference to other local groups.

In the 1860s the term *Eurasian* gained a wide currency, mainly as a result of campaigns for the separate education of children of mixed Indian and European parentage. Earlier in the century poorer Eurasian children who lived outside Calcutta or in its slums were educated in schools alongside other Indians. But in the 1860s Dr George Cotton, a civil servant in the education service, launched a campaign for the provision of schools specifically for Eurasian and *Domiciled European* children. 'Domiciled European' referred to people of unmixed parentage who resided in India permanently and owned property there (often soldiers, sailors or discharged railway workers who did not return to Europe after periods of service). Statistics were collected for the first time on the economic and social situation of Eurasians as a separate community. Cotton proposed a system of hill-station schools for the richer members of the community and plains schools for the poorer members. Canning, the Viceroy, argued that this was essential, otherwise the government would soon be 'embarrassed . . . with a floating population of Indianized English loosely brought up and exhibiting some of the worst qualities of both races'. Railway companies, charitable trusts and religious groups established schools in the hills and plains. These focused on technical education for boys and domestic education for girls. They did not equip the pupils for entry to Indian universities. The term 'Firinghee' was used again in this period in government reports on education to describe people of mixed (often Portuguese) descent in the country regions, especially around Chittagong. Firinghees were Eurasians who had become 'too Indian' for the authorities to allow them to attend English-medium schools. The term 'Eurasian' did not carry any distinct legal rights until 1883 when government-funded and controlled education for Europeans began. In order to determine who was eligible for education in the European schools a Eurasian was defined as a person of European descent, pure or mixed, who was permanently resident in India and retained European habits and modes of life.

From 1870 to 1880 Indian nationalist organizations argued for the greater employment of Indians in the lower levels of the civil service. The government responded to their demands in 1883 by ruling that 'natives' should be more widely employed. They defined 'natives' as 'any person of Pure Asiatic origin'. The newly founded Anglo-Indian and Domiciled European Association unsuccessfully protested against this definition which excluded people of mixed parentage from the category of 'native'. Although they continued to be preferentially recruited on the railways, this ruling had cut them off from positions in the civil service. The association argued for the name

Anglo-Indian to be given to people of mixed European and Indian parentage. The Secretary of State for India rejected their suggestion because this word was associated with British citizens who returned home after periods of employment in the Indian Civil Service. By the end of the nineteenth century the Bengali word *Tash*, referring to an Indian Christian or Eurasian, began to be used widely in Bengal. It carried the associations of being Anglicized, weak, impure, immoral and of low class and caste. Indian national and regional identities developed in protest against the inequalities of a Christian British Raj, therefore people of mixed parentage or with multiple cultural affiliations were increasingly seen as an anomaly.

In 1911 Lord Hardinge agreed to the use of 'Anglo-Indian' as a category in the Indian Census to distinguish people of mixed parentage who had a European ancestor in their male line of inheritance. But it wasn't until the Montagu Chelmsford electoral reforms of 1919 that 'Anglo-Indian' was more widely used as a category. These reforms gave Indians very limited powers of provincial self-government, based on principles of separate electorates and community representation. One of the communities that emerged out of this with a distinct public identity was that of Anglo-Indians. Being identified as an Anglo-Indian on the new electoral registers gave individuals contradictory rights. Their position was clarified by the secretary of state for India in 1925. For purposes of employment they were considered as statutory natives of India, but for purposes of education and internal security they were classed as European British subjects. This meant that like other Indians they were excluded from the higher levels of the civil service and railways. Yet they could not compete on an equal footing with well-educated Indians for professional posts because they had to attend English-medium schools, which did not equip them for the entrance exams for the Indian universities. But they could be conscripted into the British army. Just before Independence some Anglo-Indians campaigned to be called *Britasian*. At Independence the Indian constitution continued the definition of an Anglo-Indian as a 'person whose father or any of whose other male progenitors in the male line is or was of European descent but who is domiciled within the territory of India and is or was born within such territory of parents habitually resident therein'. Anglo-Indians are still represented in the provincial and central legislatures by nominated MPs.

A SON OF THE CIRCUS

John Irving

'IRVING HAS GIVEN US THAT TREAT OF TREATS, A
WIDE-RANGING FICTION OF MASSIVE DESIGN AND LENGTH
THAT ENCAPSULATES OUR WORLD WITH INTELLIGENCE AND
SUGARS THE PILL WITH WIT'
David Hughes, *Mail on Sunday*

Born a Parsi in Bombay, sent to university and medical school
in Vienna, Dr Farrokh Daruwalla is a Canadian citizen – a
59-year-old orthopedic surgeon, living in Toronto. Periodically, the
doctor returns to India; in Bombay, most of his patients
are crippled children.

Once, twenty years ago, Dr Daruwalla was the examining physician
of two murder victims in Goa. Now, twenty years later, the doctor
will be reacquainted with the murderer.

'DARUWALLA'S QUEST FOR THE TRUTH IS WHAT SUSTAINS
THIS BOOK . . . A WRITER WITH THE COURAGE TO FOLLOW
THIS DIFFICULT JOURNEY WHILE ALSO EXPLORING ISSUES
OF POVERTY, RACISM AND DISEASE IN A NOVEL SO FULL
OF HUMOUR IS A WRITER TO BE TREASURED'
Erica Wagner, *The Times*

'[IRVING] IS AT THE PEAK OF HIS POWERS . . . HE PLUNGES
THE READER INTO ONE SENSUAL OR GROTESQUE SCENE
AFTER ANOTHER WITH CHEERFUL VIGOUR AND A MADCAP
TENDERNESS FOR LIFE . . . ENTERTAINMENT ON A GRAND
SCALE'
Economist

'DARUWALLA IS ANOTHER ICONIC IRVING FIGURE . . . THE
GOOD MAN IN AN INEXPLICABLE WORLD . . . IRVING HANDLES
THIS INCARNADINE COMBINATION OF FARCE AND HORROR
WITH HIGH SPEED SKILL, CREATING A COMPULSIVELY
READABLE BOOK'
Elizabeth Young, *Guardian*

'IRVING'S POPULARITY IS NOT HARD TO UNDERSTAND. HIS
WORLD REALLY IS THE WORLD ACCORDING TO EVERYONE'
Time

0 552 99605 X

BLACK SWAN

SISTER OF MY HEART

Chitra Banerjee Divakaruni

'CHITRA BANERJEE DIVAKARUNI IS A TRUE STORYTELLER. LIKE
DICKENS, SHE HAS CONSTRUCTED LAYER UPON LAYER OF
TRAGEDY, SECRETS AND BETRAYALS, OF THWARTED LOVE . . .
[A] GLORIOUS, COLOURFUL TRAGEDY'
Daily Telegraph

Born in the big old Calcutta house on the same tragic night that both
their fathers were mysteriously lost, Sudha and Anju are cousins.
Closer even than sisters, they share clothes, worries, dreams in the
matriarchal Chatterjee household. But when Sudha discovers a
terrible secret about the past, their mutual loyalty is sorely tested.

A family crisis forces their mothers to start the serious business of
arranging the girls' marriages, and the pair is torn apart. Sudha
moves to her new family's home in rural Bengal, while Anju joins
her immigrant husband in California. Although they have both been
trained to be perfect wives, nothing has prepared them for the pain,
as well as the joy, that each will have to face in her new life.

Steeped in the mysticism of ancient tales, this jewel-like novel shines
its light on the bonds of family, on love and loss, against the realities
of traditional marriage in modern times.

'DIVAKARUNI STRIKES A DELICATE BALANCE BETWEEN
REALISM AND FANTASY . . . A TOUCHING CELEBRATION
OF ENDURING LOVE'
Sunday Times

'A PLEASURE TO READ . . . A NOVEL FRAGRANT IN RHYTHM
AND LANGUAGE'
San Francisco Chronicle

'DIVAKARUNI'S BOOKS POSSESS A POWER THAT IS BOTH
TRANSPORTING AND HEALING . . . SERIOUS AND ENTRANCING'
Booklist

'MAGICALLY AFFECTING . . . HER INTRICATE TAPESTRY OF OLD
AND NEW WORLDS SHINES WITH A RARE LUMINOSITY'
San Diego Union Tribune

0 552 99767 6

BLACK SWAN

FRIEDA AND MIN

Pamela Jooste

FROM THE PRIZE-WINNING AUTHOR OF *DANCE WITH A POOR MAN'S DAUGHTER*

'ONE OF THE NEW BREED OF WOMEN WRITERS IN SOUTH AFRICA WHO ARE TELLING OUR STORY WITH SUCH POWER AND TALENT'
Cape Times

When Frieda first met Min, with her golden hair and ivory bones, what struck her most was that Min was wearing a pair of African sandals, the sort made out of old car tyres. She was a silent, unhappy girl, dumped on Frieda's exuberant family in Johannesburg for the summer of 1964 so that her mother could go off with her new husband. In a way, Min and Frieda were both outsiders – Min, raised in the bush by her idealistic doctor father, and Frieda, daughter of a poor Jewish saxophone player, who lived almost on top of a native neighbourhood. The two girls, thrown together – the 'white kaffir' and the poor Jewish girl – formed a strange but loyal friendship, a friendship that was to last through the terrible years of oppression and betrayal during the time of South Africa under Apartheid.

'A NOVEL THAT EVERYONE SHOULD READ . . . HAS THAT RARE ABILITY TO BE BOTH MOVING AND FUNNY . . . DESERVES ALL THE PRAISE THAT IT WILL SURELY GET'
Pamela Weaver, *Examiner*

'HAS A GOOD STORY TO TELL AND SHE TELLS IT WELL . . . HAS LOST NONE OF THE QUALITIES THAT MADE *DANCE WITH A POOR MAN'S DAUGHTER* SO CREDIBLE'
Isobel Shepherd-Smith, *The Times*

0 552 99758 7

BLACK SWAN